"This is, in many ways, a particularly American story, and anyone interested in history or museums will find this a very satisfying read. Author Colin Davey had a life-long love affair with the museum, growing up in New York and spending many, many hours happily lost in the museum collections, and that shines through in his writing, as does his fine, in-depth research. Plenty of excellent graphics and photographs support this fascinating history." —*Seattle Book Review*

"This volume makes a valuable contribution to our knowledge of one of the most iconic American institutions devoted to science and popular education, especially regarding astronomy and space science, over the course of more than a century. Deeply researched and illustrated with 50 black-and-white period photos and numerous diagrams, the work is not only a pleasure to read but will serve as a notable reference for years to come. Planetarians everywhere can benefit from a short to an in-depth perusal of its pages." —*Planetarian: Journal of the International Planetarium Society*

"Want to learn more fascinating history about the Museum of Natural History? In honor of its 150th anniversary, Colin Davey and Thomas A. Lesser have brought out a new, definitive history of the museum. The book, *The American Museum of Natural History and How It Got That Way*, provides a history of the museum's architecture, collections, exhibitions, and research and conservation efforts, charting the institution's relationship with the natural world and with New York City. In these pages you'll find polar explorers, intrepid archaeologists, and visionary rocket scientists who devoted their lives to discovery and, in many cases, to the museum itself." —Lucie Levine, *6sqft*

"The American Museum of Natural History is one of New York City's most beloved institutions and one of the largest, most celebrated museums in the world. Since 1869, generations of New Yorkers and tourists of all ages have been educated and entertained here. Located across the street from Central Park, the huge structure, spanning four city blocks, is constructed of many buildings of diverse architectural styles built over a period of 150 years. This is the first book to tell the story of the museum from the point of view of these buildings. *The American Museum of Natural History and How It Got That Way* combines them with New York, American history, and the history of science." —*Prehistoric Times*

"A gigantic treasure chest stands next to New York's Central Park, filled with the wonders of prehistoric times, life on Earth, and deep space. For me, the American Museum of Natural History and Hayden Planetarium were like a second childhood home. I'm so glad for this book, which at last tells its remarkable story." —Andrew Chaikin, *A Man on the Moon*

D0897145

THE AMERICAN MUSEUM OF NATURAL HISTORY AND HOW IT GOT THAT WAY

THE AMERICAN MUSEUM OF NATURAL HISTORY AND HOW IT GOT THAT WAY

COLIN DAVEY
WITH THOMAS A. LESSER

Empire State Editions
An imprint of Fordham University Press
New York   2019

Fordham University Press has no responsibility for the persistence or accuracy of URLs for external or third-party Internet websites referred to in this publication and does not guarantee that any content on such websites is, or will remain, accurate or appropriate.

Fordham University Press also publishes its books in a variety of electronic formats. Some content that appears in print may not be available in electronic books.

Visit us online at www.fordhampress.com/empire-state-editions.

Library of Congress Control Number: 2019932464

Printed in the United States of America

21 20 19   5 4 3 2

First edition

Contents

Preface to the 2020 Paperback Edition

Colin Davey

I would like to use this Preface to the revised version of *The American Museum of Natural History and How It Got That Way* to update the earlier verson with events that have occurred since its release and to include some topics that didn't make their way into it.

THEODORE ROOSEVELT

Because one of the many themes of the book is President Theodore Roosevelt's connection to the Museum from its founding to his death and beyond, I want to add some topics to that theme here: one from his boyhood, one from his post-presidency, and one from a few months ago.

EARLY DONATIONS

While the earlier version of the book covers the involvement of Roosevelt's father in founding the museum, as well as the future president's earliest boyhood visit, it is also worth noting that the future president donated numerous specimens to the museum as a young teenager, including a bat, twelve mice, a turtle, and a squirrel skull.

ROOSEVELT RONDON SCIENTIFIC EXPEDITION

From December 1913 to April 1914, the fifty-six-year-old former president undertook a perilous Brazilian expedition for the museum. In 1908, as his presidency was coming to a close, Father John Augustine Zahm, a priest and old friend, proposed a joint expedition to interior of South America. Instead, Roosevelt began a yearlong expedition to

Africa in 1909–10, where he hunted one of the elephants in the muse-um's Akeley African Hall, as recounted in these pages. In 1912, Roos-evelt had run for president under the "Bull Moose" party label, was shot in the chest by a would-be assassin, and lost the election (along with Eugene V. Debs and incumbent William Howard Taft) to Woodrow Wilson.

In February 1913, Roosevelt received an invitation from Argentina's Museo Social to visit South America for a lecture tour. Ever the natu-ralist, Roosevelt contacted American Museum president Henry Fairfield Osborn about adding a scientific expedition to the tour, and in June, Roosevelt met with museum ornithologist Frank Chapman, resulting in the museum's sending two naturalists to accompany Roosevelt.

The original itinerary consisted of several well-charted rivers with a variety of landscapes and wildlife without being too strenuous or dan-gerous. However, almost immediately on Roosevelt's meeting with his Brazilian hosts in October 1913, plans were changed. The new plan was to traverse and map the uncharted River of Doubt, of which Chapman later wrote, "In all of South America, there is not a more difficult or dangerous journey." Roosevelt was to be accompanied by Cândido Rondon, who was, at the age of forty-eight, Brazil's foremost explorer. When Osborn got wind of the change, he wrote to Roosevelt that he would never consent to this trip "under the American Museum flag." Roosevelt's response: "If it is necessary for me to leave my bones in South America, I am quite ready to do so."

In December, after his lecture-tour duties were complete, the ardu-ous two-month wilderness trek to the mouth of the river began, during which specimens were collected for the museum. The journey down the river began on February 27 and lasted until April 26, 1914. There is not enough space here to relate all the hardships that expedition endured, which included extreme heat and humidity, piranha fish, unremitting swarms of attacking insects, insufficient food, and an incident in which a canoe carrying Roosevelt's son Kermit and two boatmen was swept over a waterfall, killing one of the boatmen. At the halfway point, Roosevelt gashed his leg, which quickly became infected, while he also came down with malaria—as had much of the team. From that point on, it was unclear whether he would survive the journey.

Roosevelt's health never fully recovered, and he died less than five years later. Rondon would live to the age of ninety-two, a Brazilian hero in part for his lifelong support for indigenous Brazilians. Rondônia, one of Brazil's twenty-six states, is named for him.

THE STATUE

As noted in the earlier version, the statue of Roosevelt at the museum's Central Park West entrance had been controversial for its depiction of Roosevelt on horseback towering over semi-nude figures of an African and a Native American, which can be seen as suggesting white supremacy. In July 2019, two months after the initial publication of this book, the museum launched an exhibition, curated by museum anthropologist David Hurst Thomas, called "Addressing the Statue," which also examined the museum's exhibitions on eugenics in the early twentieth century.

And on June 21, 2020, in the wake of the George Floyd killing, the museum announced that the statue was to be removed. As museum president Ellen Futter put it, "Over the last few weeks, our museum community has been profoundly moved by the ever-widening movement for racial justice that has emerged after the killing of George Floyd. We have watched as the attention of the world and the country has increasingly turned to statues as powerful and hurtful symbols of systemic racism. . . . Simply put, the time has come to move it." The ultimate fate of the statue is still to be determined.

GILDER CENTER UPDATE

As we were rushing to finish the first version of this book, it was unclear whether the museum would be allowed to build the Gilder Center for Science, Education, and Innovation, the ambitious new Columbus Avenue extension, because of a vigorous legal challenge. Judge Kotler's December 10, 2018, ruling allowing the building came just in time to be included in the book.

But the story had a few twists and turns remaining. Community United, the group opposing the construction, appealed the decision, and on December 18, the group was granted a temporary stay pending appeal. On February 5, 2019, the court overturned the stay, allowing construction to proceed. On April 18, a state appeals court dismissed the appeal, thus overcoming the museum's last legal obstacle. The museum held a groundbreaking ceremony on June 12.

On April 3, 2020, with the museum closed to the public because of the global COVID-19 pandemic, construction was suspended until further notice. On June 15, it resumed. At this point, work on the excavation and foundation is well underway.

CARTER EMMART

When I visited the museum in November 2019 to work on the museum's documentary *Stories in the Sky: A History of Planetariums*, I had the opportunity to spend some quality time with Carter Emmart, the museum's director of astrovisualization, who, besides being an original designer of the Digital Universe, directed all six space shows at the Rose Center: *Passport to the Universe*, *The Search for Life: Are We Alone?*, *Cosmic Collisions*, *Journey to the Stars*, *Dark Universe*, and the recently opened *Worlds Beyond Earth*. In the process, I realized that this book needed more information on his background. Here is my chance to correct that.

Emmart grew up in New Jersey at the height of the space race—he was eight when *Apollo 11* landed on the moon. (Later he would become *Apollo 11* astronaut Buzz Aldrin's illustrator.) He developed his interest in astronomy by visiting the original Hayden Planetarium, where he took classes from the age of ten through high school.

After a Saturday class during the winter of 1973–74, when Emmart was around 13, one of his classmates discovered that he could jimmy open a door in the back of the classroom with his mother's credit card. On the other side of the door was the planetarium library, which at the time was open to planetarium staff only. There, the boys found a stash of photographic plates from the Harvard Observatory. In the following weeks, the boys returned with gloves, flashlight, and magnifying glass in order to study the plates until, as Emmart put it, "a guard came in, threw on the lights, and we were busted." Seeing how pervasive galaxies were on those images gave Emmart an epiphany that he now feels was a career-defining moment. Later, Emmart recalls, after librarian Sandra Kitt got wind of the incident, the boys did penance by helping her move the library to the planetarium's newly built Perkin Wing. (At the time, co-author Thomas Lesser had just joined the planetarium staff, with his first assignment being to help Kitt move the library.) Kitt now recollects that Emmart, who had become a library fixture, "showed an astonishing talent in art and was really exploring his two main interests and figuring out how to combine them."

As an undergraduate at the University of Colorado Boulder, Emmart was a co-founder of The Case for Mars, a group that held a series of conferences over a 15-year period to explore the possibility of travel to Mars. Before joining the American Museum, he had careers in architectural modeling and technical space illustration. When Emmart joined the planetarium as an employee in 1998, Sandra Kitt was still the librarian.

This new version also corrects numerous typographical errors that have been discovered since the initial version's release. Finally, I would like to thank my publisher and readers for making this new version possible, and Neil deGrasse Tyson for writing the new Foreword and for his support throughout the project.

Foreword

Neil deGrasse Tyson

The American Museum of Natural History, on Manhattan's Upper West Side, sits within a school-trip distance of 30 million people. My family as natives of New York City, visited. I visited with classmates. I came by myself. I came with friends. Decades later, I would bring my own kids.

Each display hall represents the slow accretion of architectural spaces, built over time, as vision and budget allowed. Within these spaces, the AMNH pioneered the diorama and the storytelling that it enabled. Previously, museums were cabinets of curiosities—collections of tagged old things on display shelves. But artifacts have history, culture, purpose, and, most importantly, emotional or spiritual value. Why not infuse static collections with a re-created life of their own? One where the visitor could, but does not need to, read the accompanying text because the diorama shows it all—the who, the when, the why, the how, and, most importantly, the context.

And when things are not artifacts but a part of nature itself—drawn from the land, the sea, the air, or the animal and plant kingdoms—they still make excellent dioramas.

My wife, raised in Alaska, was wholly unmoved by the arctic flora and fauna of the Hall of North American Mammals, with its brown bear and caribou. In particular, the moose diorama looked exactly like her walking path to the school bus. Nor did she pause for the colorful aurora borealis, meticulously painted across the diorama back panels. "That just looks like home," she would say.

That's surely some of the best evidence that the museum got it right. But wait, I have more.

My first time in the plains of Africa, at Kruger National Park wild game reserve, I visited a watering hole (from binocular distance) that was crowded and busy with baboons, zebras, giraffes, and wildebeests, with a small herd of large elephants ambling in the distance. My first thought, at once joyous and embarrassing, was "This scene reminds me of the African watering-hole diorama in the Akeley Hall of African Mammals at the American Museum of Natural History!"

Of course not everything in AMNH lives in a diorama. What scene would you build for the fifty-eight-ton Cape York meteorite in the Hall of Meteorites? Its native habitat is the vacuum of space. Or the dinosaur halls: bones, bones, bones. Even so, from its menacing posture, there's no doubt that T-Rex wants to eat you.

This uncanny realism, rampant throughout the museum, is not bound to Earth. Urban kids foster no relationship with the night sky. City lights. Tall buildings. Air pollution. It all impedes your communion with the cosmos. So imagine a nine-year-old child, who had never seen or noticed the night sky before, imprinted by the star-filled dome of the American Museum's Hayden Planetarium. Over the decades, I have come to wonder whether it was not I who chose the universe, but instead the universe that chose me.

Into adulthood, with access to the world's greatest mountaintop observatories, I reflect on the majestic canopies of stars and I (still) say to myself, "These skies remind me of the Hayden Planetarium."

The legacy of the Hayden Planetarium, now part of the Rose Center for Earth and Space at AMNH, extends beyond its architectural footprint. More than 100 books and 1,000 research papers have been published by members of the educational and scientific staff since it was founded in 1935. Becoming its Director (in 1996) was a call to duty, to ensure that the Hayden Planetarium I oversee has no less impact on the hearts and minds of visitors today than the Hayden Planetarium that had touched me so deeply a lifetime ago.

Such was the influence of AMNH on my ambitions and my outlook on the world. And such was the influence of AMNH on generations past and present, as will continue to be its influence on countless generations to come.

Neil deGrasse Tyson is Astrophysicist at American Museum of Natural History and Director, Hayden Planetarium.

Foreword

Kermit Roosevelt III

The American Museum of Natural History is one of our nation's most iconic institutions. It's a staple visit for New York schoolchildren or families, but anyone growing up on the East Coast is likely to have visited. I spent my childhood in Washington, D.C., but still remember wandering through the exhibits. (The dinosaurs are the classic draw for youngsters, but what sticks in my mind are the gemstones in the Hall of Minerals.) As a Philadelphian, a few hundred miles closer, I've had the chance to watch my own children run around under the whale suspended in the Hall of Ocean Life.

The Museum has made its way into popular culture, featured in a number of movies and even a pop song ("Laser Show," by Fountains of Wayne, is about the Hayden Planetarium). Perhaps most famously, J. D. Salinger's alienated teenager Holden Caulfield spends a fair amount of *The Catcher in the Rye* reflecting on his visits to the Museum. He's comforted by the permanence of the exhibits: Nothing changes, no matter how many times you go back.

Holden was not alone in that sentiment. "Nothing changes" is what the Museum's president said in 1968, upon unearthing the time capsule buried in 1874 and reading the newspaper headlines it contained. His reaction was understandable. The capsule was buried during the post–Civil War Reconstruction; by digging it up during the Second Reconstruction of the civil rights era, he had caught one of history's rhymes. But it was wrong. Things do change, as this book reveals. The Museum has grown from a single Victorian Gothic building to a vast (and sometimes bewildering) set of spaces; its location, what its geologist called a "rugged, disconsolate tract of ground," is now the heart of the Upper West Side. The Museum has a Twitter account and a Facebook page. The blue whale was updated for greater accuracy; the original Hayden Planetarium was demolished and replaced. Not even the number of planets is stable. Tracing the path of the Museum's development is fascinating in its own right. But can the story of this institution tell us something more?

Ontogeny recapitulates phylogeny. It's a phrase to warm the heart of a natural history enthusiast. It means that the development of an individual organism repeats the stages of evolution of the species. As a biological hypothesis, it's not quite true, but the idea has application to other fields. Individual athletes, artists, and students, for example, often develop their skills in a manner that parallels the historical development of their discipline.

So too, in a way, with natural history. The Museum has changed, and the world around it, and it is not fanciful to see in the Museum's history some parallels to our own relationship with the natural world. It starts with mastering the environment, making the rough and inhospitable ground into a place fit for our habitation. It continues with expansion and acquisition: We take, we build, we display. In 1915, the Museum's president pronounced that its growing collections had placed it "in the position of a family that has outgrown its home." He wanted new buildings, and he got them. But at a certain point there is no more room. Since the dedication of the Roosevelt Memorial in 1936, little has been added. Instead, the Museum has renovated, modernized, and renewed its existing spaces.

That is a different kind of change, and its implementation requires a different vision, one focused not on expansion and acquisition but on conservation and improvement. It requires that we change—which, inevitably, we do. (In the end, Holden can't go into the Museum for that reason: Its stability will confront him with how much he has changed.) Our ideas of productive engagement with the natural world change; we see ourselves less as conquerors and more as custodians. "The nation behaves well," said Theodore Roosevelt, "if it treats the natural resources as assets which it must turn over to the next generation increased, and not impaired, in value." Like museums, he saw natural spaces as resources for everyone, places all could go to learn, to find themselves, or to forge new identities, as he had. (Of the Museum itself, he told his cousin

Franklin, "You can learn more about nature and life in the Museum than in all the books and schools in the world.")

There is, though, one important way in which the analogy fails. We can live without museums; we can neglect them, let them fall to pieces, and still go on. We cannot live without the environment, for the simple reason that we live within it. In that sense we are less the caretakers of the natural world than its guests. I think often these days of a story I heard about an octopus that discovered it could rearrange the contents of its tank. It shifted around some rocks; it moved a mirror. Then it pulled out the aerator, and I imagine it must have felt pretty smart for a few hours, as the water turned to poison around it.

Preservation, it turns out, requires change: change in ourselves, change in our understanding of our place in the world. We need an attitude not of conquest or idle tinkering but of respect, even awe. How can we promote that? Museums are surely part of the answer, which suggests that perhaps we cannot live without them after all. What the Museum has done, in different ways, through the different stages of its life, is to feed the human sense of wonder at the universe. And that is the one thing that must remain constant if we are to endure.

Kermit Roosevelt is a professor of constitutional law at the University of Pennsylvania Law School and the author of the novels In the Shadow of the Law *and* Allegiance.

How This Book Came to Be Written

Colin Davey

This book would have never been written if I, like so many New York City children, had not grown up visiting the American Museum of Natural History and the Hayden Planetarium countless times as a youngster.

My mother, a native New Yorker who taught science in the city's public schools, herself made regular visits to the museum and planetarium when she was young. And as was the case for so many New Yorkers, the museum and planetarium were a favorite destination for family outings for as long as I can remember. I learned to read at the museum. My mother tells the story of how, when I was three or four, I would look at the exhibits and spell out the labels: "T-i-g-e-r . . . Tiger!" "B-e-a-r . . . Bear!" "B-l-u-e m-a-r-l-i-n . . . Fish!"

When I was a student, the museum and planetarium were frequent destinations for field trips. The museum's gift shops and the planetarium's Book Corner were my parents' go-to destinations for birthday and Christmas presents. Like so many young visitors to the museum, then and now, I was enchanted by the amazingly lifelike dioramas that recreated remote terrains and their unfamiliar inhabitants. I was held spellbound by the reassembled skeletons of dinosaurs, exotic creatures who had roamed Earth tens of millions of years ago. I was mesmerized by the star show at the planetarium and the image of distant heavenly bodies arching through a dark night sky.

I began going to the museum on my own at the age of seven. I visited so often that a planetarium employee eventually recognized me and introduced himself, saying, "From now on, you get in for free. Just say you're with me, Mark Twomey. I work at the Book Corner. To remember my name, just think 'Twomey, as in sock-it-to-me.'" At the time, "sock it to me" was a catchphrase from the popular TV show *Laugh-In*, a phrase that even presidential candidate Richard Nixon had uttered during a cameo appearance on the show. I haven't seen Mr. Twomey since I was seven in 1967, but I would be delighted to remake his acquaintance. If any reader knows him, please put him in touch with me!

The first time I saw the full glory of the night sky far from the smog and light pollution of New York City, where even on a clear night only a handful of stars are visible, I remember gasping, "It's just like the Hayden Planetarium!" The visits to the museum and the planetarium awoke in me a curiosity about science and a scientific way of thinking that would stand me in good stead for my entire life.

Despite my passion for the museum, one thing I remember clearly about all those visits was that I never had any idea exactly where I was in that vast space or how to get from one place to another. For decades, being lost at the museum became a recurring dream. This, no doubt, led to my desire to better understand the museum's physical structure.

Flash forward to 2010. I had been living for three decades in Eugene, Oregon, and was working as a software engineer in the field of neuroscience. I had also developed a deep interest in New York City's history and architecture. Around this time, I began looking for information about the original Hayden Planetarium, which had been demolished in 1997 to make way for the new Rose Center for Earth and Space. To my surprise, information was hard to find. Google searches on "Hayden Planetarium" resulted almost entirely in links about the Rose Center rather than about the original planetarium.

Digging deeper, I discovered some resources on eBay and elsewhere. Most importantly, I met Thomas A. Lesser, whom I found through one of his online comments about the memorable dreamlike scene in Woody Allen's 1979 movie *Manhattan* that is set in the darkened planetarium. Dr. Lesser had been a senior lecturer at the planetarium from 1975 to 1982, after which he held various management positions at the museum. Thus began the collaboration leading to the idea for a book titled *The Heavens in the Attic: The Original Hayden Planetarium, 1935–1997*. In that process, we were encouraged by Neil deGrasse Tyson.

In the process of researching *The Heavens in the Attic*, I learned a great deal about the museum's structure and physical history. I realized that an understanding of its history and architecture could profoundly enhance the experience of visitors and be a valuable aid in navigating the exhibition halls. I also realized that much of this information was not readily available. Thus the idea for a second book: *The American Museum of Natural History and How It Got That Way.*

Perhaps inevitably, it became apparent that these were not two books but rather two halves of a single work. This book is the result.

Preface

Thomas A. Lesser

O ne could still see the Milky Way when I grew up on Long Island. My aunt lived in Queens, and every year for my birthday I would stay with her, and she would take me anywhere I wanted to go in Manhattan. Every year we went to the same place—the American Museum of Natural History and the Hayden Planetarium. Years later my dream came true: I was writing, producing, and presenting sky shows at the Hayden. After overseeing the automation of the (old) Hayden, I was asked to join the staff of the American Museum of Natural History and served in several positions there.

There are numerous people who made working at the Hayden and the museum a fantastic experience for me, too many to mention, but I would especially like to remember Dr. Thomas D. Nicholson (who served as both chairman of the planetarium and later as director of the museum), Helmut K. Wimmer (former art supervisor at the Hayden and an incredible artist), Dr. Kenneth L. Franklin (former astronomer at the Hayden), and Anne Sidamon-Eristoff (former chair of the Board of the Museum).

When Colin Davey contacted me, I realized that there were only a few of us left who knew some of the history and anecdotes about the Hayden. Then we realized that there was also a gap in the printed material about the evolution of the museum. His interest and persistent hard work has created this book, which provides just a glimpse into the history of these marvelous institutions.

Growing up, I loved the museum and the Hayden. I loved working there. Leaving the Hayden and the museum was difficult, but I am fortunate that I still have a love affair with those institutions.

THE AMERICAN MUSEUM OF NATURAL HISTORY AND HOW IT GOT THAT WAY

Introduction

The American Museum of Natural History is one of New York City's most beloved institutions and one of the largest and most celebrated museums in the world. Since 1869, generations of New Yorkers and tourists of all ages have been educated and entertained at the museum. Located across Central Park West from Central Park, the sprawling museum structure, consisting of dozens of separate buildings spanning four city blocks, is a fascinating conglomeration of diverse architectural styles built up over a period of about 150 years.

This is the first book to tell the history of the museum from the point of view of these buildings. It also contains the first history of the museum's astronomy department and Hayden Planetarium. It's a story of history, politics, science, and exploration and features many forceful, colorful, and passionate personalities, including American presidents, New York power brokers, museum presidents, polar and African explorers, dinosaur hunters, and German rocket scientists.

This emphasis on the museum's buildings is especially timely in light of the proposed addition of a major new section, the Gilder Center for Science, Education, and Innovation. The first draft of this book was written before the Gilder Center was announced, and the project is covered in the Epilogue. As this book documents, the Gilder Center is the largest new construction project at the museum since the 1930s. Compared to the previous major project, the Rose Center for Earth and Space, which largely replaced an existing building, the Gilder Center adds about 200,000 square feet for collections, exhibits, and education spaces.

Overview

A quick chronological overview of the story is as follows.

In Chapter 1, the museum's founder, Albert Bickmore, secures the rocky, hilly, swampy site, then known as Manhattan Square, for the museum in 1872.

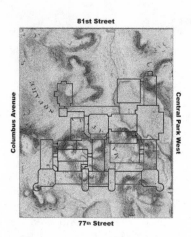

In Chapter 2, Bickmore works with the architects Vaux and Mould to design the cross-in-a-box master plan intended to govern all future building on the site, and then builds the first section, which opens in 1877.

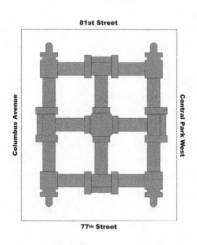
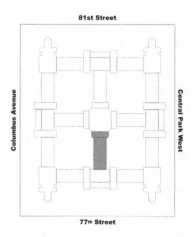

In Chapter 3, the museum's third president, Morris K. Jesup, launches a flurry of building, resulting in the completion of the museum's palatial fortress-like Seventy-Seventh Street façade in 1899. In 1905 and 1908, a couple more sections are added.

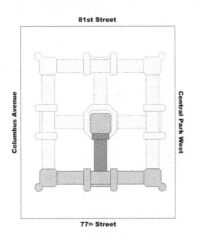
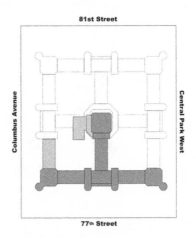

In Chapter 5, the museum's fourth president, Henry Fairfield Osborn, deviates from the master plan by allowing building in the courtyard areas, with the southern portion of Manhattan Square being filled in during the 1920s. During the early 1930s, he gets the Central Park West façade underway, including the monumental Theodore Roosevelt Memorial entrance. Plans are also put in place for building a planetarium in the northeast courtyard, although no funding is yet available.

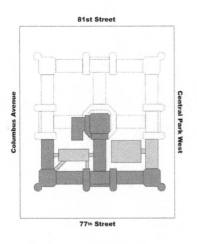
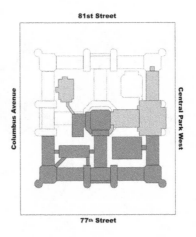

In Chapter 8, we see that from 1936 to 1999 there were no major new sections added to the museum and that buiding was limited to filling in voids in the courtyard areas.

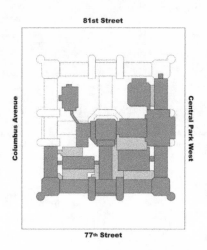

In Chapter 9, the obstacles to building the long-desired planetarium are overcome during the first year of the museum's fifth president, F. Trubee Davison, and the Hayden Planetarium opens in 1935.

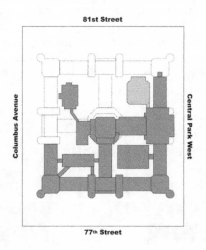

In Chapter 13, under museum president Ellen Futter, along with planetarium director Neil deGrasse Tyson, in an effort to revitalize and modernize the astronomy program, the Hayden Planetarium is replaced by the Rose Center for Earth and Space, which opened in the year 2000.

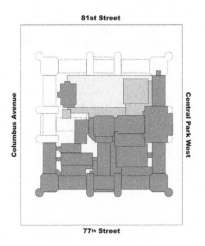

In the Epilogue, on December 11, 2014, the museum announces plans to build the Gilder Center for Science, Education, and Innovation, its largest new construction project since the 1930s.

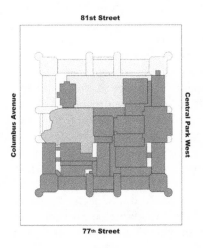

New York History

The history of the museum is so woven into the fabric of the history of New York City and State that to a large extent this is a book of New York history.

As we will see in Chapter 1, the American Museum of Natural History's origin story, including the choice of its location, is intimately tied to the growth of New York City from a small Dutch outpost to a world-class metropolis and the creation of Central Park. It involved some of the most important and colorful characters in the city's history, from the notoriously and epically corrupt and powerful William "Boss" Tweed to one of New York's unsung heroes, Andrew Haswell Green, a founder of Central Park, the American Museum of Natural History, the Metropolitan Museum of Art, the New York Public Library, and the Bronx Zoo, and who is known as the Father of New York City for his role in uniting Manhattan with the Bronx, Brooklyn, Queens, and Staten Island to form the city that we know today.

We will also meet Robert Moses, the legendary and controversial power broker who transformed the New York metropolitan area from the 1920s through the 1960s by overseeing the construction of the region's most important roads, bridges, parks, and beaches, as well as the United Nations and Lincoln Center, among other things. As we will see in Chapter 9 and Chapter 10, Moses played a significant role in the building and early years of the Hayden Planetarium. He also makes cameo appearances in Chapter 5 and Chapter 8. Despite several comprehensive books about Moses and his career, this is the first to detail his roles with the museum and especially the Hayden Planetarium.

Another theme that runs through this book is the long association between the museum and America's twenty-sixth president, Theodore Roosevelt, who spent years in New York City and State government, including a stint as governor. We first meet him in Chapter 1 as a child visiting the early museum that his father helped found. In Chapter 4 we see his support, first as undersecretary of the navy and later as president of the United States, for Robert Peary's mission to reach the North Pole, and in Chapter 6 we accompany him on a safari with Carl Akeley, in which Roosevelt kills one of the elephants on display in the Hall of African Mammals today. And in Chapter 5, we see museum president Henry Fairfield Osborn's effort to memorialize Roosevelt at the museum, an effort in which he was only partially successful.

Expeditions

But of course, the main work of the museum and planetarium is its expeditions, collections, science, research, educational outreach, and exhibits. Obviously this book can't contain a comprehensive survey of these topics. Instead, it presents a selection based on its relevance to the construction of the museum and the planetarium, combined with being personally interesting to the author, and providing an opportunity to contribute new research.

In addition to overseeing the majority of the growth of the museum's buildings, the museum's presidents Jesup and Osborn also oversaw the museum's "golden age of exploration," undertaking research expeditions to every corner of the earth. From this myriad of storied expeditions, this book selects two for in-depth chapters: Robert Peary's exploration of the Arctic during the Jesup presidency and Carl Akeley's exploration of Africa during the Osborn presidency. Incidentally, both these expeditions received critical support from Theodore Roosevelt.

Chapter 4 tells the story of the museum's role in Robert Peary's quest to reach the North Pole and in the acquisition of the thirty-four-ton Ahnighito meteorite, the largest in any museum. Peary is widely, although controversially, credited with leading the first expedition to reach the North Pole, on April 6, 1909. This was the culmination of twenty-three years of effort and eight grueling expeditions to Arctic Greenland and Canada beginning in 1886. The museum and its president Jesup began a long and fruitful relationship with Peary in 1895 when, at the behest of Peary's wife, they funded a mission to bring Peary and his crew home after they were stranded in Greenland at the end of a particularly grueling expedition. The Ahnighito meteorite has been displayed at three locations in the museum, including the original Hayden Planetarium. Each move required a feat of engineering. Although many books have been written about Robert Peary and his polar quest, this is the first detailed telling of the Peary story from an American Museum–centric point of view.

Chapter 6 tells the story of the Akeley African Hall, whose centerpiece is a group of eight elephants and which contains the Mountain Gorilla Diorama, one of the museum's most iconic images. The two-story hall was designed by Carl Akeley, the museum's African explorer, and the six-story museum section that it resides in was specially designed to accommodate the hall. The trajectory of Akeley's entire life led directly to this space, and it was his single-minded focus over the final seventeen years of his life. His work on the hall began in 1909, hunting elephants for the elephant group with Theodore Roosevelt, and it ended in 1926, when he died in Africa in the beautiful region depicted in the gorilla diorama.

The museum is probably best known for its dinosaur exhibits. The gigantic creatures that dominated the earth's surface hundreds of millions of years ago never fail to capture the public's imagination. For more than a century, the museum has been home to the world's most important collection of dinosaur fossils collected over countless expeditions. Chapter 7 traces the evolution of the museum's dinosaur halls, from the origins of modern paleontology, through the growth of its buildings, to the current exhibits, focusing on six of the museum's largest and most beloved specimens, which have historically formed the centerpieces of those halls, including the iconic *Tyrannosaurus rex* and *Apatosaurus* (formerly known as *Brontosaurus*).

Hayden Planetarium

There was no major new construction at the museum from 1936 to 1999. This is the period that spanned the life of the original Hayden Planetarium, to which Part 2 of this book switches focus. For this section, we are joined by my coauthor Thomas A. Lesser, formerly a senior lecturer at the original Hayden Planetarium. As Neil deGrasse Tyson told us when we were beginning this project, "A book on Hayden's history is long overdue." This is the first detailed history of the museum's astronomy department and Hayden Planetarium.

The grand opening of the Hayden Planetarium on October 10, 1935, was the result of many forces and events—cosmological, scientific, economic, and political. Chapter 9 tells this story, starting with early forays into astronomy at the American Museum, the invention of the Zeiss projection planetarium, and the museum's scientific Renaissance man and educator Clyde Fisher. The long-sought planetarium finally became a reality during the Great Depression thanks to the New Deal programs of President Franklin Roosevelt, the lobbying of New York's emerging power broker Robert Moses, and the philanthropy of Charles Hayden, the planetarium's namesake.

Despite the planetarium's auspicious grand opening, by 1941 attendance had been consistently disappointing, and financial difficulties threatened the planetarium's very existence. Chapter 10 describes the elaborate proposal by Robert Moses, along with the industrial and theatrical designer Norman Bel Geddes (who had designed the 1939 World

Fair's Futurama exhibit), for radically redesigning the planetarium. The chapter also describes how the planetarium's financial crisis was ultimately resolved.

As you might expect, the planetarium experienced a heyday during the space race, starting in the years leading up to it and lasting through the Apollo program's Moon landing. But the planetarium also played a significant role in igniting that race. Chapter 11 tells this story, which has its roots in the earliest days of rocket science and includes the stories of two gifted young German rocket scientists and friends: Willy Ley, who fled to America as the Nazis rose to power, and Wernher von Braun, who led the Nazi rocket program.

Chapter 12 guides you through a visit to the original Hayden Planetarium, including:

Black Light Murals, a collection of incredibly realistic, life-sized, fluorescent astronomical images as you might see them from the cockpit of a spaceship or standing on the surface of an alien world;

Your Weight on Other Worlds, a simple but popular exhibit consisting of five scales showing the visitor's weight on the Moon, Mars, the Sun, Venus, and Jupiter;

The Copernican Theater, a forty-foot-wide ceiling-mounted mechanical animated model of the solar system; and

The Sky Theater, where you would see the planetarium's main event, an astronomical topic presented using astonishingly realistic simulations of the night sky projected onto the dome by the Zeiss projector, along with other special effects and projectors.

Astronomia, an innovative, bright, and colorful exhibition hall designed in the 1960s with hands-on mechanical exhibits illustrating abstract astronomical concepts;

As the Apollo program drew to a close in 1972, the public's interest in spaceflight waned, as did the Hayden Planetarium's attendance figures. Chapter 13 tells the story of how efforts in the early 1990s to reinvigorate and modernize the planetarium evolved into plans for the first major new building at the museum in sixty years, after Ellen Futter became the museum's president in 1993 and Neil deGrasse Tyson joined the staff in 1994. The result was the Rose Center for Earth and Space, a gigantic sphere encased in a monumental glass cube on the footprint of the original Hayden Planetarium.

Now, let's start where it all began: a desolate, rocky, hilly, swampy site known as Manhattan Square.

PART I

The American Museum of Natural History and How It Got That Way

1
Manhattan Square

Let's start by looking at what life was like in New York City in 1872, the year the museum was given its home on Eighth Avenue (now Central Park West) opposite Central Park, on a site then known as Manhattan Square (renamed Theodore Roosevelt Park in 1958).

The United States comprised only thirty-seven states. Ulysses S. Grant, the eighteenth president, sat in the White House just six years after the end of the Civil War, the excruciating conflict that had made the former general a household name.

New York City consisted only of Manhattan. The boroughs beyond would not become part of the larger metropolis until 1898. Although construction had begun on the Brooklyn Bridge, it would not open for more than a decade. And even after thirteen years of construction, Central Park itself was still not quite complete. According to the New York historians Robert A. M. Stern, Thomas Mellins, and David Fishman, "though by 1865 New York was the nation's largest city, it was still provincial by international standards."[1]

Nor did Manhattan Square seem an ideal site for such an ambitious project. In his autobiography, Albert S. Bickmore, the museum's founder, wrote, "The first time I visited the square it seemed an almost hopeless task that we were undertaking" because the terrain was so forbidding, dotted with high rocky hills, and the location so desolate.[2] To someone familiar with the flat, manicured grounds on which the museum sits today, the square would hardly be recognizable. The museum geologist Louis Gratacap described "a rugged, disconsolate tract of ground . . .

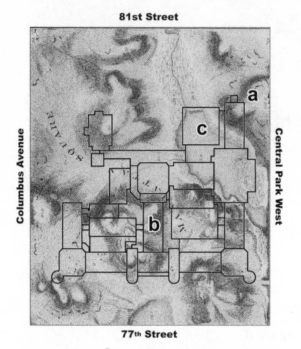

81st Street

Columbus Avenue

Central Park West

77th Street

1870 map of Manhattan Square's topography, with the current American Museum of Natural History floor plan as an overlay.
Source: First annual report of the BCDPP (1871), 276.

Albert Bickmore: "The first time I visited the square it seemed an almost hopeless task that we were under-taking. . . . There was a high hill at the north east corner [a] . . . in the north west corner another hill of solid rock rose much higher than the elevated railroad station, which now stands in its place . . . [The Columbus Avenue El train to which he refers no longer exists] In the southern and central part of the square [b], just where the first section of our building was to be erected, was a third hill, whose crest rose as high as the ceiling of our present Hall of Birds," at the time on the second floor ("Autobiography," 2:29–30).

[c] Hayden Planetarium/Rose Center for earth and space. Note the lake.

where the gneiss ledges protruded their weathered shapes . . . filled with stagnant pools."[3]

And the site was also far from the masses that Bickmore hoped to attract. The adjoining neighborhoods of the Upper East and West Sides were largely undeveloped and unpopulated, with most of the city's residents living below Fifty-Ninth Street, Central Park's southern boundary. During Bickmore's first visit, he recalled, his "only compan-ions were scores of goats," adding, "Only the temporary shanties of squatters could be seen on the north, except two or three small and cheap houses half way between Eighth and Ninth Avenues. On the west were only shanties perched on the rough rocks, and south of us there was no building near."[4] Even a decade later, when the famous Dakota was rising nearby, it was suggested that the apartment building was so named because Manhattan's Upper West Side seemed as remote as America's Dakota Territory, soon to become the states of North and South Dakota.

The Growth of Manhattan and the Creation of Central Park

Nonetheless, the early history of New York City was one of relentless northward expansion. From the time of the original Dutch settlement in 1624 to the Revolutionary War in 1776, the streets of New York occupied the southernmost sliver of Manhattan Island, scarcely stretching above Wall Street. The following decades would witness a steady northward expansion, and by 1811 the streets extended roughly to Greenwich Village, covering about a fifth of the island. Because expansion was haphazard, the resulting street organization was chaotic, and it remains so to this day in Lower Manhattan.

To rectify this, the city commissioners developed a plan, adopted in 1811, intended to guide the city's inevitable northward growth. The plan organized the undeveloped portion of the island into an orderly

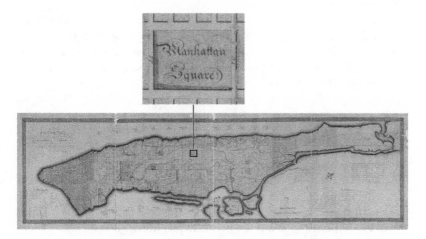

Manhattan Square in 1811, from "Map of the city of New York and island of Manhattan, as laid out by the commissioners appointed by the legislature, April 3d, 1807."
Source: Geography and Map Division, Library of Congress.

grid of rectangular blocks reaching north all the way to 155th Street. Over the next century, Manhattan developed largely as envisioned by the 1811 plan, with one major exception—the addition of Central Park.

The commissioners saw no need for a major public park, and more than four decades would pass before Central Park would be added to the cityscape. However, the plan did include several small "squares," including Manhattan Square,[5] and as a result, the future home of the American Museum existed long before the idea of Central Park was conceived.[6]

One of the earliest calls for a major public park for the city came in 1844 from William Cullen Bryant, the lawyer, poet, and editor of the *New York Evening Post*: "Commerce is devouring inch by inch the coast of the island," Bryant wrote in an editorial, "and if we would rescue any part of it for health and recreation it must be done now. All large cities have their extensive public ground and gardens, Madrid, and Mexico their Alamedas, London its Regent's Park, Paris its Champs Elysées, and Vienna its Prater."[7] As the *New York Times* architecture critic Paul Goldberger would point out a century and a half later, "New York, it was said in the 1840s . . . had nothing in the way of public open space to compare with the great cities of Europe, and if the city was truly to become the international metropolis it took pleasure in seeing itself as, something had to be done."[8]

The movement gathered steam, and on July 21, 1853, the New York State Legislature passed the Central Park Act, authorizing the city to buy the 778 acres bounded by Fifty-Ninth Street on the south, 106th Street on the north (later extended to 110th Street), Eighth Avenue on the west, and Fifth Avenue on the east.[9]

Andrew Haswell Green and the Board of Commissioners of Central Park

Nearly four years later, on April 17, 1857, the State Legislature established the Board of Commissioners of Central Park and appointed eleven men to the board, among them an exceptionally civic-minded New Yorker named Andrew Haswell Green.[10]

Green, a lawyer, was a protégé of the prominent Democratic politician Samuel J. Tilden.[11] Green's career in public office began in November 1854, when he was elected to New York City's Board of Education, serving from 1855 to 1860, a period that overlapped with his time as a commissioner of Central Park. In 1856, he was elected president of the

Board of Education and was reelected the following year. In 1858, he declined to seek or accept the presidency again.[12]

Although Green had accepted the position of Central Park commissioner reluctantly,[13] he quickly became the group's most active member.[14] Within two months of joining the body, he became its first treasurer, and on May 10, 1858, while also serving as treasurer, he became president.[15]

One of the commission's first acts was to hold a design competition for the park. There were thirty-three submissions, and on April 28, 1858, the commission chose as the winner the "Greensward plan" of Frederick Law Olmsted and Calvert Vaux. Both men already had history with Central Park. Olmsted had become the park's superintendent the previous autumn, and Vaux had been instrumental in the decision to hold a design competition in the first place.[16]

On September 15, 1859, the Central Park Commission created the position of comptroller/treasurer, the group's only paid position and one earmarked specifically for Green. At that point, he gave up his law practice to focus on the park, in the process taking control over every aspect of its construction and day-to-day operations.[17] As Green rose through the ranks, he developed a reputation as an austere, incorruptible, and persuasive public servant. He maintained an active interest in education for the rest of his life, and it showed in his vision for Central Park.[18]

Early Plans for Museums and Educational Institutions in the Park

Park planners had intended to include museums and other educational institutions in the new park even before the park's location was selected. In fact, one factor in the selection of Central Park's location was the possibility that it could house institutions of this type.

On January 2, 1852, a special committee released a report comparing the merits of two sites for a public park: Central Park and an area near the East River known as Jones Park.[19] One point in Central Park's favor, the committee concluded, was that the "grounds admit numerous adaptations for ornamental or scientific purposes (as the erection of observatories, or museums, or the formation of a botanic garden, and various other objects), for which 'Jones' Wood' would be too small, and, by reason of its proximity to the river, ill adapted."[20]

The specifications for the Central Park design competition had required "at least one institution of cultural uplift or practical knowledge."[21] Four of the submissions had included a museum in the park, and two had featured a zoo.[22] The winning Greensward plan included a museum but no zoo.[23]

The Greensward plan was among several submissions that identified the Arsenal, located at Sixty-Fourth Street facing Fifth Avenue and one of the few structures that predated the park, as a potential home for a museum or zoo. Built by the state between 1847 and 1851 to store munitions, the Arsenal still stands today, serving as headquarters for the New York City Department of Parks and where, until recently, the original Greensward plan was on display.

On April 15, 1859, the State Legislature passed an act that provided for the establishment of "museums, zoological or other gardens, collections of natural history, observatories, or works of art" in the park.[24] The Central Park Commission's third annual report, published in January 1860, reflected this intent, noting the public's desire for such institutions.[25] The report, however, "deemed it proper that the means for their establishment, maintenance and arrangement should be derived from private sources."[26] The legend to the map that accompanied the report suggested that the Arsenal be altered to accommodate a museum.[27]

Throughout the 1860s, Green and his fellow commissioners focused on bringing to the park both America's first zoo and a museum in which the New-York Historical Society, one of the city's venerable cultural institutions, could display its collections.

The Central Park Zoo

The modern zoo emerged in the early nineteenth century in London, Paris, and Dublin. But by 1859 America still had no such institutions. The Philadelphia Zoo, considered by some to be America's first zoo, was chartered in 1859, but its opening was delayed until 1874 because of the Civil War. Through the early 1860s, Green, along with the park commissioners and the newly formed American Zoological and Botanical Society, strove to create the first American zoo and locate it in Central Park.[28]

In 1860, Olmsted recommended setting aside an area for this purpose on the east side of the park between Seventy-Third and Eighty-Sixth Streets. This site was selected because structures there would not encroach on Vaux and Olmsted's pastoral vision for the park, being isolated from the park proper by two reservoirs.[29] (At the time, it was bounded on the west by the Lower Reservoir, which was located where the Great Lawn now sits. The reservoir was converted to the Great Lawn

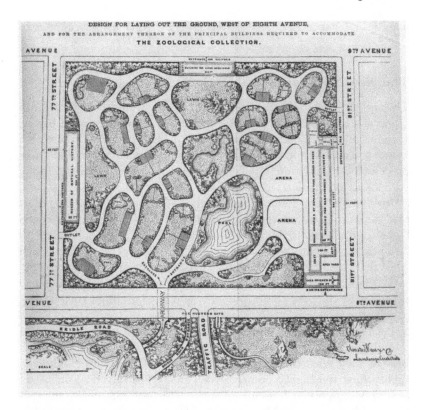

Olmsted & Vaux's design for the proposed zoo on Manhattan Square.
Source: Tenth annual BCCP report (1866), 42.

in the 1930s, with the American Museum controversially involved in the process.) But by 1864, Olmsted and Vaux had become deeply opposed to locating a zoo in the main body of the park.[30]

On April 23, 1864, the State Legislature passed an act annexing Manhattan Square to Central Park and giving the park commissioners the power to establish a botanical and zoological garden. Olmsted and Vaux promptly started drawing up plans for locating a zoo on the site,[31] and in 1868 work began on the foundation and enclosing walls.[32] But even as officials argued about where and how to create the zoo, an ad hoc zoo started forming under their noses, thanks to donated animals. In 1865, the park commissioners placed the menagerie by the Arsenal, where the Central Park Zoo has remained in various incarnations to this day.[33]

The New-York Historical Society

Throughout the 1860s, it appeared that there would be a New-York Historical Society museum in Central Park. The Historical Society, founded in 1804, housed the city's only public art museum, but it no longer had room for its collections. In 1860, the society expressed interest in establishing a museum of antiquities and science in the park, along with an art gallery.[34]

In 1862, the park commissioners indicated in their fifth annual report that the Historical Society's organization, reputation, and collections "would add greatly to the attractions and utility of the park . . . perhaps on a plan somewhat similar to that of the British Museum."[35] On March 25 of that year, the State Legislature passed an act authorizing the Historical Society to use the Arsenal and adjoining grounds as deemed necessary by the park commissioners, with any building expense to be paid by the society.[36]

By 1868, the park commissioners and the Historical Society had thought better of the Arsenal as a location for the society's museum.[37] Instead they selected the eastern portion of Central Park between Eighty-First and Eighty-Fourth Streets facing Fifth Avenue, the site of today's Metropolitan Museum of Art.[38] This was part of the site that Olmsted had nominated for a zoo in 1860. Originally a playground in the Greensward plan,[39] the area was now fenced in for a deer park.[40] The new site was approved by the State Legislature on April 29 of that year.[41]

In 1869, partly for reasons of cost, the Historical Society's project fell through.[42] According to the Central Park Commission's 1869 annual report, "The Board has not been advised of any progress by the New-York Historical Society toward establishing a Museum of Natural History and Gallery of Art, as authorized several years since by an Act of the Legislature."[43]

On May 5 of that year, the State Legislature passed an act authorizing the park commissioners to erect in the park a "Meteorological and Astronomical Observatory, and a Museum of Natural History and a Gallery of Art." The act did not name any specific location or institution. And unlike the earlier acts, which had required the Historical Society to pay building expenses, this one allowed the Central Park Commission to cover these costs.[44]

The map that accompanied the commission's 1869 annual report showed a large complex, designed by Calvert Vaux and assistant Central Park architect Jacob Wrey Mould, on the site previously reserved for the Historical Society and generically labeled "Proposed Art Museum and Hall."[45]

The Historical Society bought its permanent site on Central Park West across Seventy-Seventh Street from the American Museum in 1891. Construction began in 1902, and the opening took place in 1908.[46]

The Paleozoic Museum

As debate over the Historical Society was going on, Green and his fellow commissioners took on a new educational project for Central Park: the Paleozoic Museum, a set of life-size models of dinosaurs from the American continent, similar to those developed for the Sydenham Crystal Palace in London by Benjamin Waterhouse Hawkins and Richard Owen, the superintendent of the natural history department of the British Museum, who first coined the word "dinosaur." By this time, Hawkins and his models had developed an international reputation, and he had become a prominent lecturer and illustrator. In March 1868, he arrived in New York City for a lecture circuit that included the Lyceum of Natural History and Cooper Union.[47]

On May 2 of that year, Green wrote to Hawkins on behalf of the Central Park Commission, asking him to help with the project. Hawkins promptly replied that he was ready to start immediately.[48]

Over the next seven months, Hawkins threw himself fully into the task. He began by making a thorough study of the available fossils found in America. He traveled to Washington, New Brunswick, Albany, New Haven, Philadelphia, and Chicago before settling down to work at the Academy of Natural Sciences in Philadelphia. There he found two of the nation's preeminent paleontologists—Joseph Leidy and Edward Drinker Cope—along with the first nearly complete dinosaur skeleton ever found, a *Hadrosaurus* ("powerful lizard"). The *Hadrosaurus* had been discovered in Haddonfield, New Jersey, in 1858, several years after the opening of the Sydenham Crystal Palace, and it was Leidy who both supervised its excavation and named the beast.

While at Philadelphia, Hawkins created the world's first dinosaur mount, a dinosaur skeleton assembled into a lifelike posture for public display (a technique later perfected at the American Museum), with the *Hadrosaurus* as the subject. The result was three stories tall. This process included drawing and describing every bone fragment, scrubbing off rock debris that was still clinging to many of them, modeling missing bones, devising a way to make molds and create casts of the bones, mounting the actual bones and casts of the modeled missing bones, and shipping the molds to Central Park for his work there—all at his own expense. He also did substantial work with other fossilized specimens. As Edwin Colbert, curator of vertebrate paleontology at the American Museum for forty years, summed up Hawkins's achievements: "He must truly have been a Victorian Hercules performing prodigious labors with fossils, plaster, and clay."[49]

On December 4, Hawkins returned to New York, and three days later he took possession of the upper floor of the Arsenal as a temporary studio. By the following March, he had created a large model of a *Hadrosaurus* in a recumbent position.[50] As Hawkins was starting work in the Arsenal building, the nascent stirrings of the American Museum were taking place.

Albert S. Bickmore

The American Museum of Natural History was the brainchild of the naturalist Albert S. Bickmore. Born on March 1, 1839, Bickmore developed a love of natural history as a child growing up on the coast of Maine. After graduating from Dartmouth in 1860, he began studying under Professor Louis Agassiz at Agassiz's Museum of Comparative Zoology in Cambridge, Massachusetts.

One day in 1861, while working at the museum, Bickmore had the opportunity to talk to Dr. Henry Wentworth Acland, who just that year had founded the Oxford University Museum. In his autobiography, Bickmore recalls asking Acland, "Does it seem strange to you, sir, that Agassiz, our great teacher, should have located his museum of natural history out here in Cambridge, while in Europe the institutions of this character are placed in the political or monetary capitals of the several empires, as London, Paris, Berlin, Vienna?" He went on: "Now New York is our city of greatest wealth and therefore probably the best location for the future museum of natural history for our whole land." Acland's response: "My young friend, that is a grand thought." Bickmore recalled, "I at once determined that I would work for nothing else by day and dream of nothing else by night until I had, at least in some degree, aided in establishing a museum of natural history upon Manhattan Island." However, it would be years before he would realize his dream.

After an expedition to Bermuda in the summer of 1862 to collect tropical marine life specimens for P. T. Barnum's museum, Bickmore volunteered to fight as a Union soldier in the Civil War. After the war, he raised money for an expedition to the Far East, an undertaking that would last from 1865 to 1867.[51] Before his departure, Bickmore made a stopover in New York City, where he lobbied wealthy New Yorkers on behalf of the museum he hoped to create. One of the men he visited was William E. Dodge Jr., a prominent New York businessman and philanthropist with whom Bickmore maintained a correspondence throughout his expedition.[52] By the time he departed, Bickmore had also designed the layout of the future museum. He took this design with him so that when he passed through London toward the end of his journey, he could show it to Richard Owen. Bickmore was gratified to receive Owen's approval.[53]

"Immediately on my arrival back to New York, in December 1867, from three years travel in the Orient, and over Siberia," Bickmore recalled in his autobiography, "I called upon the gentlemen, who had previously expressed the generous hope that when my proposed journeys were completed . . . favorable conditions would then exist for founding" the museum.[54] For Bickmore, the following year would be occupied by the writing and publication of his book *Travels in the East Indian Archipelago* and campaigning for the museum, which consisted of rounding up wealthy and influential New Yorkers to lend their political support and contribute money for the purchase of collections.

William Dodge Jr. was unable to participate actively at that time because he was occupied with the construction of a YMCA building. He did, however, introduce Bickmore to Theodore Roosevelt Sr., a prominent New York City businessman and philanthropist, whose namesake son would be the twenty-sixth American president. Roosevelt joined the cause and recommended inviting a young lawyer named Joseph H. Choate to help with the legal work.[55]

On March 2, 1868, P. T. Barnum's American Museum was destroyed in a fire.[56] This resulted in a March 18 article in the *New York Times* that asked, "Why cannot we now have a great popular museum in New York, without any 'humbug' about it?" The article continued: "In respect to this type of thing, our city is, and always has been, a marvel of poverty. Compared with any one of the hundred larger cities of Europe, we are beneath contempt."[57]

Bickmore's year-long campaign for just such an institution culminated in a letter that he sent to the Central Park Commission on December 30:

"A number of gentlemen have long desired that a great Museum of Natural History should be established in Central Park," the letter began, "and having now the opportunity of securing a rare and very valuable collection as a nucleus of such Museum, the undersigned wish to enquire if you are disposed to provide for its reception and development." The letter was signed by nearly a score of notable New Yorkers, among them J. Pierpont Morgan, the department-store magnate Alexander T. Stewart, Theodore Roosevelt Sr., museum president John David Wolfe, and the future presidents Robert L. Stuart and Morris K. Jesup. Two weeks later, on January 13, 1869, the group received an enthusiastic reply from Commissioner Green in support of the project.[58]

Having secured the support of New York's aristocracy, Green, and the Central Park Commission, Bickmore's next step was to get the State Legislature to pass a law officially establishing the museum. He and Joseph Choate prepared a draft of a charter to present to the museum's newly formed board of trustees at a meeting on February 26. This meeting was held at the home of John David Wolfe, by now the museum's first president. The trustees approved the draft unchanged.

The name "American Museum of Natural History" makes its first appearance in this document.[59] Bickmore wanted a name that echoed that of the British Museum, something that, as he put it, "will indicate our expectation that our museum will ultimately become the leading institution of its kind in our country."[60] Bickmore also paid homage to the British Museum in the title he chose for himself—superintendent—which was Richard Owen's title at the British Museum.[61]

Boss Tweed

It quickly became apparent to all parties that to get a law passed by the State Legislature, it would be necessary to secure the support of William Magear Tweed, also known as Boss Tweed, "whose influence was said to be growing so rapidly," Bickmore wrote in his autobiography, "that it promised soon to become of paramount importance upon the fate of all laws relating to our metropolis."[62] And Choate would later recall: "When it had finally been resolved to establish the American Museum, the first thing was to get a charter from the state, and I went in company with the late William E. Dodge to Albany to consult with members of the Legislature about granting it. To our surprise we found that the matter of granting us a charter depended upon the decision of William M. Tweed, who was then practically in supreme control of the Legislature."[63]

Bickmore's autobiography continues: "A friend of Mr. Samuel J. Tilden procured from him a favorable letter of introduction for me to this senator, and later when I learned the exact situation, I realized that the letter was the one credential I needed to insure the success of my mission."[64] Tilden, Green's longtime friend and mentor, was chairman of the state Democratic Party at the time.

Tweed had begun his career as a chair maker, brush maker, bookkeeper, and firefighter. He then became the foreman of the Americus "Big Six" firefighting company and leveraged this position into a political career. He served in Congress from 1853 to 1855, after which he took control of New York's notorious and powerful Tammany Hall political machine, the muscle of the local Democratic Party, and was elected its chairman in 1863.[65]

Tweed's rise to power continued in meteoric fashion through political skill, graft, and other forms of corruption. In 1867, he was elected to the New York State Senate. And in 1868, the year Bickmore was campaigning for the museum, Tweed's grip on power tightened further as his handpicked Tammany Hall cronies (who became known as the "Tweed Ring," or just the "Ring") attained positions of power. These included John Hoffman and Abraham Oakey Hall, who were elected governor and mayor of New York City, respectively, to be sworn in on January 1, 1869. Hoffman was Tweed's previous handpicked mayor. The voting irregularities in the election were so blatant that a special congressional select committee concluded that the 1868 election had been grossly manipulated, with the total vote count being 8 percent greater than the number of possible voters.[66]

It was probably in late March or early April 1869 that Bickmore made his pitch to Tweed in the senator's Albany hotel room.[67] Bickmore found the political boss to be "a man of portly dimensions and comfortably seated in a large arm chair."

Bickmore: "Senator I am honored by your friend Mr. Samuel J. Tilden, with this letter, and I have also these other letters from other leading citizens in New York City."

Tweed: "Well, well; what can I do for Mr. Tilden?"

Bickmore: "These gentlemen, Senator, whose names are on this paper, have asked me to state to you that they desire to found a Museum of Natural History in New York, and if possible on Central Park . . ."

Tweed: "All right, my young friend, I will see your bill safely through."[68]

Bickmore remained in Albany to keep an eye on matters as the bill establishing the museum worked its way through the legislature and its ultimate signing into law by Governor Hoffman on April 6. It was formally accepted by the trustees at a meeting at Theodore Roosevelt's residence on April 8. The final version was unchanged from the draft that Bickmore and Choate had presented to the museum's trustees.[69]

On November 23, 1869, a meeting took place at the Union League Club that led to the founding of the Metropolitan Museum of Art. This meeting was the result of the activism of many prominent New Yorkers, including William Cullen Bryant; John Taylor Johnston, who became the institution's first president; the Central Park commissioners Green and Stebbins; Central Park's designers Vaux and Olmsted; the New-York Historical Society's William J. Hoppin; and several supporters of the American Museum, including William E. Dodge Jr., Joseph H. Choate, and Alexander T. Stewart. Within five months, on April 13, 1870, the museum was formally established by an act passed by the State Legislature.[70]

The timing was fortunate. Plans for the Historical Society's museum had just fallen through given its cost, thus freeing up the site previously reserved for that institution, and the State Legislature had just agreed to allow the Central Park Commission to pay for the building of a museum. (This was not lost on the Historical Society, whose president would write in 1954 that his institution was "instrumental in fostering the establishment of its great competitor across the park.")[71]

As of the second half of 1869, the Central Park Commission had not yet decided on a site for the Paleozoic Museum. So, the work was put on hold, and Hawkins was asked to make designs and scale models for the zoo planned for Manhattan Square.

In January 1870, a site for the Paleozoic Museum was selected, and excavation and foundation work began for a building designed by Olmsted and Vaux working with Hawkins.[72] The location was inside the park, alongside Eighth Avenue (Central Park West), starting around Sixty-Third Street and extending a half-block to the north.[73] According to the paleontologist Edwin Colbert, "Unfortunately no drawings of what the building was to look like on the outside have come to light, but a lithograph published in the Thirteenth Annual Report of the Board of Commissioners gives us an idea." Colbert added, "It is evident that the influence of the two Crystal Palaces dominated the thinking."[74]

On December 23, 1869, W.A. Haines, chairman of the executive committee of the American Museum, wrote to Commissioner Green, by now also a member of the museum's executive committee, requesting use of the upper two stories of the Arsenal. Green replied approving the request on January 21, 1870.[75]

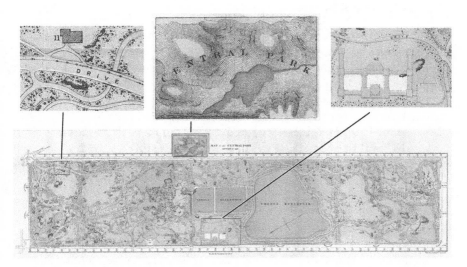

Plans for the development of Central Park, showing the Paleozoic Museum, Manhattan Square, and proposed Art Museum site.
Source: Thirteenth annual BCCP report (1869), 28.

Hawkins described what happened next:

As the Arsenal was required for the Museum of Natural History, it became necessary that my large model and the moulds should be removed, and a small temporary shed was built with a forge. . . . I now had hopes for the commencement of my real proper work, for the comptroller [Green] promised me that the platform on which alone I could erect my models, might reasonably be expected from week to week. But sundry administrative-changes were then taking place which appeared to postpone the advancement of this platform . . . until in the month of May, the total change of the commissioners again presented a barrier to the hoped-for commencement of my own legitimate work.[76]

The change in commissioners that Hawkins referred to stemmed from a power grab by Boss Tweed that would shake up New York city and state politics, including Central Park and all the projects associated with it.

The Tweed Charter

On April 5, 1870, a bill that became known as the Tweed Charter was passed into law. Tweed pushed through the legislation under the pretext of establishing home rule for New York City, an issue that united city residents who had grown resentful of the State Legislature's control over their local affairs. But hidden in the bill was language that further tightened Tweed's grip on power.

The charter abolished the state-controlled commission that had been steadily building Central Park since 1857 and replaced it with a new city-controlled Department of Public Parks—with its own board, ready to be packed with members of the Ring. The department's jurisdiction covered not just Central Park but all the city's parks.

In moving decision-making powers from Albany to Manhattan and in the process stripping powers from the city's elected aldermen, the legislation specifically bestowed those powers on a Board of Apportionment that consisted of the mayor, the comptroller, the president of the Department of Public Parks, and the commissioner of public works.

The Board of Apportionment was filled as follows: The mayor was Tweed's handpicked crony, Oakey Hall. The comptroller since 1867 was Tweed's longtime crony Richard B. Connolly. Shortly after the bill was signed, Mayor Hall appointed Tweed's longtime right-hand man, Peter "Brains" Sweeny, president of the new Department of Public Parks. And the man Mayor Hall appointed commissioner of public works was Tweed himself.

Furthermore, the bill was packed with language that would allow the Ring to maintain their hold on power. For example, once in place, board appointees could not be fired, even by the mayor, short of an act of impeachment.[77]

During the lead-up to the vote on the bill, Samuel Tilden stood out as the bill's most outspoken opponent, arguing that the bill bestowed too much unaccountable power on a small number of public officials. The day before the vote, Tilden spoke at length, including a contentious exchange with Tweed. Green spoke as well, urging that the management of Central Park not change hands.[78]

The Park and Its Museums under the Ring

On April 20, 1870, the Central Park Commission was officially disbanded and replaced by the Board of Commissioners of the Department of Public Parks, which met for the first time on May 3.[79] Green was allowed to remain on the board because removing him would have been politically untenable. But the top two posts, president and vice president, went to Tweed loyalists. Sweeny was named president, and the former judge Henry Hilton became vice president and treasurer. As it happened, Hilton was the lawyer, friend, and right-hand man of Alexander T. Stewart, a supporter of both the American Museum and the Metropolitan Museum.[80]

Green's relations with his new fellow commissioners can be seen in his blistering introduction to the department's first annual report, in which he wrote: "As the name of the undersigned appears on its title page, he deems it due to the public, to his colleagues of the earlier Board, and to himself, to submit this brief disavowal of responsibility for this report, which he never saw till it was in print."[81]

Over the next year, the board of the American Museum had two main tasks: preparing for its grand opening in the Arsenal and working toward a permanent home. Within the first month of the new regime, the museum's board contacted the new Department of Public Parks to verify that the previous arrangements for the use of the Arsenal would be honored. The board was gratified to receive the department's full cooperation, with Commissioner Hilton personally arranging the construction of cases and suggesting improvements and modifications to the building, including workrooms for the curators.[82]

One day, as Bickmore and the museum curators were preparing the exhibits, the elder Theodore Roosevelt brought his twelve-year-old son to the Arsenal. This visit would mark the beginning of the future president's lifelong association with the museum.[83]

On April 27, 1871, the museum held its opening reception in the Arsenal building.[84] By August, the exhibits had expanded into the octagons at the corners of the Arsenal.[85] However, the Arsenal was always intended to be a temporary home for the museum. On November 14, 1870, as the Arsenal was still being prepared for the museum's grand opening, its board members had begun plans to obtain a permanent building. The timing was fortunate, since the Metropolitan Museum, which had been established earlier in the year and shared many supporters with the American Museum, was also seeking a home. In February 1871, the two museums combined forces to petition the State Legislature for land and buildings. They succeeded in gathering forty thousand signatures, including those of some of New York's wealthiest and most influential citizens.

And so once again, it became necessary to secure the support of Boss Tweed in Albany. Four decades later, George F. Comfort, a member of the board of the Metropolitan Museum, recalled that he "and a representative of the Museum of Natural History [Bickmore] took the petition to Albany. Tweed and Sweeny were in power then." Tweed looked at the petition a moment, and, Comfort continued, "instantly, with that celerity of action for which he was noted, he took it to a room, and said: 'You will see Mr. Sweeny. He will take charge of this.' Then Mr. Sweeny took the paper and . . . when he saw the names attached to it . . . as I watched his face, there was not the quiver of an eye, or twitch of the muscles, but he turned quickly and said: 'Please inform these gentlemen that we are the servants of the people.'"[86]

By this point, the Department of Public Parks had already determined that Manhattan Square was inadequate for a zoo because its terrain presented insurmountable drainage and sewage problems.[87] On April 5, 1871, three weeks before the American Museum's grand opening in the Arsenal, the State Legislature passed an act authorizing the park commissioners to construct "in and upon that portion of the Central Park, formerly known as Manhattan Square, or any other public park . . . suitable fireproof buildings" for the Metropolitan Museum and the American Museum.[88] The need for fireproof buildings reflected the fact that the Lyceum of Natural History and P. T. Barnum's American Museum had recently been destroyed by fire.[89]

Tweed and his cronies were far less kind to Professor Hawkins and his Paleozoic Museum. Through 1870, Hawkins continued to get assignments unrelated to the Paleozoic Museum. Fearing that his project was in danger, on September 5 he proposed an alternative plan, incorporating an aquarium into the structure.[90] Despite this, on December 13, the Department of Public Parks resolved to discontinue the Paleozoic Museum and directed "that the present foundation be covered over; and that the site, as far as possible, be converted to the growth of grass and trees."[91]

The commissioners justified the cancellation by noting that the excavations and foundation had already cost $30,000 and that an additional $300,000 would be needed to finish the building, "which was deemed too great a sum to expend upon a building devoted wholly to paleontology—a science which, however interesting, is yet so imperfect as not to justify so great a public expense for illustrating it; certainly not until the living animals in [the] charge of the Department have been properly cared for." The commissioners also feared that the structure would block the view of the park for residents of Central Park West.[92]

Hawkins nonetheless campaigned to revive the project. On March 6, 1871, he brought his case to a meeting of the Lyceum of Natural History where Commissioner Green was in the audience, resulting in the Lyceum passing a resolution in support of Hawkins and his project. The next day, the *New York Times* ran an article about the meeting, including sarcastic remarks by a Mr. E. G. Squier that the only way the museum could be successful "was to elect Tweed as president, Sweeny as Treasurer, and the rest of them as directors" and adding that "the idea of his [Hawkins] trying to get up a museum in this City without a corresponding scheme for dividing the profits was an absurdity." A Dr. Walz "objected to the manner in which the last gentleman had spoken, having a tendency to do more harm than good to their project."[93]

Dr. Walz's remarks proved prophetic. On May 3, 1871, under orders of Commissioner Hilton, all of Hawkins's work of the previous two and a half years was destroyed by sledgehammers and buried. The shattered items included two gigantic dinosaur models, molds, sketches, and sketch models.[94]

In a few months, the Tweed Ring's downfall would begin. By the end of the year, Tweed would be arrested, and Sweeny and Hilton would resign from the Department of Public Parks in disgrace. But it was too late for the Paleozoic Museum.

The Fall of the Ring

Although the political cartoonist Thomas Nast had been skewering Tweed and the Ring in *Harper's Weekly* since 1867 and the *New York Times* had begun an editorial campaign against them in late 1870, these efforts had scant effect on the Ring's continuous rise to power.

The Ring's downfall began abruptly when James O'Brien, a former sheriff and disgruntled former crony, got his hands on documents from Comptroller Connolly's office showing massive theft by the Ring through overcharges, kickbacks, fraud, and money laundering. O'Brien handed the evidence to the *New York Times* on July 18, 1871. Starting the next day and continuing daily through July 29, the newspaper published devastating exposés.[95] The reporting ignited a firestorm of anti-Ring sentiment. The drama mounted when, on the evening of Saturday, September 9, there was a mysterious burglary of the comptroller's office.

The only thing stolen was evidence relating to the *New York Times* articles, suggesting a cover-up.

As the calls for reform mounted, Samuel Tilden remained quiet publicly. But when an opportunity to deliver a fatal blow to the Ring presented itself, he pounced. Comptroller Connolly must have seemed the obvious choice for fall guy, and Mayor Hall began calling for his resignation. But Connolly had other ideas. He decided to hire a lawyer and throw in with the reformers. The former mayor William Havemeyer suggested that Connolly hire the reformer Tilden to represent him.

On September 14, Tilden was surprised to receive a request from Connolly for an appointment. They met the next day, and after Connolly asked Tilden to represent him, Tilden made a counteroffer. He would not be Connolly's lawyer, but he would help Connolly if he stayed in office and cooperated with the reformers. After Connolly left, Tilden hatched his plot. He found a provision in the Tweed Charter that allowed the comptroller to transfer his powers to a deputy, and no one could fire either man. And Tilden had just the person in mind for the position of the deputy who would become acting comptroller: his longtime friend and protégé, the comptroller of Central Park, Andrew Haswell Green.

That evening, the men had planned to meet again, but Connolly didn't show up. Havemeyer rushed to Connolly's residence and found him in a panic, ready to back out of the deal. But Havemeyer managed to buoy up Connolly's courage. The next morning, September 15, Connolly, Tilden, Green, and Havemeyer met to execute the plan. By five o'clock that evening, Green had been sworn in as deputy and taken control as acting comptroller, and announcements had been sent to the newspapers. With this maneuver, Tilden and Green had quietly used Tweed's own charter and Ring member against him to take control of the most powerful office in city government. Tweed and the other Ring members wouldn't learn what happened until they read about it in the newspapers.[96]

As city comptroller, Green had his work cut out for him. Between January 1869 and the summer of 1871, the city's debt had had ballooned from $36 million to $97 million.[97] A $2.7 million interest payment was coming due in November, and the city coffers only contained $2.5 million.[98] Thousands of municipal employees, unpaid for weeks, were clamoring for their money.[99]

On October 27, Tweed was arrested.[100] On October 31, Connolly resigned as comptroller, and on November 18, Green became the city's permanent comptroller. On November 25, Connolly was arrested, shortly after which he jumped bail and fled the country.[101] In November, Sweeny and Hilton resigned from the Department of Public Parks, and Sweeny fled to Paris.[102] Green regained control of the Park Commission, and despite his awesome responsibilities as city comptroller, continued as park commissioner until May 1, 1873.[103]

The Museums Get Their Homes

As late as February 5, 1872, the plan was for both the American Museum and Metropolitan Museum to be located in Manhattan Square, the site selected during the Tweed regime.[104] Acting under this understanding, representatives of both museums met with architects to prepare a set of recommendations, and it was determined that since the two museums had very different needs, the buildings should be designed independently.

After Green regained control of the Park Commission, the trustees of both museums and the park commissioners revisited the issue of the museums' locations, holding meetings and site-inspection trips. The first site offered the American Museum was the site the Metropolitan Museum occupies today.[105] Also considered as a possible site for both museums was Reservoir Square on Forty-Second Street and Fifth Avenue, where the Main Branch of the New York Public Library and Bryant Park are now located. In fact, it was the unanimous choice of the Metropolitan Museum's executive committee, given its centralized location in the developed portion of Manhattan, despite the limited space for expansion.[106]

But the ultimate decision rested with Green, and on March 20, he offered a resolution, passed by the Park Commission, selecting the final sites for both institutions.[107] The Metropolitan Museum was placed on the site Green and the park commissioners had proposed in 1868 for an art museum, and Manhattan Square and the American Museum were finally united.

John David Wolfe, president of the American Museum, died May 17, 1872, just months after seeing his efforts to establish the museum come to fruition. He was replaced by Robert L. Stuart.

Epilogue: What Became of Them?

Here's how life unfolded for some of the major players in this drama:

William Tweed spent the rest of his life in and out of jail. In 1875 he slipped past his guards and escaped to Spain, but the Spanish police recognized him and turned him in. He died in prison on April 12, 1878.

Richard Connolly spent the rest of his life in exile, dying in Marseilles in 1880 a broken man.[108]

Peter Sweeny lived in exile in Paris until 1886, when he negotiated a deal allowing his return to the United States after paying $400,000 in exchange for being officially exonerated.[109] He lived the rest of his life in the shadow of the Tweed Ring, unsuccessfully trying to clear his name.[110]

From 1872 to 1876, Benjamin Waterhouse Hawkins appealed unsuccessfully to the Park Commission for compensation for unpaid salary, expenses, interest, breach of contract, lost opportunities, and damage to his reputation.[111] In the meantime, he created a major dinosaur mural and *Hadrosaurus* reconstruction for Princeton University and continued to lecture around the country before retiring to England, where he died at the age of eighty-six.[112]

Samuel Tilden led the prosecution of the Tweed Ring and became governor of New York in 1875. In 1876, he ran against Rutherford B. Hayes for president, and although he won the popular vote, he lost in the Electoral College.

Andrew Haswell Green went on to become one of the most consequential, yet unsung, figures in New York City history. He remained city comptroller until 1876, after the city's finances had been repaired. He helped found the New York Public Library, chartered in 1895, when, as an executor of Samuel Tilden's estate, he arranged for the library bequeathed by Tilden to be combined with the existing Astor and Lenox Libraries. And he played a leading role in the founding of the Bronx Zoo (originally named the New York Zoological Park) in 1895. But perhaps Green's most important contribution to the city's history was his effort to unite Manhattan with the Bronx, Brooklyn, Queens, and Staten Island. Green first articulated the vision of a united New York City in 1868 (during the early stirrings of the American Museum), and he lobbied for the plan until it became a reality in 1898. For this achievement, he is known as the Father of New York City.

2

The Master Plan and the Bickmore Wing

The building of the American Museum of Natural History's first section, now known as the Bickmore Wing, involved two ceremonies led by two US presidents. On June 2, 1874, President Ulysses S. Grant led the cornerstone-laying ceremony. And on December 22, 1877, five years after the museum received its home in Manhattan Square, President Rutherford B. Hayes led the grand-opening ceremony.

Once the Manhattan Square site was selected for the American Museum, the next order of business was designing the building and preparing the grounds. In the summer of 1872, the park commissioners assigned the Central Park architects Calvert Vaux and Jacob Wrey Mould the job of designing buildings for the two sister museums, the American Museum and the Metropolitan Museum. This team was the natural choice. Vaux had co-designed the park's Greensward plan with Frederick Law Olmsted. Mould, the park's assistant architect from 1858 to 1870 and its architect in chief during 1870 and 1871, had collaborated with Vaux on the design of Bethesda Terrace and Fountain, the park's architectural heart, among many other park features. And in 1869, before the Metropolitan Museum was founded, the two men had worked together on designs for an art museum on the site that would later be occupied by the museum. On June 12, 1872, the park board requested that Vaux consult with the American Museum's executive committee and report back to the board with a design for the institution.[1]

Vaux and Mould invited Bickmore to meet with them and bring the initial design he had shown to Richard Owen of the British Museum in 1865. That plan envisioned a central dome with two wings radiating from it, similar to the Capitol Building in Washington, DC. The wings were designed to provide space for a series of T-shaped display cases and would each contain an end section with staircases and rooms for curators.[2]

The architects came up with a master plan that extended this initial design. Two wings were added, forming a Greek cross. The end sections were extended to form broad façades fronting on Seventy-Seventh Street, Eighty-First Street, Central Park West, and Columbus Avenue. Each façade was a sort of replication of the initial design and formed a square. This design resulted in four courtyards that would provide natural lighting to the interior sides of the halls. In this way, the design would fill Manhattan Square, resulting in a building that would be the largest on the North American continent and the world's largest museum.[3] Visitors would be able to circulate around the museum's perimeter as well as cross from east to west and north to south.

The design was cleverly broken into modular sections (central, entrance, and corner pavilions; wings, and transepts) that could be built one at a time, allowing the final structure to take shape gradually, with new sections being added as the need and funding arose. Since money was available only for one building, the museum chose to build the south transept first, as opposed to a street-facing façade, so as to lay claim to the entire Manhattan Square.[4]

The architectural style Vaux and Mould selected for the façade was a medieval Gothic style from Venice from the fourteenth century. This style, characterized by polychromatic brickwork, vertical lines, and gothic arches, had experienced a revival during the Victorian era thanks to the writings of the British architecture critic John Ruskin and is often described as Ruskinian Gothic, high Victorian Gothic, or Gothic Revival.

In August 1872, Vaux and Mould submitted their plan to the park board, the board approved the plan, and cost estimates were made and approved.[5] At the same time, the site was being prepared. This included removing squatters, along with their herds of goats and pigs,[6] leveling the grounds, removing rocks, and filling in the sections that were below ground level.[7]

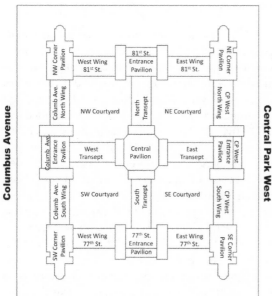

81st Street

Vaux and Mould's
1872 master plan.

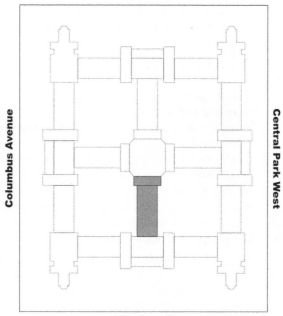

81st Street

The museum's first wing,
aka the Bickmore Wing.

The Laying of the Cornerstone

In the spring of 1874, after the foundations and walls of the first floor were completed, the trustees invited President Ulysses S. Grant for a formal cornerstone-laying ceremony.[8] Shortly after four o'clock on June 2, a beautiful spring Tuesday, Grant arrived, accompanied by Secretary of State Hamilton Fish, Secretary of War William W. Belknap, and Secretary of the Navy George M. Robeson. The festivities included live music provided by the Dodworth Band, a celebrated brass ensemble. Attending the event were Mayor William Frederick Havemeyer; Andrew Haswell Green; members of the museum's board of trustees, including J. P. Morgan;[9] a group of squatters who had recently been removed from the site;[10] and a herd of goats.[11]

After an opening prayer, speeches were made by the museum's president, Robert L. Stuart; the Parks Department's president, Henry G. Stebbins; Governor John Alden Dix; and Joseph Henry, secretary of the Smithsonian Institution. After the speeches, a time capsule was placed into the cornerstone—a copper box containing documents related to the museum and Central Park, fifteen newspapers and periodicals, some currency, and other odds and ends.[12]

President Grant smeared mortar over the cornerstone with a specially engraved ivory and silver trowel ordered for the occasion from Tiffany's. (The trowel was presented to Grant as a souvenir and is now in the Smithsonian's National Museum for American History.)[13] The ceremony was followed by a visit to the museum at its Arsenal location.

The Grand Opening

Several years later, as the museum's grand opening approached, once again the president of the United States, now Rutherford B. Hayes, was recruited for the ceremony. In the week preceding the opening, the museum was lit up so brilliantly it could be seen from New Jersey.

On the afternoon of the event, Saturday, December 22, 1877, the *New York Times* reported that "much of the available ground in the neighborhood was filled with carriages" that had carried "many of the best known and most distinguished ladies and gentlemen of the city." The ceremony took place on the second floor, which seated eight hundred. The third-floor gallery, which overlooked the space, seated several hundred additional guests, and it was standing room only for hundreds

The cornerstone of the Bickmore Wing, being laid by President Grant on June 2, 1874.
Source: *Leslie's Illustrated Newspaper*, June 20, 1874, 32.

more. Outside milled countless spectators who could not gain admission but hoped for a glimpse of the president.[14]

At 2:30, after President Hayes and his party were given a private tour of the museum, the ceremonies began. The speakers sat at a platform assembled for the occasion while a band played at the opposite end of the hall. After an opening prayer, speeches were delivered by the museum's president, Robert L. Stuart; the Parks Department's president, William R. Martin; Charles W. Eliot, president of Harvard University; and the paleontologist Othniel C. Marsh.[15] Finally, President Hayes spoke: "Mr. President and ladies and gentlemen," he began. "Without introduction, I now proceed to perform the honorable but brief and simple duty assigned to me. This enterprise, so noble, so splendid, which the country owes to the enlightened liberality of the city and citizens of New York,

The Bickmore Wing viewed from the location of the current planetarium in 1878, shortly after its opening. Note the rough landscape.
Source: Harroun & Bierstadt/Museum of the City of New York. X2010.11.1234.

The Bickmore Wing, as seen from the roof of the Dakota, 1880.
Source: Photography © New-York Historical Society.

is now ready to be opened to the public; and I now declare, the opening ceremonies having been completed, that the American Museum of Natural History is now opened."[16]

Epilogue: The Time Capsule

Around 1919, the year of the museum's fiftieth anniversary, an interest developed in the time capsule that had been placed in the cornerstone back in 1874. However, no one could find it.

On September 17, 1941, perhaps with the museum's forthcoming seventy-fifth anniversary in mind, museum director Wayne M. Faunce tried to pick the brain of the only person still alive who had attended the cornerstone-laying ceremony sixty-seven years earlier. That day, Faunce wrote to Edward Ringwood Hewitt, the son of one of the museum's early trustees, who had been seven at the time of the ceremony. "It is a source of chagrin that no one now connected with the museum knows the location of this cornerstone," Faunce wrote. "Can you throw any light on the matter?" Hewitt replied that "the whole place was covered with a cloth except the stone," adding, "There would be no way in which a small boy could tell where it was as there was a wooden stand erected all over the place."[17]

Around 1965, with the museum's 1969 centennial approaching, interest in finding the cornerstone was renewed yet again, and Robin Smith, the museum's librarian and archivist, was asked to keep an eye out for any new information. Aware that the search had been going on for about half a century, she was not confident.

But then a clue surfaced in the form of a June 3, 1874, article in the *New York Times* that stated that "full Masonic rites were observed in the ceremony." This detail suggested that the cornerstone was in the northeast corner, as called for by Masonic tradition. In the summer of 1968, a museum volunteer named Richard Weil found another article about the ceremony in a copy of the *Daily Graphic* from June 4, 1874. An accompanying sketch also suggested the cornerstone was in the building's northeast corner.

Then, one day when Smith was doing research in the Bickmore archives, she found a 1910 letter in which Bickmore recalled the "striking scene" of the cornerstone laying. "So many of my former associates have passed away," he wrote, "that I find that I am probably the only person still living who can tell you from his own personal observation, the exact stone which the general placed in the exterior of our first section on that historic occasion . . . under my office window." Bickmore indicated that the stone had a cross carved into it.

With this new information, drilling through the children's cafeteria began at eight in the morning on November 19, 1968. By four that afternoon, workers found a stone carved with a faded cross, inside of which was a copper box, which was immediately placed in a safe. Two days later, the capsule was opened in the presence of several descendants of the museum's founders, including J. P. Morgan's great-grandson and Joseph Choate's grandnephew.

After reading headlines of the 1874 newspapers about cabinet shakeups, civil rights, criticism of the police, and concern about communism, the museum's president, Gardner D. Stout, remarked, "Nothing changes."[18]

The museum celebrated its hundredth anniversary in 1969 with a yearlong exhibition called "100 Years of Wonder," which included the items from the time capsule.[19]

3

The Jesup Years (1881–1908) and the Seventy-Seventh Street Façade

Despite an upbeat opening ceremony, the newly opened museum was immediately in trouble. The day after the opening ceremony, Albert Bickmore, the museum's founder and superintendent, found the exhibition halls deserted because of the museum's isolated location.[1] Only a few hundred people a week made the long trip from Lower Manhattan by horse car.[2] Bickmore pinned his hopes for improved attendance on the rumored northward extension of the Columbus Avenue elevated train line,[3] and on June 9, 1879, the extension was complete, including an Eighty-First Street station.[4] Yet in 1880, the museum's Arsenal location, which remained open until 1886 to house collections that would not fit in the main building,[5] still attracted double the attendance of the main building.[6] Even the attendance at the museum's trustees meetings fell off during these years.[7]

As a result of its extravagant spending on collections, the museum also faced financial problems. For example, in 1874 the museum bought the Hall collection, a trove of tens of thousands of fossils so important that they inspired the nomenclature of the geological structure of North America.[8] But as a result of this spending, the museum remained in debt for years.

By February 1880, Bickmore faced a mutiny among the trustees, who, disappointed with the museum's attendance and financial state, clamped down on spending. They also assigned Morris Ketchum Jesup, a museum founder and member of the executive committee, to study the institution's future needs,[9] assuming that he would propose to curtail the museum's operations and expenses. Because his background was in business rather than science, he seemed the right man for the job.

Early that spring, Jesup began visiting the museum daily.[10] After carefully examining every aspect of its work, he surprised the trustees, and perhaps himself, by urging expansion rather than contraction of the institution. He recommended increasing the museum's income, preferably through an endowment, reorganizing the business office, and making the exhibits more interesting to the public by adding, as he put it, "lions and other big animals." The trustees were impressed with Jesup's enthusiasm. And when Robert Stuart resigned from the museum presidency on February 14, 1881, because of ill health, Jesup was the unanimous choice to replace him.[11] Stuart died the following year.[12]

Although Jesup's twenty-seven-year administration transformed the museum, he had an unlikely background for this role, having only a sixth-grade education and no training in science. He had been born into wealth, but when he was seven, his family's fortune was wiped out in the Panic of 1837. This was followed almost immediately by the death of his father, leaving his mother with eight children to support. All but one sibling eventually died of tuberculosis. When Jesup was twelve, he dropped out of school to support his mother by working as a Wall Street messenger boy. From this humble beginning he learned the ropes of business. By the time he became a museum founder in 1869, he had amassed a fortune in the banking and railroad businesses and had become a generous philanthropist.[13]

Unlike the museum's first two presidents, who were happy to leave the running of the institution to Bickmore, Jesup took an active role in the institution's affairs.[14] His enthusiasm, along with large contributions of his own money, invigorated the spirits of the trustees, and by 1882, they accepted his report urging construction of another section of the museum.[15]

The Sunday Issue

After winning over the trustees, however, Jesup hit a wall in gaining political support for any new construction or, indeed, any funding. Over the next decade a controversy would erupt over whether the American Museum (along with the Metropolitan Museum) should open on Sundays. Neither museum did so because their Presbyterian trustees believed in keeping a "strict old-fashioned Sabbath." As a result, most New Yorkers, who worked six days a week, were unable to visit those institutions.

The sabbatarians (those opposed to Sunday openings) included the majority of trustees of both museums, many of the museums' contributors, conservative religious leaders, and much of the city's elite. Jesup was regarded by the *New York Times* as the "life and soul of the opposition" to Sunday openings.[16] In addition to being president of the American Museum, he was president of the New York City Mission and Tract Society and of the American Sunday School Union, and he was a founder of the Presbyterian Hospital and the Brick Presbyterian Church.[17] The sabbatarian camp also included Bickmore.[18]

The antisabbatarians (those in favor of Sunday openings) included labor activists, secularists, women's groups, progressive Christian religious leaders, and Jewish, German, and Irish organizations, representing three of the city's major immigrant groups. Since they composed a substantial voting bloc, the antisabbatarians had the support, throughout the 1880s, of the mayors William Russell Grace, Abram S. Hewitt, and Hugh J. Grant. The antisabbatarian camp also included Joseph Choate, the trustee of both museums who wrote many of their founding documents.[19]

The sabbatarians argued that opening on Sundays would "desecrate and secularize the Sabbath."[20] They also couched their argument in prolabor, nonreligious terms, proposing that Sunday openings would actually be a slippery slope toward workers, who were already working six days a week, losing their only day of rest.[21]

In summarizing the antisabbatarian position, the *New York Times* concluded, "New York is too varied and cosmopolitan and its foreign and liberal element too large to admit of the strict application of the old-fashioned idea of the Sabbath."[22] The antisabbatarians also pointed out that Sunday openings would uplift the community by giving the masses access to educational opportunities otherwise unavailable to them, adding that with the museums off-limits, these same masses would be more likely to turn to saloons for their Sunday recreation.[23]

The antisabbatarians also argued that the workers' tax dollars supported the museums, so it was only fair that they should be able to enjoy those institutions. The sabbatarians argued that opening on Sundays would increase the museums' expenses. At the very least, the extra expense would need to be made up.

The sabbatarians most potent argument, however, was that three-quarters of the museums' revenues came not from the tax-funded state coffers but from private donors, many of whom gave on the condition that the museums would observe the Sabbath, and they predicted that much of this income would disappear if the museums opened on Sundays. For example, in 1886, the trustees of both museums suspected that Mary Stuart, the widow of former American Museum president Robert L. Stuart, was planning on leaving large gifts for both museums in her will. But they were worried that she would cancel the gifts if the museums opened on Sundays. After she died in 1891, the trustees learned that her will had indeed contained generous gifts to both museums but that she had revoked the gifts when she came to believe that the museums would probably open on Sundays eventually.[24]

A similar controversy—whether concerts should be allowed in Central Park on Sundays—raged on through the 1860s and 1870s.[25] As early as 1877, a letter writer to the *New York Herald* asked why is it "that the museum at Central Park is kept closed on Sundays as if to exclude the working classes, the real payers of all the burdens?"[26]

Late in 1880, several politicians attacked the trustees of the museums, accusing them of closing the institutions on Sundays to "keep the people down."[27] On April 20, 1881, the parks commissioners received a petition from ten thousand citizens asking that the museums be opened on Sundays.[28] In 1882, Mayor William Russell Grace adamantly opposed any spending for new construction at the museum, so Jesup and the trustees decided to wait until Grace was out of office before pushing the issue again.[29] Attacks on the trustees by various New York politicians continued from 1881 to 1884.[30]

In the spring of 1885, the city's park commissioners and the Board of Aldermen passed resolutions asking the trustees of the two museums to open on Sundays.[31] That October, New York's Board of Estimate and Apportionment asked the presidents of both museums to come to Mayor Grace's office to make their cases for remaining closed on Sundays. Jesup spoke for both museums. His arguments were published in pamphlet form as *The Museums in the Park: Should They Be Opened on Sunday?*

Pressure to open Sunday quickly mounted, yet Jesup and the trustees refused to relent. In late November, Samuel P. Putnam, secretary of the American Secular Union, responded by circulating a petition on behalf of Sunday opening. Putnam's petition received extensive coverage by the *New York Times*, and by March it had gained nine thousand signatures as well as the support of the Central Labor Union, representing fifty thousand workers.[32]

By that time, the collections of the American Museum had grown so large that the institution desperately needed a new wing, and on January 1, 1887, the *New York Times* reported that the American Museum's trustees were proposing to go to the State Legislature for funding for a new building. But there was little chance of success without the consent of the city.[33] That day, Abram Hewitt, a supporter of both museums since their inceptions, succeeded the obstructionist William Grace as mayor. Yet even Hewitt told Jesup that unless the museums opened on Sundays, "he personally doubted if either museum would ever again be granted public funds for any purpose."[34]

Several days earlier, on December 27, 1886, the Board of Estimate and Apportionment had offered both museums an additional $5,000 a year if they would open on Sundays.[35] The trustees debated accepting the board's offer for about a month before deciding to postpone the decision.[36] The issue was finally resolved two years after the original offer, on December 26, 1888, with a compromise: Each museum would get an additional $10,000 a year, but they would *not* open on Sundays. Instead, they would add two evenings a week to their schedule, installing new lighting technology for this purpose.[37]

Plunkitt and Cady, Berg & See

In their quest for money for a new building, the American Museum finally found an ally at the State Legislature in the powerful Democratic senator George W. Plunkitt. On January 20, 1887, he introduced a bill allowing the city's Board of Estimate and Apportionment to finance the project. After several attempts by legislators to amend the bill to require Sunday openings, the bill passed without any such amendment a month later.[38]

Early the following year, it was decided that the new section would be the Seventy-Seventh Street entrance pavilion.[39] By the fall of 1888, excavation was complete, and the design and architects had been chosen.[40] Calvert Vaux consulted on the design,[41] Jacob Wrey Mould having died in 1881, and at least two designs were considered, both based on Vaux and Mould's master plan. The architect R. H. Robertson submitted a design similar in style to Vaux and Mould's original building.[42]

But the design selected was the one submitted by the firm of Cady, Berg & See (the partners were Josiah Cleaveland Cady, Louis DeCoppet Berg, and Milton See).[43] Cady, Berg & See had already done some work

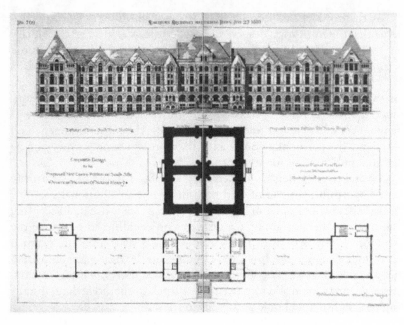

R. H. Robertson's design for the Seventy-Seventh Street façade, 1889.
Source: American Architect and Building News 26, no. 709 (July 27, 1889): 37.

for the museum, having designed a renovation of the entrances of the original buildings in 1881.[44] The firm had also previously designed the original Metropolitan Opera House, which opened in October 1883. (It was demolished in 1967, after the opening of Lincoln Center.)

Cady, Berg & See created a palatial fortress-like design based on the Richardsonian Romanesque style popular at the time. The original Romanesque style, dating from approximately AD 700 to 1100, had its roots in classical Roman architecture and was the predecessor to the Gothic style in Europe. The influential architect Henry Hobson Richardson popularized his interpretation of Romanesque architecture, which was faithful to the classical tradition.[45]

Each façade (on Seventy-Seventh Street, Eighty-First Street, Central Park West, and Columbus Avenue) would have a central entrance pavilion with an wide arched carriage entrance (porte-cochère) framed on each side by a staircase curving up to meet a porch with seven arches above the entrance. The stories above the porch would be divided into three bays by narrow turrets, and the pavilion would be framed on each side by a forward-projecting turret tower with a conical roof.

The corner pavilions would feature a turret tower rising above the rest of the façade with carved eagles perched on wreaths distributed around the base of steep conical roofs. The wings connecting the entrance pavilion to the corner pavilions would, like the upper portion of the entrance pavilion, be divided into three bays by narrow turrets. The design also featured a sky-scraping tower at the museum's center.

To create exhibition spaces uninterrupted by columns, the building's design called for twenty-eight of the largest girders ever used in the construction of a building, each sixty-two feet long and weighing twenty tons. In May 1889, the longest and strongest available trucks were used to transport the girders to Manhattan Square from the Hudson River near Fiftieth Street, each pulled by twelve horses. During the journey, several of the trucks collapsed under the weight of their load.[46]

The Sunday Issue Redux

While the horses were struggling with the girders, Jesup and the trustees again found themselves struggling with the Sunday issue. That May, Mayor Hugh J. Grant, who had succeeded Hewitt, tried to block the Board of Estimate and Apportionment from giving the museum a new round of funding needed to complete the building unless the institution agreed to Sunday openings. Jesup and the trustees were saved once again when the city's corporation counsel reported that the board lacked the authority to issue such a requirement. Reluctantly, the mayor relented and voted for the funding while declaring, "I think it's an outrage to deprive a large portion of the public of the only opportunity they have to look upon . . . the exhibits of the museum."[47]

In the spring of 1891, as the new wing of the American Museum was being built, the antisabbatarians mounted a fresh attack on the Metropolitan Museum, resulting in a petition with thirty thousand signatures and a pledge of enough money to pay for the extra Sunday expenses for an experimental four months. On May 18, after prolonged deliberations, the Metropolitan Museum's trustees finally agreed to start opening on Sunday afternoons.[48]

Two days later, a New York Times headline declared, "Only a Question of Time: When the Natural History Museum Will Open Sunday Too."[49] That event, however, would not take place until more than a year later, on August 7, 1892, after the trustees were able to observe the

Metropolitan Museum's successful experiment and resolve how the Sunday openings would be paid for.[50]

To his credit, Jesup subsequently recanted his opposition to Sunday openings, telling a friend years later: "For a long time I stoutly opposed opening the city museums on Sundays . . . I frankly acknowledge my opposition to the plan originally to have been caused by ignorance pure and simple." Jesup attributed his change of heart to what he described as the "satisfaction to me to watch the weekly returns registered in the museums of the Sunday afternoon attendance, knowing that it is made up of persons who are too busy to enjoy these pleasures on other days."[51]

Renewed Building

The new wing formally opened on November 2, 1892,[52] and the next eight years proved a boom time for construction at the museum. Once the museum started opening on Sundays, there was much less resistance to new funding. New buildings were needed thanks to the rapid growth of the collections, and the alliance with State Senator Plunkitt was highly productive. He passed bill after bill for funding new construction.[53]

During this period, with help of the architects Cady, Berg & See, the museum completed the entire Seventy-Seventh Street façade, along with a central auditorium. This included the east wing, built from 1894 to 1895; the west wing (1895–1897); the southeast corner pavilion (1897–1899); the southwest corner pavilion (1897–1899); and the auditorium (1899–1900).[54]

After Plunkitt's decline in power, building slowed. However, Jesup managed to get two more sections built, both designed by the architect Charles Volz. The Power House and Boiler House, built from 1903 to 1904 (with an extension to the Power House built in 1905), represented a slight departure from the master plan. The Power House occupied only a portion of the area earmarked for the west transept, while the adjoining Boiler House encroached on the southwest courtyard. The south wing on Columbus Avenue, which was faithful to Cady, Berg & See's original concept, was built from 1906 to 1908.[55] In addition, Volz designed the astronomy-themed renovation of the foyer of the Seventy-Seventh Street entrance that opened in 1906.[56]

Cady, Berg, and See's vision for master plan.
Source: Copyright Moses King.

Seventy-Seventh Street façade, showing new entrance pavilion, 1893.
Source: AMNH ID 474.

Seventy-Seventh Street façade, showing new east wing, April 17, 1895.
Source: AMNH ID 475.

Seventy-Seventh Street façade completed in 1900.
Source: Detroit Publishing Company photograph collection, Library of Congress.

Seventy-Seventh Street façade showing south wing on Columbus Avenue completed in 1908. Note tracks of Columbus Avenue elevated train line.
Source: Art and Picture Collection, New York Public Library.

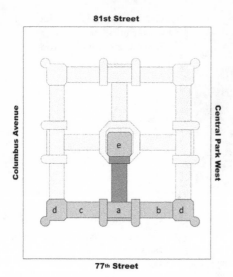

Museum sections built from 1890 to 1900: (a) Entrance Pavilion, 77th Street (1890–1891), (b) East Wing, 77th Street (1894–1895), (c) West Wing, 77th Street (1895–1897), (d) SE and SW Corner Pavilions (1897–1899), (e) Central Pavilion, Auditorium (1899–1900).

Museum sections built from 1903 to 1908: (a) Power House and Boiler House (1903–1905), (b) South Wing, Columbus Ave. (1906–1908).

Jesup's Enduring Impact

Under Jesup, the museum didn't just grow physically. From 1884 to 1907, annual attendance increased from 250,000 to 537,000,[57] and from 1881 to 1907, the staff increased from six to twenty-eight and the number of departments from three to eleven.[58]

But Jesup's lasting imprint on the museum was not limited to the institution's growth. Museums have always struggled to balance the seemingly conflicting goals of serving the general public and advancing scientific research. Jesup aggressively pursued both, believing they worked hand in hand, an approach that has made the museum what it is today. He insisted that the exhibits be attractive and accessible to the general public, and he pursued an energetic outreach to the city and state school systems. But, according to the museum historian Douglas Preston, he also "recognized that the foundation for good exhibitions was good research and active collection."[59] As Jesup's successor, Henry Fairfield Osborn, put it, Jesup was determined "that the museum should be as famous for its scientific research and explorations as for its popular exhibitions of educational work."[60]

Improved Exhibits

Under Jesup's leadership, the museum's exhibits became more accessible and attractive, turning his lack of scientific background to the museum's advantage. "I am a plain, unscientific business man," he often said. "I want the exhibits to be labeled so that I can understand them, and then I shall feel sure that others can understand."[61]

Jesup led the museum to develop its signature exhibition technique, the habitat diorama. The American Museum, like natural-history museums in general, had previously consisted largely of dark hallways filled with crowded and dusty cases of specimens. But on an 1885 trip to Europe, Jesup saw the British Museum's exhibits of stuffed birds perched on models of their native plants, which were known as "habitat groups." Impressed, he hired a pair of British taxidermists to work with the American Museum's staff to create similar exhibits.

In 1888, the museum hired a young ornithologist named Frank M. Chapman, and around 1900, Chapman started adding painted backgrounds to these groups, in the process turning them into "habitat dioramas." (This technique had been pioneered in 1889 at the Milwaukee Public Museum by Carl Akeley, who would later become an important figure at the American Museum.) In 1902, the Hall of North American Birds hall opened under Chapman's direction—the world's first museum hall entirely devoted to the habitat-group method of display.[62]

Educational Outreach

Jesup was not content simply to produce great exhibits and wait for people to come. He also helped create an ambitious outreach program targeting the public schools of the city and state. With Jesup taking over the reins of museum administration, Bickmore was able to focus on education. The education program began modestly in 1881, with Bickmore delivering lectures to thirty New York City schoolteachers. By 1883, his audience had grown to 150 teachers, and the following year, New York State hired him to teach at teacher-training colleges throughout the state. Bickmore created a teaching method that became known as "visual instruction," pioneering the use of photographic slides, a technology still in its infancy, and traveling the world collecting photographs.

In 1904, when Bickmore started lightening his load because of ill health, the museum strengthened its connection to the schools by hiring several instructors and providing lectures for schoolchildren at the museum to supplement their classroom work. The museum also began preparing "nature cabinets" for loan to schools. The cabinets included preserved birds, insects, mollusks, crabs, starfish, worms, sponges, corals, minerals, and samples of wood, and each year, this material would reach nearly a million students.[63]

Expeditions

Under Jesup's watch, the museum launched its so-called golden age of exploration, which lasted until the early twentieth century, taking museum representatives on expeditions to every continent on the globe. This marked a transition from simply buying existing collections to active collecting,[64] beginning in 1888 with an expedition in search of the fast-vanishing bison.[65] As a result, the new buildings constructed during Jesup's time were quickly filled with the new collections.

The most ambitious expedition, the Jesup North Pacific Expedition, was a series of grueling journeys to the northwest coast of North America and Siberia that took place between 1897 and 1902. These expeditions had two main purposes: to determine whether native Americans had originally come to the American continent from Siberia across the Bering Strait and to document the life of the vanishing cultures of the North American Indians and of Siberia.

This project was the result of Jesup's reinvigoration of the museum's anthropology department, including the hiring of Franz Boas, who has been called the father of modern anthropology and who proposed the project. Artifacts from this project, including numerous towering and colorful totem poles, have filled the Hall of Northwest Coast Indians on the first floor of the museum's first building (the south transept) since 1899, making this display the museum's oldest surviving exhibition area.[66] An offshoot of this new emphasis on anthropology was the 1926 hire of Margaret Mead, who had studied under Franz Boas at Columbia University and who would become one of the best-known American Museum employees and popularizers of anthropology.

Jesup also supported Robert Peary's attempts to reach the North Pole starting in 1895. Jesup did not live to see Peary make his claim on the Pole in 1909, but the museum benefited through the acquisition of many wildlife specimens, Eskimo artifacts, and the Cape York meteorites, a trove that included the Ahnighito meteorite, the largest in any museum.

In May 1891, Jesup established the museum's department of vertebrate paleontology and hired Henry Fairfield Osborn to be the curator. This ultimately led to the museum having the world's leading dinosaur collection, starting with the spoils from an 1897 expedition to Wyoming where Osborn and Barnum Brown found the museum's first dinosaur specimen. Osborn would go on to succeed Jesup as president of the museum and in that role would make formidable contributions to the institution.

The Gift That Keeps on Giving

Last but not least, Jesup's enduring contributions to the museum also included massive sums of money. The gifts he made during his lifetime, including collections purchased and expeditions sponsored, amounted to $450,000. In his will, he left the museum $1 million, to be used as a permanent fund, with the principal to be invested and the income used for scientific purposes only. When his widow, Maria DeWitt Jesup, died in 1914, she left the museum an additional $5 million from the estate she had inherited from her husband.[67]

4

Robert Peary, the Journey to the North Pole, and the Cape York Meteorites

Weighing thirty-four tons and measuring 11' by 7' by 5½', the Ahnighito meteorite is the largest meteorite in any museum and one of the American Museum's most massive objects. It has resided in three locations in the institution, one of them being the original Hayden Planetarium. The meteorite, which arrived during the early days of the museum's astronomy department and golden age of exploration, is intimately tied to Robert Peary's quest to be the first human to reach the North Pole, a project that was deeply important personally to the museum's president Morris Jesup. Theodore Roosevelt also took an intense personal interest in Peary's quest.

Long ago in the history of our solar system, an asteroid was shattered by a collision. Thousands of years ago, one of the fragments, a two-hundred-ton mountain of iron-nickel alloy, was swept up by Earth's gravity and plunged through the atmosphere. Traveling tens of thousands of miles an hour, the fragment shattered into smaller pieces from the rapid surface heating caused by friction with the atmosphere.

Three fragments ended up near Cape York in the Melville Bay region of northwestern Greenland and for this reason are called the Cape York meteorites. The two smallest meteorites landed on the mainland about one hundred feet apart. The largest of these meteorites, which would come to be known as the Ahnighito, landed six miles away, on an island near the coast.

Greenland is the world's largest island, and more than three-quarters of its surface is covered by an ice sheet one to two miles thick. The surface of the ice is constantly shifting, depending on snowdrifts and weather patterns, and only the ice-free fringes of the coast are populated. Cape York's latitude is 75° north, where the sun remains above the horizon from approximately April 20 to August 20. The sea surrounding Cape York is frozen solid most of the year, and the cape is only approachable by boat from late July through September, and that only semireliably.

Around AD 1000, the Thule people, who lived in Alaska and Arctic Canada, migrated to northwestern Greenland, becoming the world's northernmost living people, the people we now know as Polar Eskimos, or Inuit, meaning "the people" in the native language.

The Inuit discovered the Cape York meteorites and started chipping off pieces of the metal, making tools and weapons from them. To the Inuit, the meteorites looked like, from largest to smallest, a tent, a woman, and a dog, and they named them thusly. So according to legend, the Evil Spirit hurled a woman, a dog, and a tent from the sky.

At one time, the Woman resembled an actual woman even more. But after the discovery that the material could be used for tools and weapons, one tribe separated the head to bring back to their home base up north by dog sled. But the sled carrying the head broke through some soft ice, taking the sled, dogs, and iron with it. The Inuit considered this to be a punishment from the Woman's spirit and never tried to move the meteorites again.[1]

Starting around 1600, European explorers developed an intense interest in exploring the northern regions of the globe. One reason was economic: These explorers were looking for a Northwest Passage, a sea-based trade route connecting the Atlantic and Pacific Oceans. Another reason was scientific. The poles were a total mystery. One theory that endured through the mid-1800s was that the North Pole consisted of a temperate, ice-free ocean. In addition, the northernmost boundary of Greenland had not yet been found, and some people believed that it extended all the way to the pole.

In fact, the North Pole lies in the Arctic Ocean, with the closest points of land being the northernmost point of Greenland (about 450 miles away) and the northernmost point of Canada's Ellesmere Island (about 500 miles away). The Arctic Ocean is frozen during the winter, but even during the coldest winter, the surface of the ice shifts constantly in a random fashion, with the formation of pressure ridges and breaks in the ice sometimes as wide as a river.

By the 1800s, Arctic fever approached space-race proportions, with the explorers being the astronauts of their time and hundreds of them losing their lives in the process. In 1818, while in search of the North-west Passage, the British explorer John Ross discovered a community of about 250 Inuit near Cape York. According to Ross, these people, the northernmost peoples known, believed that they were the only humans on Earth. Ross discovered that they had iron tools, and they told him that they had been making these tools since time immemorial from a "mountain of iron," which Ross correctly guessed to be a meteorite.

After Ross's discovery of the meteorite's existence, numerous Arctic expeditions tried unsuccessfully to locate the so-called Iron Mountain. But its location was a closely guarded secret, and no Westerner was to set eyes on it until Robert Peary, a civil engineer with the US Navy, did so at 5:30 a.m. on May 27, 1894.[2]

Robert Peary

Peary is widely, although controversially, credited with leading the first expedition to reach the North Pole on April 6, 1909. But that expedition was preceded by a series of grueling and drama-filled polar expeditions, starting in 1886.

Peary, born on May 6, 1856, had grown up in Portland, Maine, and graduated from Bowdoin College in 1877 with a degree in civil engineering. He then joined the US Navy and in 1881 was promoted to lieutenant. He was in many respects a remarkable man, known for his almost superhuman stamina, determination, and physical courage. And in 1885, at the age of twenty-eight, he set his sights on Greenland and the North Pole.

On April 23 of the following year, he presented a paper at the National Academy of Sciences suggesting two possible routes for cross-ing the Greenland ice sheet from west to east. One was a four-hundred-mile southern route. The other, a more ambitious journey, started in northwestern Greenland and headed northeast. This would allow the explorers to determine Greenland's northernmost boundary.[3]

The next month, Peary departed alone on his first expedition to Greenland, attempting the southern route he had described in his paper. After arriving in Greenland, he was joined by Christian Maigaard, a Danish government official, and together they succeeded in traveling one hundred miles, turning back only when they had barely enough food for the return trip. It was the second deepest penetration of the Greenland ice sheet.

Peary's next Arctic expedition would not take place until 1891 because his naval duties took him to Nicaragua to survey possible routes for a canal linking the Atlantic and Pacific Oceans. During the period between the two expeditions, Peary formed two key relationships that would have a major impact on his polar exploration.

In 1887, when Peary was in Washington, DC, preparing for his Nicaragua mission, he met a remarkable twenty-one-year-old African American named Matthew Henson while buying a hat. Henson, who worked in the hat store's stockroom, had spent five years at sea as a cabin boy, traveling to China, Japan, Africa, Spain, France, and Russia, in the process learning to do most of the jobs on the ship. In the evenings, the ship's captain taught him to read. Peary hired Henson as his personal assistant for the Nicaragua mission, and they maintained this relationship for the next twenty-three years, with Henson accompanying Peary on all his subsequent Arctic expeditions.

And on August 11, 1888, Peary married Josephine Diebitsch, whom he had met six years earlier while attending dancing school in Washington, DC.[4] Mrs. Peary would accompany her husband on several Arctic expeditions, despite resistance from crew members to the presence of a female member. She also provided critically needed home-front support and wrote several important books about her Arctic experiences.

The 1891–1892 Expedition

In 1888, the Norwegian explorer Fridtjof Nansen bested Peary by successfully crossing the southern portion of the Greenland ice sheet. So for his 1891 expedition, Peary set out to accomplish the second, more ambitious crossing described in his 1886 paper, a trek from northwestern Greenland traveling northeast, with the goal of determining the northernmost boundary of Greenland. He also hoped to include a side mission to look for the meteorite.

The strategy was for a boat to drop off the crew in the summer. The crew would then build a house, set up headquarters, establish relationships with the local Inuit, do some local exploration, and prepare for the northeast crossing, which would begin when the sun rose in the spring. The following summer, a boat would return to bring the crew back to the United States. The expedition would be subsidized partly by bringing a team of scientists each summer to do exploration until the boat's departure.

The cultivation of relations with the Inuit would become a key part of Peary's method. This included bartering for their labor and adopting their survival methods, such as hunting, building igloos, wearing furs, and using sled dogs and sledges (low sleds) for transportation. Henson would become the most proficient team member when it came to learning the Inuit's skills and language.

His crew consisted of seven people. Along with his wife and Henson, the team included Eivind Astrup, a ski expert; John Verhoeff, a meteorologist; and Frederick Cook, an ethnologist and medical doctor. Decades later, Cook and Peary would become archrivals in the goal to reach the North Pole.

The crew set sail from Brooklyn aboard the *Kite* on June 6, 1891. Shortly before their arrival in Greenland on July 23, Peary broke his leg in a freak accident, and the injury did not completely heal until the following February. During his convalescence, Peary's thoughts turned to the Iron Mountain, and he made a deal with an Inuk (Inuit individual) named Qisuq[5] in which, in exchange for a gun, Qisuk would guide Peary to the site of the meteorite after Peary returned from the main mission, the northeast crossing.[6]

Peary and four men set out on the crossing on May 3, 1892. Henson turned back early because of a frostbitten heel. Some 150 miles later, two more men turned back. Peary and Astrup continued on alone. On July 4, looking out over a fjord from atop a thousand-meter cliff, they determined, incorrectly, that they had reached Greenland's northernmost point. Because of the date, Peary named the spot Independence Bay. The party arrived back at headquarters on August 6, having traveled 1,250 miles, four times the previous record for the Greenland ice sheet.

By the time they returned, the *Kite* had arrived to take Peary and the crew home, and given the unfavorable weather conditions, Peary determined that a journey to the meteorites was not advisable. However, he spent about a week exploring the nearby Inglefield Gulf with his wife, a few crewmembers, and some Inuit. On this expedition, which coincided with the Pearys' fourth wedding anniversary, the explorers discovered a bay, which Peary named Bowdoin Bay after his alma mater. Peary determined that it was "an ideal site for an arctic house." This location would become the headquarters of Peary's next Greenland expedition.[7]

The expedition ended on a tragic note. In its final days, John Verhoeff set off to explore some glaciers and never came back. Peary, along with the remaining crewmembers and several Inuit, spent six days searching for him. His footprints were finally found at the edge of a glacial cliff, and it was assumed he had fallen to his death.

The 1893–1895 Expedition

On July 2, 1893, Peary and his crew left New York aboard the ship *Falcon*, setting out to replicate and extend the accomplishments of their previous expedition. The basic strategy was the same, but for this mission Peary brought a larger crew of fourteen. The plan was to take eight men to Independence Bay, and from there Peary and two men would cross the bay and proceed north as far as they could—all the way to the pole if possible. Another team of three men would explore along the coastline to the southeast. Two men would camp at Independence Bay, hunting and preparing for the return trip. From the 1891 mission came Mrs. Peary, Henson, and Astrup. This time, Mrs. Peary was seven months pregnant and was accompanied by a nurse, Susan Cross. Also making the trip was a young man named Hugh Lee.

As on the previous expedition, the plan was to set up headquarters in the summer and prepare for the trek to take place the following spring. On August 3, the *Falcon* arrived at Bowdoin Bay, the spot where the Pearys had spent their anniversary the previous year and where they would celebrate it again in a few days. There the crew proceeded to build the house that would become their home, naming it Anniversary Lodge.[8]

On September 12, Mrs. Peary gave birth to a baby girl believed to be the most northerly born white child. The baby was named Marie Ahnighito Peary—Marie for the girl's aunt (Mrs. Peary's sister) and Ahnighito for an Inuit woman who had made the baby a fur Inuit suit.[9] Marie Ahnighito became a local sensation, with Inuit traveling from far and wide to see her.[10]

But after this joyous event, the team's luck took a turn for the worse. On October 31, a tidal wave sent a wall of water almost to the door of Anniversary Lodge, causing the party to lose most of their fuel, smashing two boats, and carrying away a number of sled-dog puppies.[11] And the northward trek that began on March 6, 1894, with eight crewmembers including Peary, five Inuit, and about eighty dogs, was beset with disasters. Several dogs developed piblokto, a mania caused by cold temperatures, and had to be shot. Several of the men had to return to Anniversary Lodge, suffering from frostbite and food poisoning. With the team already weakened, they were trapped by a blizzard that brought blinding snow, fifty-mile-an-hour winds, and temperatures by some accounts as low as minus 60° F. On April 10, after traveling only 128 miles, Peary admitted defeat and decided to turn back.

Before doing so, the explorers buried a huge cache of supplies for use in the next attempt, marking the site with a fourteen-foot pole. Pre-positioning caches of supplies on the ice cap was a strategy Peary generally used in order to avoid having to carry all the supplies from the start of the journey. On April 18, the expedition arrived back at Anniversary Lodge.[12]

Finding the Meteorites

After this string of defeats, Peary was ready for a success, and his thoughts returned to the meteorite. On May 16, Peary and Lee set out on a journey of about 120 miles from Anniversary Lodge to Cape York to find the Iron Mountain. They hoped that once they were near Cape York they would find Qisuq, the young man who had agreed to lead Peary to the Iron Mountain two years earlier.

Three days into their journey, at a small village, they ran into a trusted acquaintance named Aleqatsiaq.[13] It turned out that Aleqatsiaq knew the location of the Iron Mountain and agreed to guide Peary and Lee to the site. Aleqatsiaq explained that there were actually three "great irons" of various sizes.

When the explorers arrived at Cape York after a week of battling fierce storms, they did indeed find Qisuq, who was happy to join the team. At 5:30 in the morning of May 27, after a full day of travel, the expedition arrived at the site. There, Aleqatsiaq dug a pit in the snow three feet deep and five feet wide, allowing a Westerner to see one of the great irons (the Woman) for the first time.

After scratching his initial on the surface of the metal, Peary left a note nearby saying: "This record is deposited to show that on the above date [Sunday May 27, 1894] R. E. Peary, U.S. Navy, and Hugh J. Lee of the North-Greenland Expedition of 1893–94, with Aleqatsiaq, an Inuit guide, discovered the famous 'Iron Mountain,' first mentioned by Capt. Ross, and have carefully examined the same." The team arrived back at Anniversary Lodge on June 6 to await the return of the *Falcon*.[14]

The Return of the *Falcon*

The *Falcon* returned on July 31. Peary, unwilling to accept failure, determined to try for the pole again the following year, even though there were no funds or plans for a ship to bring him back to the United States. But there was not enough food or supplies for the entire crew, and dissension had developed among the ranks. So Peary sent the entire crew home, with the exception of Hugh Lee and Matt Henson. Also sent home were Mrs. Peary, the couple's baby daughter, and a twelve-year-old Inuit girl named Eqariusaq,[15] who had cared for the baby. The Pearys gave Eqariusaq the nickname "Miss Bill," and she would subsequently spend an eye-opening year in the United States.

Initially, the Pearys had planned to raise money for a ship to pick up Peary, Henson, and Lee a year later by sending one or two of the Cape York meteorites back to the United States aboard the *Falcon* for sale or exhibition.[16] Peary accompanied the *Falcon* as far as Cape York to attempt to put the Dog and Woman meteorites aboard the ship. However, when the craft arrived on August 27, Melville Bay was frozen, so they could not get near the prizes. Peary returned to Anniversary Lodge, and the *Falcon* and its passengers returned to the United States.[17]

Before Peary had parted ways with his wife and baby daughter, the couple devised a plan for bringing the crew home. Mrs. Peary would embark on a fundraising drive to hire a ship to return for the crew, with the aim of meeting at Anniversary Lodge in mid-August the next year.[18] If the plan proved unsuccessful, Peary and his crew would proceed on foot and sledge along the west coast of Greenland to the Danish settlements seven hundred miles south and take a Danish supply ship to Copenhagen.[19]

The 1895 Peary Relief Expedition

The *Falcon* arrived at Philadelphia on September 25, where much public attention was focused on baby Marie Ahnighito.[20] Mrs. Peary returned to her mother's home in Washington, DC, with her daughter and Miss Bill, with the latter astonished to see for the first time such sights as trains, large buildings, trees, and a sun that rises and sets every twenty-four hours.

Back in Washington, Mrs. Peary sprung into action, organizing and raising money for an expedition to rescue her husband. Fortunately, she had the support of a tight-knit family, with her brother Emil Diebitsch becoming the business manager of the fundraising project and her mother and sister doting on the children.

Mrs. Peary began by appealing to the American Geographical Society and its president, Charles P. Daly, who had supported Peary in the past.

On December 7, Daly and the society sent a request to the secretary of the Navy asking that the Navy send a ship to Greenland to bring home Peary, Lee, and Henson. On January 18, 1895, the request was denied.[21]

Meanwhile, back at Anniversary Lodge, after the *Falcon* had left, Peary, Lee, and Henson began making preparations for the Arctic winter and the planned expedition of the following spring. Their main concern involved food: hunting enough to get through the winter and making sure that the pre-positioned food caches were in order for the spring.

In October 1894, the Arctic winter was particularly harsh as the explorers trekked out to examine the caches. They were shocked to find that the snow was so deep that they couldn't find any of the caches, undoing much of the previous year's efforts. They would have to use lower-quality food and carry it with them from the start. But more importantly, they would not have enough for the entire trek. They were gambling that they would be able to hunt enough food to survive. In effect, they were risking starving to death on the Arctic ice hundreds of miles from the nearest humans.

In December, when the Arctic night was bright with moonlight, Peary and Lee tried to revisit the meteorites. But they were blocked at Cape York by stormy weather, and their grueling return trip included an arduous forty-six-hour forced march without food or sleep.[22]

In the United States, having failed to get satisfaction from the Navy, Mrs. Peary came up with a new plan. The rescue mission would double as what was called the Greenland Scientific Expedition of 1895. For $1,000 per person, scientific societies, educational institutions, and individuals would be offered the opportunity to send a scientist to Greenland to collect specimens and do research. The total cost was estimated at $12,000. The expedition was scheduled to depart on July 5, 1895, from St. John's, Newfoundland, and last three months.

On March 2, 1895, the American Geographical Society resolved to contribute $1,000 to the cause. Mrs. Peary's brother wrote a lengthy pitch for the expedition, touting the opportunities for research in the fields of glacial geology, zoology, ethnology, and botany. To sweeten the deal, Peary himself was offered as a guide for the scientists' explorations.[23]

At this point, on the recommendation of Daly, Mrs. Peary secured an appointment to meet with Jesup and the American Museum board. After making her pitch, the museum pledged $1,000 to the cause, with Jesup adding, "I believe that you are doing all you can to raise this money, and I don't want you to do any less, but if you do not succeed in raising it all, come back to me again. You must understand that while

I am interested in the scientific aspects of your expedition, my chief interest is that I want you to get your husband back." This pledge marked the beginning of the Pearys' lifelong friendship and collaboration with Jesup and his institution.[24]

Despite this guarantee, the fiercely self-reliant Mrs. Peary did not let up on her fundraising efforts. Although she suffered from severe stage fright, she raised several thousand dollars by giving public slideshow lectures on the subject of "Life in Greenland" during May, with her brother operating the projector. The photograph of Marie Ahnighito swaddled in Inuit garb prompted the biggest applause.[25]

Jesup ended up footing most of the bill for the expedition.[26]

Lewis Lindsay Dyche, a professor of natural history from the University of Kansas, went on behalf of the American Museum and his university. The previous summer, Dyche had joined an expedition to Greenland aboard the ship *Miranda*, organized by Peary's future rival Frederick Cook, an expedition beset with mishaps, culminating with the ship sinking along with the hundreds of specimens Dyche had collected. Fortunately, all the passengers survived, having transferred to a crowded fishing boat earlier when the *Miranda* became damaged.[27]

The expedition departed aboard the *Kite* from St. John's on July 11.[28] Miss Bill was also on board, returning home from her year in the United States. When the *Kite* arrived back in St. John's on September 21 with Peary and the crew, Mrs. Peary and the public first became aware of the tribulations Peary and his team had endured after the *Falcon* departed the previous year.[29]

On April 1, 1895, Peary, Henson, and Lee had left Anniversary Lodge with forty-one dogs, accompanied by a support team of Inuit, until they arrived at the vicinity of the huge food cache, in another unsuccessful attempt to find it. At this point, the Inuit turned back. Early into the trek, Lee suffered from a frostbitten toe, one of many ailments that would plague him during the journey. After about four hundred miles, only seventeen dogs remained, and a week later, just eleven. At this point, Henson and Peary left the ailing Lee with the dogs and went off to hunt for musk oxen. After several days of brutal snow and fog, they returned to Lee empty handed.

The explorers now had a choice. If they turned back at this point, they had barely enough food to survive. If they went forward, their survival would depend on being able to hunt musk oxen successfully. Peary would later write: "We were Americans. One of us carried about him the Red, White and Blue. We could not turn back."[30] Once again,

Peary and Henson left Lee and went off to hunt. This time, they were able to track and shoot ten musk oxen, but this would be the last food they would find for the rest of the journey. Ultimately, they reached Independence Bay, replicating the feat of Peary's 1891–1892 expedition, but they lacked the food or energy to progress further.

On June 1, when they began their six-hundred-mile return trip, they had only nine dogs remaining and very little food. They were able to survive only because the men and dogs supplemented their diet with the meat of the weak and dead dogs. They ran out of food and had only a single dog remaining when they were one day and twenty-one miles from Anniversary Lodge, to which they returned on June 25, starving and debilitated. All they could do was pray that Mrs. Peary's fundraising efforts back home had been successful.

On August 2, Peary fell asleep after reading until midnight. The next thing he knew, he was being shaken awake by his brother-in-law, Emil Diebitsch. The *Kite* had arrived off the coast on July 31, but the ice had prevented her from entering Bowdoin Bay. Diebitsch and an expedition scientist made the long Arctic trek to Anniversary Lodge on foot.

Around August 21, the *Kite* and crew headed toward Cape York and the meteorites. The ice conditions were far more favorable this time around, and they were able to get the ship within a mile of the shore. Unlike the first time Peary had set eyes on the Woman, the snow had now melted so that the entire rock was exposed, as was the Dog, which was found about a hundred feet away. What followed was a several-day engineering effort, led by Diebitsch.

The giant rocks were moved to the shore using a system of jacks, sledges, and rollers. Then they were ferried across the expanse of water separating the shore from the frozen bay using huge chunks of ice as rafts. Finally, they were dragged across the frozen bay to the ship and hoisted aboard. As the team was preparing to hoist the larger of the two meteorites aboard the *Kite*, the ice supporting it gave way, submerging the meteorite and tipping the ship to its side. But ultimately they succeeded in wrestling it aboard. As Diebitsch and his team were moving the Dog and the Woman, Peary and his team were working to excavate the giant Tent, located on the nearby island. However, after four days of effort, they were unable to budge it.

On September 1, the *Kite* headed west and ultimately found its way to St. John's on September 21.[31] A Red Cross steamer, the *Silvia*, took Peary, Henson, and Dyche to Halifax, where Mrs. Peary was waiting to see her husband for the first time in more than a year.[32] From Halifax, the Pearys and the *Silvia*, with Henson and Dyche aboard, went their separate ways.

Back in America

On September 30, the Pearys took a train from Halifax to the home of Peary's mother in Portland, Maine. When reporters caught up with the explorer there, he admitted his discouragement. "I shall never see the North Pole," he said, "unless someone brings it here." Peary, now a few months short of forty, continued, "I am too old to snowshoe twenty-five to thirty miles a day for weeks, and to carry a heavy load during most of the time. . . . I am not an old man . . . but I am too old for that sort of work."[33] Peary had another reason to be discouraged. As he wrote in *Northward over the Great Ice*, his 1898 account of his journeys, "the fact that there were two well-equipped expeditions still in the field [Frederick Jackson's and Fridtjof Nansen's], with a good chance of accomplishing their objects [of reaching the pole], made me feel as if my life-work had been a failure."[34] The Pearys then proceeded to the home of Mrs. Peary's mother in Washington, DC, where their daughter was waiting.[35]

After separating from the Pearys in Halifax, Henson and Dyche headed for New York aboard the *Silvia*. With them, bound for the museum, were the specimens Dyche had collected, along with the two meteorites.[36] They arrived on October 1.

According to *Dark Companion*, the 1947 biography of Henson written with Henson by Bradley Robinson, before Henson left the boat, a curator from the museum showed up to inspect the walrus and musk oxen specimens. The curator was so impressed with Henson's preparation of the skins that he offered him a job with the museum, where Henson worked steadily until 1898 when not accompanying Peary on his arctic missions. While there is evidence that Henson did some work at the museum during this time, Robinson's account appears to be highly exaggerated.[37]

Shortly after his return to the United States, Dyche began expressing his own aspirations for mounting an expedition to the North Pole, and, much to the irritation of Peary, he also stated his intention to bring back the great Tent meteorite himself. This led Peary to write to Dyche on December 12, "The large meteorite which I left last summer . . . is mine by the right of discovery just as much as those that I did bring back. Further I shall send a ship for the meteorite next summer. As for the North Pole, if it be true that you are going after it, you have my best wishes for your success and safety." However, Dyche's expedition never materialized, and he gradually stopped mentioning it.[38]

Despite his discouraged state, Peary still hoped to bring back the meteorite. To do so, he needed six months leave, which the Navy was reluctant to grant. After Jesup pulled a few strings, Peary secured the leave in the spring of 1896.[39] Once again, to help subsidize the trip, Peary took several scientific teams that did additional exploration while he and his team focused on landing the Tent meteorite.[40]

The 1896 Expedition

Peary returned to Greenland with Lee, Henson, and a few other men. This time, they sailed aboard the *Hope*, a much larger ship, bringing with them four hydraulic jacks, two with a maximum lifting capacity of thirty tons, one that could lift up to sixty tons, and one with a capacity of one hundred tons.

Rounding up as many able-bodied Inuit as possible, they proceeded to work on retrieving the great Tent meteorite. Work proceeded round the clock for ten days. The sixty-ton jack gave out after the first lift, and the two thirty-ton jacks gave out over the following days.

"Never have I had the terrific majesty of the force of gravity and the meaning of the terms 'momentum' and 'inertia' so powerfully brought home to me, as in handling this mountain of iron," Peary wrote in *Northward over the Great Ice*. "Had the matter been a subject of study for weeks by the celestial forge-master, I doubt if any shape could have been devised that would have been any more completely ill suited for handling in any way, either rolling or sliding or lifting." Peary estimated that the meteorite weighed ninety to one hundred tons, perhaps because it broke the sixty-ton jack but not the hundred-ton one. His conclusion would later be shown to be incorrect.

After ten days, the men managed to excavate the meteorite and maneuver it the distance to the shore, but they weren't able to bring it aboard the ship before the *Hope* had to flee during a fierce gale to avoid being trapped by ice for the winter.[41] Peary had failed to bring home the meteorite, but he did return with two live polar bears and a hundred cases of collections for the American Museum.[42]

A New Plan

Despite the failure to bring home the meteorite, Peary returned from the expedition in high spirits. "The summer's voyage and the Arctic atmosphere had brushed away the last vestige of the previous year's exhaustion and morbidness," Peary wrote in *Northward over the Great Ice*. Along with the bracing Arctic air, Peary's spirits were buoyed by the fact that his two competitors' polar expeditions had failed. Peary continued: "The fact that . . . the plan nestling fully developed in my mind before my return was now proven to be not merely the most practicable but the only remaining practical one by which to reach the yet unscaled apex of the Earth, filled me with new hopes and courage."[43]

Peary chose January 14, 1897, the occasion of his being awarded the American Geographical Society's Cullum Medal, to reveal his latest plan. In his acceptance speech, he announced that he proposed to take a ship as far north as possible up the forty-mile-wide channel separating Greenland and Canada's Ellesmere Island, aiming for the Arctic Ocean. The team would then wait for the winter conditions to come together to sledge north on the frozen Arctic Ocean and head for the pole. While waiting for these opportunities, they would explore uncharted areas of northern Greenland and Ellesmere Island. They would remain at the task for years, until they reached their destination or died trying. On February 20, the society resolved to support the plan.[44]

The Navy, in the meantime, had become adamantly opposed to allowing Peary the five years of leave that the expedition required. Jesup led a prolonged campaign to obtain the leave for Peary, including appeals to President McKinley and the museum's old friend, Theodore Roosevelt, who at the time was the undersecretary of the Navy. Peary received the leave on May 25.[45]

By then it was too late to get the main expedition underway. So a summer expedition was planned for the purpose of bringing home the Tent meteorite and recruiting Inuit for the main expedition planned for the following year. On May 24, Franz Boas, then the museum's assistant curator of anthropology, wrote to Peary requesting that he bring back an Inuk for the purpose of anthropological study.[46]

The 1897 Expedition

In August, Peary returned to the Arctic aboard the *Hope*, this time bringing Mrs. Peary and their daughter, now four, as well as Henson, several other men, and some scientific teams. Before heading toward Cape York and the meteorite, the *Hope* went north to visit and recruit Inuit to help with the following year's expedition. This led to the joyful reunion between Marie Ahnighito Peary and Miss Bill, who was now married.[47]

Peary selected a group of Inuit to accompany him to the site of the great meteorite to help with the task ahead. This group included Miss Bill's parents and adopted sister and an Inuk named Qisuk (not the individual of the same name who helped Peary find the meteorites), with his son, Minik,[48] whose mother had recently died.[49]

This time they were able to pull the *Hope* right up to the shore near where the behemoth lay. The team created a bridge of rails extending from the shore to the ship. Then they hoisted the meteorite onto a mighty makeshift trolley and fastened it down. Finally, they drove the trolley across the bridge onto the ship. As the ship's captain and Mrs. Peary pumped the jacks, starting the meteorite toward the ship, little Marie Ahnighito Peary dashed a bottle of wine against it and christened it "Ahnighito." The entire process would require more than five days of precise, painstaking, and dangerous work.[50] Henson would later write in his autobiography, "My back still aches when I think of the hard work I did to help load that monster aboard the *Hope*."[51]

After the meteorite was safely on board, Peary requested that some of the Inuit return to the United States with him to spend a year there, both serving as subjects for the museum's anthropologists and helping the museum arrange the exhibits of the Inuit material that Peary was bringing home.[52] Having had their daughter pass a pleasant year in the United States with the Pearys, Miss Bill's parents agreed to go, along with their adopted daughter. Qisuk also agreed, bringing Minik with him.[53] After departing, the *Hope* moved on to some of the area's Inuit villages to deliver instructions for the preparation for the following year's expedition. Along the way, they picked up another Inuk named Uisaakassak for the trip to the United States.[54]

Home with the Ahnighito and Six Inuit

The *Hope* arrived with the Ahnighito at the Brooklyn Navy Yard on October 2, and the meteorite was unloaded using a hundred-ton crane. Some twenty thousand people watched, and many came aboard the *Hope* to see the six Inuit who had made the journey.[55]

In one of the museum's more controversial and tragic episodes, by the following May, four of the visiting Inuit had died, succumbing to the unaccustomed warm climate and diseases to which they had no resistance. As was common practice at the time, their remains were placed in the museum's anthropological collections. In 1993, the remains were returned to Greenland to receive a ceremonial burial. The two survivors were Uisaakassak, who would return to Greenland with Peary the following summer, and the newly orphaned Minik, who was adopted by the museum's superintendent of building and would later become a fierce critic of Peary and the museum.[56]

In December 1897, while Peary was in London, the publisher Alfred Harmsworth offered him the ship the *Windward*, which had been on a previous Arctic expedition, for the upcoming expedition. Unfortunately, when the ship arrived in May, it didn't have the new engines that were promised, because of a machinists strike in England. As a result Peary needed to bring the *Hope* as an auxiliary ship.[57]

The 1898–1902 Expedition

In July 1898, Peary's next expedition finally got underway, handicapped by the *Windward*'s condition. By 1902, when he and his team returned to the United States after four years, they had made two northward pushes toward the pole. Although they failed to reach their destination, they attained the latitude of 84.17 north, the most northerly on the Western continent. They also accomplished much groundbreaking exploration of Greenland and Ellesmere Island, including finding the true northernmost point of Greenland (and northernmost point of land on Earth, except for some tiny islands off Greenland), which Peary named Cape Morris Jesup.[58]

As always, the expedition did not lack for punishing adventure. According to Henson: "During the four years from 1898 to 1902, which were continuously spent in the regions about North Greenland," Henson wrote, "we had every experience, except death, that had ever fallen to the lot of the explorers who had preceded us, and more than once we looked death squarely in the face."[59]

The team left the *Windward* on December 20, 1898, to explore the northeastern coast of Ellesmere Island by sledge. By January 6, 1899, Peary's feet had become frostbitten, and in March, after returning to the *Windward*, all but two of his toes had to be amputated.[60]

Back in New York and unaware of Peary's tribulations, on January 29, Jesup and a group of wealthy and influential New Yorkers met at Jesup's office at 44 Pine Street and officially created the Peary Arctic Club for the purpose of supporting the explorer's polar exploration.[61] The following summer, Jesup and the club members dispatched a mission to send supplies to Peary in Greenland and bring the *Windward* home for much-needed refurbishment.[62]

When the *Windward* returned to the United States, it brought the news of Peary's loss of his toes. As a result, when the refurbished *Windward* returned to the Arctic with supplies in the summer of 1900, Mrs. Peary and Marie Ahnighito, nearly seven, were on board, hoping to persuade Peary to return home with them in the fall.[63]

The *Windward*, with Mrs. Peary and Marie Ahnighito aboard, spent the summer chasing Peary's trail but failed to make contact with him. In the fall, when the time came for them to return to the United States, the *Windward* became locked in by ice and was forced to remain in Greenland an extra year. During this time, Marie Ahnighito was home-schooled by her mom and would play with her new and old Inuit friends. Peary finally showed up on May 6, 1901, along with Miss Bill and her husband.[64] Despite the recent death of her parents in New York, Miss Bill would remain loyal to Peary, serving as a seamstress for the remainder of his expeditions, including sewing the thick fur clothes worn by Henson on the final trip to the pole.[65]

In the summer of 1901, when the *Windward* failed to return, Jesup and the Peary Arctic Club sent another ship, the *Erik*, to investigate. Aboard the *Erik* was Peary's future rival, Dr. Frederick Cook, who was sent to check on Peary's medical condition. Alarmed by what he found, he, along with Mrs. Peary, beseeched Peary to return home. But Peary would hear none of it. The *Erik* and *Windward* returned to the United States with Cook, Mrs. Peary, and Marie Ahnighito. Peary remained in the Arctic to continue his quest.[66]

On April 21, 1902, he and a team aboard eighteen sledges attained the latitude of 84.17 north. The following summer, the *Windward* sailed north, again with Mrs. Peary and Marie Ahnighito on board, to finally bring the explorer home.[67]

Farthest North, 1905–1906

Almost immediately after returning home from his four-year mission, Peary was already planning his next expedition. This time his plan was to build a ship especially designed by him for Arctic travel.[68] The idea was to take the ship farther north than any ship had gone before, thus avoiding the long and exhausting sledge trips previously necessary to get to that point. Jesup and the Peary Arctic Club paid for the ship, which was built in Maine during 1904 and 1905, with Jesup personally contributing $50,000.[69] Peary relayed a request to President Roosevelt, through Jesup, to allow the ship to be named the *Roosevelt*, and on March 23,

1905, Mrs. Peary christened the ship with a bottle of champagne before a crowd of five thousand.[70]

In October 1904, as Peary was in Maine overseeing construction of the *Roosevelt*, the Ahnighito, which had been stored at the Brooklyn Navy Yard since 1897, was finally delivered to the museum. It was transported to the West Fifty-First Street pier on a huge derrick and then traveled north aboard a truck pulled by a team of thirty-five horses and deposited on a pedestal that had been constructed for this purpose.[71] Two years later, the museum assembled eleven of its largest meteorites, including the three Cape York meteorites and the newly acquired Willamette meteorite, into an exhibit circling the foyer of the newly renovated Seventy-Seventh Street entrance pavilion.[72]

Peary's 1905–1906 expedition began with a departure from New York City in July 1905, stopping briefly at Jesup's summer home in Bar Harbor, Maine.[73] Peary's cabin aboard the *Roosevelt* contained a pianola with a large framed portrait of Jesup, flanked by an etching of President Roosevelt and a photograph of Judge Darling, assistant secretary of the Navy.[74]

Once again, Peary failed to attain the pole, although a few weeks before his fiftieth birthday he did establish a new record, 87.6 north, on a mission, once again, as Henson described it, beset with "incredible hardships, hunger and cold."[75] The *Roosevelt*, badly damaged, returned to New York on Christmas Eve, 1906.

The Final Push

On March 30, 1907, Jesup announced that Peary and the Arctic Club had resolved to prepare the *Roosevelt* for another attempt at the pole.[76] Then came a series of devastating setbacks. Despite assurances that the *Roosevelt* would be ready by July 1, work was delayed until September, forcing the expedition to be delayed until the following summer.[77] And on October 2, 1907, while Peary was cooling his heels, the *Boston Herald* reported a new threat: Frederick Cook was in Greenland, about to launch his own assault on the pole.[78]

Next came what Peary called "the heaviest calamity encountered in all my arctic work": the death of Jesup on January 22, 1908. "In him we lost not only a man who was financially a tower of strength in the work," Peary wrote in *North Pole: Its Discovery*, "but I lost an intimate personal friend in whom I had absolute trust. For a time it seemed as if this were the end of everything; that all the effort and money put into the project had been wasted. . . . Mr. Jesup's death, added to the delay caused by the default of the contractors, seemed at first an absolutely paralyzing defeat."[79]

Nonetheless, Peary managed to muster the necessary support, including a generous donation from Jesup's widow.[80] The *Roosevelt* departed from New York on July 6, stopping at President Roosevelt's summer home in Oyster Bay, Long Island, where the president was given a tour of the ship and told Peary, "I believe in you, Peary, and I believe in your success."[81]

On March 1, 1909, Peary, Henson, five crewmembers, and fourteen Inuit set off in teams from the northernmost point of Ellesmere Island. As the teams worked their way north relaying supplies, they reduced the size of the party. Peary, Henson, and four Inuit[82] made the final push. On April 6, Peary claimed that the team had reached the North Pole.

Peary honored Jesup by naming the location he determined to be the pole Camp Morris K. Jesup and named the sledge on which he reached the pole the *Morris K. Jesup*.[83]

Upon returning to Greenland, Peary learned that Cook claimed to have reached the pole a year earlier, on April 21, 1908. Cook made his claim public on September 1, 1909, as soon as he could send a wire to the *New York Herald*.[84] When Peary reached Labrador on September 6, he in turn announced his achievement through wires to the press, supporters, his wife, Roosevelt (who was in Africa at the time), and the museum's director, Hermon Bumpus. To Mrs. Peary: "I have the old Pole. Am well. Love, Bert." To Roosevelt: "Your farewell was a royal mascot. The Pole is ours, Peary." To Bumpus: "The Pole is ours. Am bringing large amount material for Museum."[85]

Nevertheless, despite these triumphant messages, the controversy over whether Peary or Cook (or either) was the first to reach the North Pole would rage for the next century and continues to this day.

The Exhibit of the Peary Arctic Club

On October 12, 1909, a temporary exhibit of the Peary Arctic Club opened on the first floor of the museum's new south wing on Columbus Avenue. The exhibit brought together materials from the explorer's past expeditions as well as from the most recent one. The centerpiece of the exhibit was a thirty-foot-by-fifty-foot map that showed the route of the 1909 expedition, including the points where the supporting parties turned back and the place where a flag was planted at the final destination. A small model of the *Roosevelt* was placed at Cape Sheridan, where the *Roosevelt* remained during the push to the pole.

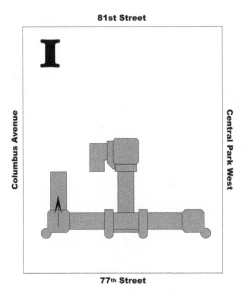

81st Street

Columbus Avenue

Central Park West

77th Street

The Peary Arctic Club exhibit, located on the first floor of the south wing on Columbus Avenue, October 1909.
Source: Bain News Service photograph collection, Library of Congress.

In front of the map were three wax figures depicting Inuit in tradi-tional garb, two of them building parts of a sledge and one of them sewing. Among the wax figures were sledges from the last three Peary expeditions, including the *Morris K. Jesup*, the sledge Peary took to the pole and subsequently donated to the museum. On the far side of the map on a platform covered with white cotton material to simulate snow was a stuffed polar bear flanked by two stuffed musk oxen. The exhibit also contained skulls, skins, and other specimens of Arctic wildlife, along with navigation instruments and photographs from Peary's expeditions.[86]

The Cape York Meteorites at the Museum

Until 1909, the Cape York meteorites were officially on loan from the Pearys to the museum. That year, after long negotiations, they became the property of the museum, bought for $40,000, with money provided by Jesup's widow.[87] They remained on display in the foyer of the Seventy-Seventh Street entrance pavilion until the week of July 8, 1935, when they were moved, along with the Willamette meteorite, to the Hayden Planetarium, then under construction. The *New York Times* described moving the Ahnighito as the museum's most difficult engi-neering feat in years.[88]

Peary had estimated its weight at between sixty and ninety tons. Museum scientists estimated the weight at 36.5 tons. But no one knew for sure until February 14, 1956. In the weeks preceding that date, the meteorite was hoisted while a custom-made Toledo scale was installed for the purpose of this measurement. The scale became a permanent part of the exhibit, and visitors could join the meteorite on the scale and observe how little the needle moved. Its weight was determined to be 34 tons, 85 pounds.[89]

In September 1979, the Ahnighito was moved from the planetarium to the museum's southwest corner pavilion, there to become the center-piece of a new exhibition hall—the Arthur Ross Hall of Meteorites. The move involved cutting a hole in the planetarium's west wall and the use of a fifty-five-foot crane, along with special supports built into the museum's new hall and extending to the bedrock of Manhattan Island to handle the weight. The new hall opened April 30, 1981,[90] and was revamped in 2003, reopening on September 2 of that year.[91]

While many visitors to the museum are awed by the great meteorites, few are aware of the connection between the museum, the meteorites, the conquest of the North Pole, and the extraordinary nature of Peary's undertakings.

5
The Osborn Years (1908–1933)

In 1908, when Henry Fairfield Osborn succeeded Morris K. Jesup as the president of the American Museum, the institution largely consisted of the Bickmore Wing and the southern façade on Seventy-Seventh Street. Osborn began by creating a detailed plan for the museum's growth, which would combine his vision of natural history and the building's original master plan. By the time he resigned twenty-five years later, the mold was set for the shape the museum has to this day. He achieved this, despite frustrating economic difficulties, through perseverance and compromise.

Osborn, born August 8, 1857, came from a well-connected New York family. He called the banking and finance tycoon J. P. Morgan "Uncle Morgan" because Morgan had at one time been married to Osborn's maternal aunt, Amelia Sturges. Amelia died the year after their marriage, when Henry Osborn was about five, and Morgan remained close to the Osborn family after her death. Morgan was also a founding member of the American Museum's trustees.[1]

Osborn's younger brother Frederick and future president Theodore Roosevelt frequently visited the American Museum together. In his autobiography, Albert Bickmore remembered Frederick Osborn as his favorite pupil, adding that when Frederick drowned in the Hudson River at the age of fifteen, Henry tried unsuccessfully to save him, narrowly escaping with his own life.[2] Another Osborn brother, William Church Osborn, became president of the Metropolitan Museum in 1941. After Henry Osborn's death, one of his sons, A. Perry Osborn, became acting president of the American Museum.

Henry Osborn earned a bachelor's degree from Princeton in geology and archaeology, where he was mentored by the noted paleontologist Edward Drinker Cope. After additional study at Cambridge, Osborn received a doctoral degree in paleontology from Princeton in 1880, where he taught until 1891. That year, he was hired jointly by Columbia University, as a professor of zoology, and by the American Museum, as curator of its new department of vertebrate paleontology. Within six years, Osborn had greatly expanded the museum's vertebrate fossil collection. In 1896, Osborn helped found the Bronx Zoo (originally named the New York Zoological Park) along with Andrew Haswell Green.[3]

Osborn was a prolific scientist, with hundreds of academic publications to his credit, and he would eventually come to be called the father of American paleontology. Less impressively, he also espoused controversial racialist theories that have long since been discredited. Shortly after Jesup's death on January 22, 1908, Osborn succeeded him as the museum's president.

History, Plan, and Scope

One of Osborn's first acts as president was to write a thorough study of the museum's past and future, titled *History, Plan, and Scope of the American Museum of Natural History*. Published in 1910, the study included Osborn's plans for the growth of the buildings and the future scope and arrangement of the exhibitions. The study also included a detailed outline of the subjects Osborn believed that the museum should cover and the state of their coverage at the time (for example, "Astronomy—Star System and Evolution of the Worlds: No exhibitions ready"; "Anthropology, Archeology, and Ethnology—Japan: Practically nothing"; "Siberian Tribes: Extensive collections"; "Zoology and Paleontology—Shells: Extensive series"; and "Reptiles: Extensive series").[4]

His plans included expanding the museum to fields not already covered, including astronomy, geography, and thalassography (the study of the sea and sea life).[5] Based on this list, Osborn made plans for filling gaps in the collections through expeditions and purchases and for creating a logical organization of the exhibition halls in conjunction with future construction.

While the report called for eventually completing the master plan, the primary focus was on filling in the southern half and adding a new auditorium in the north transept. This plan consisted of the following structures:

A west entrance pavilion facing Columbus Avenue and connected to the existing structure with a wide transept that would be an extension of the existing power plant;

An architecturally imposing east entrance pavilion on Central Park West, facing the park, connected to the existing structure with an east transept and a south wing on Central Park West;

A replacement of the existing central auditorium with a new five-story central pavilion, with a new larger auditorium in the north transept space;

Southeast and southwest courtyard buildings.

For the first time, the possibility of building in the negative spaces of the original master plan's courtyards was proposed.[6]

In conjunction with the proposed Central Park West entrance pavilion, Osborn proposed connecting the museum with Central Park by building a new concourse from the park's West Drive that would open

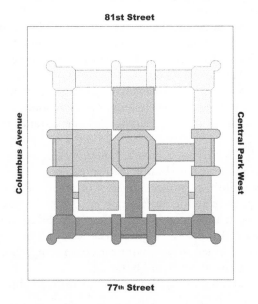

Sections proposed by Osborn in *History, Plan, and Scope of the American Museum of Natural History, 1910.*

onto Central Park West opposite the new entrance. This approach to the museum first had been proposed by Frederick Law Olmsted and endorsed by the Parks Board in 1875.[7]

As for the museum's interior, Osborn proposed what he described as "two principal ideas in sequence" for arranging the exhibits, namely "geographical" and "evolutionary."[8] As he wrote in *History, Plan, and Scope*: "Fortunately, the original plan of the American Museum by Calvert Vaux in 1873, of a great square with intersecting transepts, admirably provides for such sequence."[9]

Another principle he followed was to have exhibits about man (anthropology and archeology) located on the museum's western half and scientific exhibits (the physical and biological sciences) on the east. As an example of evolutionary arrangement, Osborn proposed locating the Astronomic Hall in the central pavilion because, as he explained, "It is obvious from the laws of the unity of nature, taught by Humboldt and Darwin, that all causes are ultimately astronomic and physical."[10] On the first floor, you would proceed from the Astronomic Hall to the earth sciences—geology and mineralogy—in the east transept and entrance pavilion, followed by thalassography (in the Central Park West south wing), followed by Darwin Hall, with a synopsis of the animal kingdom (in the southeast corner pavilion).[11]

As an example of geographical arrangement, Osborn proposed that on the first floor, as you passed through the Seventy-Seventh Street entrance pavilion to the west and circled the west court, you would encounter displays focusing on New York Indians (in the Seventy-Seventh Street west wing), Plains Indians (in the southwest corner pavilion), Southwest Indians (in the Columbus Avenue south wing), Mexico and Central America (in the Columbus Avenue entrance pavilion), and California and the South Pacific Coast (in the west transept).[12]

Based on the recent rate of growth, *History, Plan, and Scope* called for the construction of six new buildings over the next twelve years.[13] To assist with the building planning, the firm of Trowbridge & Livingston was hired to prepare architectural drawings.[14] For the next two years, Osborn and the trustees considered different building orders. *History, Plan, and Scope* called for starting with the west entrance pavilion, but ultimately they decided to start with the south wing on Central Park West and the southeast courtyard building.[15]

Osborn had another grand idea. In 1911, working behind the scenes, he hatched an ambitious plan concerning the approach to the museum from Central Park. It was becoming apparent that the Lower Reservoir, at the location of today's Great Lawn just to the west of the Metropolitan

Museum, was no longer necessary to the city's water supply. The secretary of the museum's board, Archer M. Huntington, suggested to Osborn that the space occupied by the reservoir be converted to park space and include an Intermuseum Promenade connecting the Metropolitan Museum and the American Museum by way of the proposed new concourse leading from the park's West Drive to the American Museum. He first revealed this plan in the museum's 1916 *Annual Report*.[16]

A False Start

The 1911 *Annual Report* looked ahead to the museum's fiftieth anniversary in 1919 and called for completing the proposed buildings described in *History, Plan, and Scope* for the occasion. And the report announced that money had been approved for the excavation and foundation for the first two buildings—the south wing on Central Park West and the southeast courtyard building—with the understanding that additional funds would immediately follow for completing the buildings. The southeast courtyard building was now slated for whale exhibits and was referred to as the Whale Court.[17]

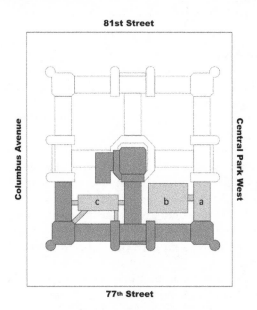

Museum sections built from 1922 to 1928:
(a) South Wing, Central Park West (1922–1924),
(b) Hall of Oceanic Life (1922–1924),
(c) Educational Services Building (1924–1928).

Excavation began on March 18, 1912, and was completed in November. But money for construction was not forthcoming. As excavation was underway, the city's financial condition worsened, and construction was halted in 1913.[18] The uncertainty increased as Europe entered World War I in July 1914. By 1916, it became apparent that construction would remain halted for some time. "The city is in such a bad way financially," one city official told Osborn, "that I don't see how we can do much for you until 1925 or thereabouts."[19] The excavation sites would remain yawning holes for a decade.

During this period, Osborn argued strenuously for new construction, emphasizing how the growth of the collections was outpacing available space. In 1915, he claimed that the museum's collections had doubled since the previous section was added a decade earlier:

> The museum is in the position of a family that has outgrown its home, of a business that has outgrown its offices, of a manufacturing concern that has outgrown its factory building, of a college or university that has outgrown its halls and dormitories. All available space of the present building, from attic to basement, has been utilized and collections have been retired from two large halls, formerly used for exhibition purposes, in order to make provision for the care and preparation of accumulating material.[20]

Compounding his frustration was the fact that Carl Akeley, the museum's African explorer, had conceived of a breathtaking design for an African Hall in the east transept that Osborn and the trustees were anxious to begin work on.

Over the next few years, Osborn responded to this state of affairs with four strategies.

First, he continued to urge the city to come up with the necessary money, economic conditions notwithstanding. His efforts were based on the belief that the lease agreement recorded in 1878 between the museum and the city was that the museum's trustees would pay for the collections and the city would pay for the building. Osborn argued that the city wasn't meeting its obligation of keeping up with the spending of the trustees or keeping up with the ability to house the collections provided by the trustees.[21]

Second, he solicited donations from private sources. The 1915 *Annual Report* explored this idea, stating that the trustees worried that this would set a bad precedent and lead to relieving the city of its obligation for future construction.[22] This concern was resolved on July 27, 1916, when the museum and Mayor Mitchell worked out a formal agreement that, given the emergency conditions, private funding of museum building would not affect the city's obligation to provide for future building.[23] The museum promptly began seeking money from the Carnegie Corporation to subsidize the new central pavilion, with its Rotunda of Astronomy, for presenting the discoveries of the Carnegie-funded observatories.[24]

Third, Osborn emphasized the museum's relationship with the city's public schools. During his administration, the educational outreach that had begun under Jesup continued to expand. In 1919, Osborn proposed building facilities to support this work. His argument included the fact that the 1878 lease agreement between the museum and the city required that city teachers have free access to the museum's facilities.[25] In 1920, Osborn's plan became more specific. He proposed building a School Services Building in the southwest courtyard to meet the needs of the rapidly growing number of schoolchildren visiting the museum.[26]

Finally, he solicited funds from New York State for a Roosevelt Memorial. Within a few months of the death of Theodore Roosevelt on January 6, 1919, Osborn recast the desired Central Park West entrance pavilion as a memorial to the former president and offered the city and state the opportunity to fund it.[27] This was a fitting gesture because of the former president's deep connections to the museum and his years in city and state government, including a stint as governor.[28] This led Governor Al Smith and the State Legislature to create a Roosevelt Memorial Commission in 1920, charged with making a formal proposal for a state-funded Roosevelt Memorial. The six-member commission included two state senators, two assemblymen, and two members at large, the latter consisting of Osborn and Peter D. Kiernan of Albany. Osborn was promptly elected the group's chairman.[29]

Up to 1921, Osborn's relentless campaigning to fund his grand vision was unsuccessful. But then began a reversal in the museum's fortunes.

Momentum Builds

The museum's 1921 *Annual Report* announced the good news: "The outstanding event of 1921 was the decision of the present City Government to renew the building construction of The American Museum of Natural History, which has been suspended for the last sixteen years owing to financial depression, to the suspension of all activities during the war, and to the high cost of building following the war."[30] On May

6 of that year, state law was amended so that construction at the museum would be "placed on precisely the same financial basis as School Buildings in the City of New York."[31]

Plans were promptly prepared for finishing the two buildings whose excavations had been completed a decade earlier. The money was appropriated on December 28,[32] and the buildings were finished in 1924.[33] Next up was the School Service Building, occupying the southwest courtyard. The five-story building was funded in 1922 and 1923,[34] construction began in 1924,[35] and it was completed two years later,[36] officially opening to the public on January 17, 1928.[37]

Despite the fact that Osborn had initiated the Roosevelt Memorial Commission for the purpose of creating a memorial at the American Museum, it immediately emerged that Kiernan and the upstate members, comprising half the commission, were pushing instead for an Albany location. In early 1924, the commission was still deadlocked, so they decided to leave the decision to the governor and legislature.[38]

By March 11, two competing bills had been introduced in the State Senate, one in favor of the American Museum and one in favor of Albany. The New York City representatives Nathan Straus Jr. and James Walker, a future mayor of New York City, drafted the bill supporting the American Museum location.[39] On April 9, after a heated debate, the

Aerial view of the American Museum of Natural History, c. 1926.
Source: AMNH ID 326167.

bill supporting the American Museum location was voted in, and on May 6 Governor Smith signed it into law.[40]

Early in 1925, the Memorial Commission held an architectural competition for the memorial's design. Participating architects were instructed that the design was to conclude an "Intermuseum Promenade connecting the eastern and western portions of the city across Central Park" and include an equestrian statue of the former president.[41]

Entries were submitted by eight firms, including Trowbridge & Livingston and John Russell Pope.[42] On June 2, 1925, Pope's Roman Revival design was selected.[43] The contract for the statue was awarded to the sculptor James Earle Fraser, who had designed the Buffalo nickel, and by December 22, 1926, plans, specifications, and a model of the memorial had been completed.[44] Then came three years of bureaucratic delay.[45]

Things finally turned around in 1929. In the museum's 1928 *Annual Report* (released May 1, 1929), Osborn beamed:

> Nineteen years ago the President laid before the Trustees the plan of the African and Grand Entrance Halls facing Central Park West. Fifteen years ago the future African Hall plan of Carl E. Akeley was presented to the Trustees. Ten years ago, January 6, 1919, Theodore Roosevelt passed away. . . . The ensuing years were crowded with difficulties which often seemed insurmountable, with repeated delays and disappointments, ending finally . . . in the complete triumph of the American Museum building program as first set forth in the year 1910.[46]

What had happened? On January 8, 1928, Jimmy Walker, by then the city's mayor, suggested a plan of concurrently building three new projects for the museum: the east transept, now known as the "Akeley Wing" (aka "African Hall"), the state-funded Roosevelt Memorial, and a Power and Service Building in the northwest courtyard.[47] (In 1926, the existing power plant had become filled to capacity, and the new building was deemed necessary. It was also to include space for exhibit preparation.)[48]

By March, it was clear that no private donor was forthcoming to fund a new central pavilion for the desired Astronomical Hall. So museum officials decided to raise money for a building in the northeast courtyard to house a temporary planetarium, hoping that it would be easier to find a donor for this less ambitious project.[49]

From January 3 to January 15, 1929, Osborn lobbied the state for funding for the Roosevelt Memorial, emphasizing the concurrent building plan of Mayor Walker. On January 15, they closed the deal, with funding appropriated for the foundation and promises of more to come.[50] On January 10, as Osborn was negotiating with the state, Harry Payne Whitney offered to pay half the cost of the north wing on Central Park West as a memorial to his father, William C. Whitney, if the city matched the gift. Until then, this wing had not been part of Osborn's plan for the foreseeable future.

William C. Whitney had been a museum trustee from 1891 until his death in 1904. His son was the sponsor of the museum's Whitney South Sea Expedition, which explored hundreds of islands in the South Pacific between 1920 and 1932, researching bird life and collecting specimens. The new wing would house the museum's ornithology department and would be called the Whitney Hall of Birds, or just the Whitney Wing. Appropriations by the city followed that year, including matching funds for the Whitney Wing.[51] Henry Payne Whitney would not live to see this building completed. He died on October 26, 1930.[52] In 1932, his widow bought the Rothschild bird collection for the museum, consisting of 280,000 specimens, the largest gift in the institution's history.[53]

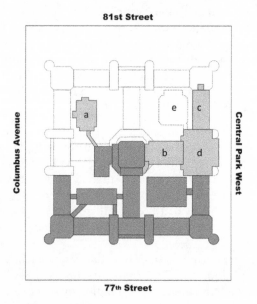

Museum sections built from 1930 to 1936:
(a) Power and Service Building (1930–1931),
(b) Akeley or African Building (1930–1934),
(c) Whitney Wing (1931–1933), (d) Theodore Roosevelt Memorial (1931–1936), (e) Proposed planetarium.

Beyond the Osborn Years

In 1931, Osborn announced his plans to retire in early 1933.[54] He was able to look back on his tenure knowing that three buildings had been added to the museum, with four more on the way. During the final years of his administration, work progressed relentlessly but slowly, with delays caused by the Great Depression. But before Osborn turned over the reins to his successor, he saw several momentous achievements met.

The cornerstone of the Roosevelt Memorial was laid by the former president's distant cousin, New York governor Franklin Delano Roosevelt, on October 27, 1931, which would have been Theodore Roosevelt's seventy-third birthday.[55] At the time, the structure had been built up to the second floor.[56] The construction of the Power and Service Building and the Akeley Wing was completed in 1932.[57] And construction of the Roosevelt Memorial and Whitney Wing was well underway. The strategy that would eventually prevail for building a planetarium was also in place. Thanks to these achievements, the shape the museum has today was set firmly in place.

Despite these accomplishments, during the height of the Depression no less, he was not satisfied. In the museum's 1932 *Annual Report*, the last of his presidency, he pushed for the construction of four additional buildings.[58]

On January 1, 1933, Osborn handed the museum's reins to his successor, F. Trubee Davison. Upon his retirement, the museum board unanimously elected Osborn honorary president for life.[59] That same year, Governor Franklin Roosevelt ascended to the presidency of the United States.

During the remaining years of the 1930s, the building projects begun during Osborn's final years rolled to completion.

On May 2, 1933, the Hall of Ocean Life opened in the southeast courtyard building. The iconic life-size ninety-four-foot blue whale model that hangs from its ceiling today would not be completed until 1969. But when the hall opened, there were numerous skeletons and models of smaller whales and other ocean creatures suspended from the ceiling.[60]

During Davison's first year, the long-sought planetarium finally became a reality, thanks to the New Deal programs of President Roosevelt, the lobbying of New York's emerging power broker Robert Moses, and the philanthropy of Charles Hayden, the planetarium's namesake. The Hayden Planetarium opened on October 10, 1935.

Osborn died on November 6, 1935, just a month after the planetarium's opening night and two months before the dedication of the Roosevelt Memorial.

Aerial view facing southwest, 1933. The Akeley and Whitney wings are complete, and the Roosevelt Memorial is under construction.

Aerial view facing southwest, 1933. Roosevelt Memorial under construction.

Aerial view facing northeast, 1937. The planetarium has been completed.

Sources: (*top*) Aerial Explorations Inc.; (*center*) McLaughlin Aerial Surveys; (*bottom*) McLaughlin Aerial Surveys.

On January 19, 1936, Franklin Roosevelt returned for the dedication of the Roosevelt Memorial, this time as the nation's president. After a rendition of "America" led by the Boy Scouts of America, speeches were made by President Roosevelt, Governor Herbert H. Lehman, and Mayor Fiorello H. La Guardia, among others.[61] The NBC Symphony Orchestra played "In Memoriam Theodore Roosevelt," a symphony commissioned for the event, at Radio City. The work was broadcast over the radio station WNYC and played through loudspeakers at the memorial.[62]

On May 19 of that year, the Akeley African Hall was dedicated, and it opened to the public the next day.[63] Only ten of the twenty-eight planned dioramas had been completed. The remaining ones were not fully installed until 1942.[64] On June 6, 1939, three halls in the Whitney Wing were formally opened.[65]

But the continuing Depression spelled the end of bold new building projects for the museum. According to the museum's 1936 *Annual Report*, "an exhaustive survey was made by the Trustees and the scientific and administrative staffs . . . to establish a program of development for the next ten years which could be confined to existing building facilities."[66]

The Finished Roosevelt Memorial

On October 27, 1940, the final touch was added to the Roosevelt Memorial when Roosevelt's widow, Edith, unveiled Fraser's equestrian statue on what would have been her husband's eighty-second birthday.[67]

Roosevelt Memorial.
Source: AMNH ID 336362.

Roosevelt Memorial and Central Park West façade.
Source: Wikimedia, author: Ihgfbruno.

The memorial, whose design had evolved slightly from Pope's original proposal, features a sixty-foot entrance arch above a 350-foot-long
plaza with steps funneling into the arch. On each side of the arch are
two Ionic columns supported by a pedestal that extends laterally, forming a low curving parapet wall. The two parapet walls delineate the
plaza and include twelve panels with bas-reliefs of animals native to
America and Africa, carved by Edward Field Sanford Jr. Atop the columns are statues by James Earle Fraser of Daniel Boone, John James
Audubon, William Clark, and Meriwether Lewis.

At the center of the plaza on a high pedestal in front of the entrance
arch is Fraser's equestrian statue, with Roosevelt seated on his horse and
towering over two half-nude figures on foot—a Native American on his
right and an African on his left. Originally described as "suggestive of
Roosevelt's interest in the original peoples of these widely separated
countries," in 2017, in the wake of a recent wave of removals of Confed-
erate monuments, these figures came under the scrutiny of a commission
appointed by Mayor Bill de Blasio to consider several controversial New
York City landmarks.

The 120-foot-by-sixty-seven-foot interior, known as the Roosevelt
Rotunda, features a barrel-vaulted ceiling reaching a height of one
hundred feet and is adorned by three large murals by William Andrew

Mackay representing important events in Roosevelt's life. As you enter the rotunda, looking straight ahead above the entrance to the Akeley African Hall, you see a mural depicting Roosevelt's African expeditions. To your right is a mural depicting the construction of the Panama Canal. And to your left is a mural depicting the signing of the Treaty of Portsmouth in 1905 to end the Russo-Japanese War. For his role in resolving the conflict, Roosevelt was the first American awarded the Nobel Peace Prize.[68]

Epilogue: The Road Not Taken

Crucial to Osborn's vision for the Roosevelt Memorial was the Roosevelt Concourse (as the approach to the memorial from Central Park's West Drive had become named) and the Intermuseum Promenade through the space occupied by the obsolete Lower Reservoir. The concourse would give the Roosevelt Memorial the grandeur of the Lincoln Memorial, allowing it to be seen from the vantage point it was designed for, and the promenade would provide a safe and easy connection between the sister museums, making it easier for visitors to see both on the same day.

Osborn's aim was for these to be finished simultaneously with the Roosevelt Memorial, and on January 23, 1930, as construction was beginning on the Roosevelt Memorial, the draining of the Lower Reservoir began in preparation for its demolition.[69] However, the concourse and promenade faced substantial opposition, starting immediately after Osborn first revealed his plan in the museum's 1915 *Annual Report*.[70]

The main issue was whether the plan fit with the park designers' original vision. A continuing issue for Central Park development had been a conflict between creating natural pastoral settings and creating playgrounds or monuments. Those favoring the pastoral settings, who became known as the preservationists, sought to maintain the park as originally intended by Olmsted and Vaux. Their ranks included the Park Association of New York City, dedicated to battling encroachments into the park, and the American Society of Landscape Architects, founded by sons and associates of Olmsted and Vaux. The preservationists viewed the proposed concourse and promenade as such an encroachment.[71]

Both sides had their points. Osborn argued that the sister museums, and implicitly the concourse and promenade, were not encroachments but instead "integral parts of the original Central Park system." The inclusion of museums and educational institutions was indeed integral

Proposed Roosevelt Concourse, 1930.
Source: *AMNH Annual Report* (1930), inside front cover.

to early park plans. To support his proposal for the concourse, Osborn cited the approach to the museum proposed by Olmsted in 1875. On the other hand, Olmsted and Vaux were resistant to encumbering the park with structures, which is why they wanted the zoo, and later the American Museum, placed on Manhattan Square and why the site for the Metropolitan Museum was selected: to be in peripheral locations not easily visible from within the park.[72]

Interestingly, Osborn's opponents in the preservationist camp included Mayor Walker and Nathan Straus Jr., both of whom had been Osborn's allies in 1924, being instrumental in getting the State Legislature to choose the American Museum site over Albany for the Roosevelt Memorial. Walker was inaugurated mayor in 1926. Straus by this time had become the president of the Park Association of New York City. Also in the preservationist camp was Walker's new park commissioner, Walter Herrick.

Another issue concerned the importance of the promenade and concourse in the 1924 legislative debate. According to Peter D. Kiernan, a member of the Roosevelt Memorial Commission who fought for the Albany location, doubt was expressed at the debate as to whether the American Museum could provide a suitably dignified setting. "Then Professor Osborn produced his masterpiece of a magnificent promenade connecting the Metropolitan Museum and the Roosevelt Memorial and the American Museum of Natural History. All the New York legislators endorsed this and it answered all our objections."[73] However, according

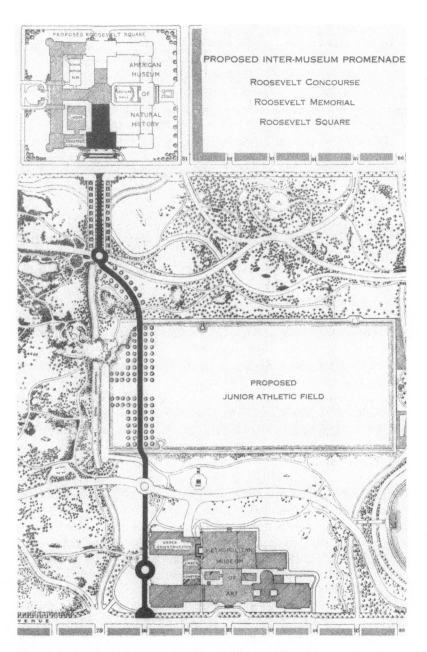

Museum's plan for the Intermuseum Promenade, April 3, 1922.
Source: AMNH Annual Report (1922), 18.

to Straus, he did "not recall mention of a proposal to build a highway through Central Park connecting the two museums" during the debate.[74] And of course another issue was that the project had to compete with other potential city, state, and park projects for scarce funds. Osborn championed his plan over the following year through bureaucratic infighting and by arguing for it in the court of public opinion via frequent letters to the editor of the *New York Times*.[75]

As the draining of the Lower Reservoir began, the American Society of Landscape Artists was drawing up a plan for the reservoir area that consisted of a great oval meadow and did not include the promenade. On April 21, the society submitted its plan to Commissioner Herrick, and he adopted it on June 1.[76]

Osborn's next move was to bypass the parks commissioner and go directly to the city's Board of Estimate and Apportionment for funding for the concourse and the promenade. On October 21, the opposing parties clashed at a meeting of the board. The board ended up sandbagging Osborn's proposal by consigning it to a committee for further consideration.[77]

President Roosevelt expressed his support for the project at the cornerstone-laying ceremony on October 27, 1931, saying: "When soon, from a great plaza in Central Park, we look up to this veritable arch of triumph, and to the heroic figure of Theodore Roosevelt at its front, let us say in our hearts, 'Hail, Leader and Friend, we greet you, we about to live!'"[78] Two months later, Roosevelt met with members of the Memorial Commission to try to resolve the controversy.[79] With Roosevelt's approval, Frederick Law Olmsted Jr., the son of the park's designer, was enlisted to complete an engineering study of the concourse and promenade.[80]

Because of the Depression, work on the plan for the reservoir stalled both from lack of money and because the area had become populated by colonies of homeless men.[81] "Only recently has a kindly Providence intervened as the only truly beneficent result of the financial depression, by suspending the execution of an opposing plan for the old Croton reservoir space," Osborn said in the museum's 1932 *Annual Report*.[82]

After Osborn retired from the museum presidency in 1933, he continued to maintain a keen interest in the concourse and promenade. With work on the reservoir stalled and with Olmsted Jr.'s study in hand, the museum pinned its hopes for the concourse and promenade on the incoming mayor, Fiorello La Guardia, who was inaugurated on January 1, 1934, and strongman Robert Moses, La Guardia's new parks commissioner.[83]

Almost immediately upon taking office, Moses vigorously resumed work on the reservoir plan, which had become known as the Great Lawn. The plan now included his own twist, namely more athletic fields than the strict preservationists would have preferred,[84] a change that did not bode well for Osborn's hopes for the promenade.

Regarding the concourse, the news was slightly better. Moses's landscape architect Francis Cormier drew up a plan for a scaled-down version of the concourse, and it was described in the *New York Times* on March 20 and 22, 1935. It provided an eastern approach to the memorial but did not extend all the way to the West Drive, rendering it useless in terms of connecting to points east within the park.[85]

Predictably, Osborn found the proposal unacceptable, and on March 29 he wrote a letter to Moses asking to discuss the matter. As Osborn put it: "Why should not a Yale graduate, 1909, meet a Princeton graduate, 1877, who is also an Honorary Doctor of Yale, and talk over the arrangements for the completion of the Memorial to a great Harvard graduate?"[86] Moses sent Cormier to discuss the plan with Osborn on April 2,[87] but on May 16, the *New York Times* reported that Moses had decided to shelve even the scaled-down approach to the memorial.[88]

Never one to admit defeat easily, Osborn persisted, writing to Davison, the museum's new president, on June 3: "Without the easterly approaches to the west driveway of Central Park the superb design has no meaning. . . . I trust, therefore, that you will back me a hundred percent in the vitally important and most pressing matter to which I have devoted the past quarter century of my life."[89]

Osborn died on November 6 that year. Although he did not have the satisfaction of attending the dedication of the Roosevelt Memorial, which occurred two months later on January 19, 1936, he lived to see the project taken to the point of certain success. He was less lucky with the concourse and promenade. However, he managed to persist from the grave. His son A. Perry Osborn served as the museum's vice president under Davison and continued to campaign for the cause.

This led Moses to write to Davison on February 15, 1937:

You will recall that while the Professor was still living, I told you that the Park Department would not agree to any such crazy, expensive, and objectionable plan as the Professor proposed for a formal architectural mall or esplanade connecting the two museums, or for any new formal entrance in the Park leading to the American Museum of Natural History. You will recall that we

went over this thoroughly, and you will also remember how persistent the Professor was about it. . . . Apparently Perry Osborn has
simply taken up his father's old scheme.

He concluded, "I am getting a little sick of this subject and suggest that
we . . . stop raking up old ashes." And that was that.[90]

6

The Akeley African Hall
From the Elephant in the Room
to the Seven-Hundred-Pound Gorilla

When you enter the American Museum of Natural History from Central Park West, cross the Theodore Roosevelt Rotunda, and pass into the Akeley Hall of African Mammals, the first thing you see is a magnificent herd of eight alarmed African elephants (*Loxodonta africana*) atop an elevated platform. Two of the elephants have their trunks raised, as if testing the air. At the back of the herd, a younger male has wheeled around to guard the rear. At the center of the group, a baby female has wrapped its trunk around the trunk of its mother.

Akeley Hall elephant group.
Source: Wikimedia, author: InSapphoWeTrust.

97

Akeley Hall mountain gorilla diorama.
Source: Wikimedia, author: Thom Quine.

Along with the elephant group, the best-known display in the African Hall is the mountain gorilla (*Gorilla beringei beringei*) diorama in the
southeast corner, to your left as you enter the space. This diorama depicts
a gorgeous forest setting with towering volcanoes in the background. A
giant silverback male dominates the scene while other amiable gorillas
lounge around nearby. Four gorillas are readily visible; a fifth is hidden
by heavy vegetation. But contrary to what many people believed, the
giant male did not weigh seven hundred pounds. That was one of the
myths about the gorilla that Carl Akeley, the creator of the hall that bears
his name, dispelled. The creature actually weighed just 360 pounds.

The trajectory of Akeley's entire life led directly to this hall, and it
was his single-minded focus over the final seventeen years of his life.
The space opened on May 19, 1936, ten years after his death, on what
would have been his seventy-second birthday. His work on the hall had
begun with the elephants and ended when he died in Africa while
working on the gorillas.

Carl Akeley

Carl Akeley was born on May 19, 1864, in upstate New York. At the
age of thirteen, he took up taxidermy,[1] and at sixteen he printed up

business cards advertising "Artistic Taxidermy in all its Branches."[2] Before he had turned twenty, he was combining his stuffed animals with painted backgrounds[3] and had landed a job in the taxidermy department of a company called Ward's Natural Science Establishment. While there, in 1885, he was assigned the task of stuffing Jumbo, P. T. Barnum's famous elephant, after it was hit by a train.[4] Akeley also mounted Jumbo's skeleton, which was given to the American Museum in 1889.[5] Akeley's Jumbo skeleton was kept on display at the museum until the 1960s and was brought out for temporary exhibits in 1974 and 1993.[6]

Around 1886, Akeley applied for a taxidermy position with the American Museum, but nothing came of it.[7] He instead began working for the Milwaukee Public Museum, where in 1889 he created a muskrat diorama that is believed to be the first habitat diorama, that is, a lifelike habitat scene set within a display case containing mounted specimens in a foreground that merges with a realistic background painting. Akeley's muskrat diorama is still on display today.[8]

In 1896, Akeley moved to the Chicago's Field Museum to head the institution's taxidermy department.[9] That year, the Field Museum sent Akeley on his first African expedition, to British Somaliland (now part of Somalia), where he obtained specimens for fifteen groups for the museum. By the time he returned, he recalled, "I had determined upon Africa as the country whose superb animals I would re-create through museum groups for the benefit of the American public." During this trip, he famously survived a leopard attack by strangling the creature with his bare hands.[10]

After returning from Africa, Akeley developed a set of deer groups, called the Four Seasons, showing the animals in spring, summer, autumn, and winter. The project took four years, during which Akeley refined his innovative taxidermy techniques—techniques that would continue to evolve throughout his entire career.

In 1902, while Akeley was visiting the American Museum, Hermon Bumpus, the institution's director, introduced him to James L. Clark, a young sculptor he had just hired. This meeting led Akeley to invite Clark to Chicago for several months to study Akeley's secret taxidermy methods.[11]

Elephants, Roosevelt, and the American Museum

Akeley first made the acquaintance of the African elephant when he returned to Africa for the Field Museum in October 1905, this time to British East Africa (now Kenya). He was accompanied by his first wife,

Delia, an experienced explorer and hunter in her own right. Akeley killed an elephant on July 27, 1906, and on August 31, Delia shot the largest elephant ever killed on Mount Kenya. The couple brought back the skins of both animals, along with the skull from Mrs. Akeley's record breaker.[12] From the skins, Akeley created the Fighting African Elephants, to this day one of the Field Museum's iconic exhibits.[13]

Upon returning from Africa in December 1906, Akeley was greeted in New York by Illinois congressman James L. Mann, who carried with him an invitation to visit President Roosevelt at the White House. Apparently, on a visit to the Field Museum, Akeley's Four Seasons deer groups had caught Roosevelt's eye.

As Akeley recounts the meeting in *In Brightest Africa*, his 1923 account of his travels to the continent, as Roosevelt, Akeley, and the rest of the party entered the dining room, spurred on by a visitor from Alaska, Roosevelt announced, "As soon as I am through with this job, I am going to Alaska for a good hunt." During dinner, Akeley regaled Roosevelt with tales of Africa, and as the party left the dining room, Roosevelt announced, "As soon as I am through with this job, I am going to Africa."[14]

By this point, Akeley had become determined to create a five-elephant display, but he was unable to get support for the plan from the Field Museum. So he brought the idea to Henry Fairfield Osborn at the American Museum. Osborn, then head of the museum's department of vertebrate paleontology—and who had been interested in elephants for as long as he could remember—supported Akeley's proposal. But Akeley and Osborn couldn't get support from the museum's trustees.[15]

In November 1908, as Roosevelt was approaching the end of his presidency, Akeley again visited the president at the White House, this time to consult on Roosevelt's planned expedition to Africa.[16] Since Akeley was trying to organize a trip of his own to collect elephants for a museum group, the two men agreed that they should try to meet in Africa. In March 1909, three weeks after leaving office, Roosevelt departed for Africa with his son Kermit, his main objective being to collect specimens for the Smithsonian Institute.[17]

In 1909, after Osborn had become president of the American Museum, Akeley joined the institution, and that August he was sent on an expedition to Africa to collect elephants.[18] When Akeley's party, which included his wife and the famous cartoonist John T. McCutcheon, arrived in Nairobi in September, he found waiting for him a letter from Roosevelt, renewing the ex-president's desire to help collect elephants.[19] (While in Nairobi in September, Roosevelt received the cable from Robert Peary announcing Peary's attainment of the North Pole.)[20]

Once in Africa, Akeley reunited with James Clark, the young man who had been dispatched to Chicago by the American Museum in 1902 to study Akeley's taxidermy methods and who had been adventuring in Africa for about a year, having quit his job at the American Museum to do so.[21]

By chance, the safaris of Akeley and Roosevelt crossed paths on Mount Kenya in British East Africa (now Kenya) on November 14. Also by chance, the Roosevelt party had sighted a herd of elephants that very morning. The next day, Akeley and the two Roosevelts set out with the goal of collecting a female elephant (cow) and a baby elephant (calf). By noon, they had caught up to the herd the Roosevelts had sighted the previous day.

Akeley selected a cow for Theodore Roosevelt to shoot. But when Roosevelt approached the target and shot, the herd charged. The other members of the party joined in the shooting, and by the time the slaughter was over, three cows were dead. Later that day, Kermit Roosevelt shot a bull calf that Akeley had selected. It then fell to Akeley, Clark, and a team of native assistants the grueling work of preparing the hides of the four elephants.[22] On Christmas Eve, McCutcheon shot a young bull.[23]

About a year into the expedition, things took a turn for the worse. While following an elephant trail, Akeley sensed an elephant charging him from behind. He wheeled around and found a tusk at his chest. Acting quickly, he grabbed both tusks and swung himself on them like a pair of parallel bars while the elephant buried the points of the tusks in the ground on either side of him. This quick reaction, which Akeley had mentally rehearsed in case of just such an emergency, saved his life.

However, he did not escape unharmed. From this position, which Akeley described as being used as a "prayer rug," the elephant swiped its trunk upward from its position curled underneath the beast, tearing open Akeley's cheek and breaking his nose. The incident also crushed several of his ribs into his lungs. Some of Akeley's native assistants guarded his body—they thought him dead—while others went off to summon his wife. Akeley was bedridden for the next three months, giving him plenty of time to think about the African Hall.[24] After a long convalescence, in spite of not being fully recovered, Akeley shot an old bull.[25]

Four of the eight elephants in the centerpiece of the African Hall are from this expedition. The mother in the mother-baby pair was the elephant killed by Theodore Roosevelt, and the baby was the one killed by his son. The elephant guarding the rear was the one killed by McCutcheon, and the old bull with the extended trunk (to the left of the group if you are standing near the room's entrance) was the one killed by Akeley.[26]

The Roosevelt African Hall

Akeley returned from Africa in 1911 with his mind "saturated with the beauty and wonder of the continent," as he described his emotions in *In Brightest Africa*. He also returned with a vision for the museum's African Hall that he would spend the rest of his life trying to fulfill.[27]

He fleshed out his plan and brought it to Osborn the following year. The two men then presented the plan to the museum's trustees, who determined that it could move forward as soon as money was available.[28] This was not a trivial precondition, since there had been no new building since 1908 and, because of economic conditions, none on the horizon.

Akeley's plans consisted of a sixty-foot-by-152-foot hall on the second floor of the east transept. (In 1910, well before Akeley conceived of his vision, Osborn had already planned a hall devoted to the life of Africa in this location.)[29] At the center of the hall, on a four-foot-high base, would stand the elephant group, built from the hides of the four elephants Akeley had brought home from the 1909–1911 expedition. At each corner of the elephant group would be a group of rhinoceroses, with white rhinos at one end and black rhinos at the other. On the third floor, there would be a gallery overlooking the hall. The second- and third-floor spaces would be framed by twenty major diorama groups, each a window onto a different region of Africa and featuring different wildlife.

Akeley believed that it was the ideal time to create such a space. Twenty-five years earlier, the necessary taxidermy and museum techniques had not yet been developed. Twenty-five years later, extinction and the spread of civilization would make collecting the necessary specimens impossible.[30]

The next step was to create a scale model of the proposed hall and to start mounting the elephants. In 1913, a workspace known as the Elephant Studio was created for Akeley on the museum's second floor, in

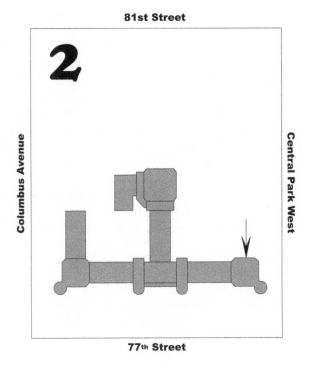

Location of Akeley's elephant studio.

the southeast corner (now part of the Stout Hall of Asian Peoples). To create this studio, the exhibits previously in that location (Mammals of the Polar Region and Reptiles and Amphibians) were moved to other already overcrowded areas of the museum.[31]

On April 22, 1914, Akeley unveiled his plans at a joint meeting of the National Sculpture Society, the Architectural League of New York, and the MacDowell Club. After an illustrated talk on hunting in Africa, Akeley led a tour of his Elephant Studio, showing the model of the hall and his work in progress mounting the bull elephant he had killed.[32]

The beginning of World War I, on July 28, 1914, slowed the progress of the project in several ways. It stymied the museum's ability to obtain money for new building, and it made it impossible to conduct new expeditions to do research and collect more specimens. In addition, Akeley joined the war effort. Among his many talents, Akeley was an inventor, and he was recruited as a specialist on mechanical devices and optical equipment in the Division of Investigation, Research, and Development of the Engineer Corps, a position that took him from New York to Washington on a weekly basis.[33] He also lost his chief assistant, Louis Paul Jonas, for several years when Jonas joined the army in 1917.[34]

Nonetheless, even during the war, work proceeded on the elephant group. According to the museum's 1917 *Annual Report*, "The close of the year finds the young male nearly finished, the female and young well advanced, and the huge male about one half done."[35] The group was completed in 1920 and put on display on January 1, 1921, in the Elephant Studio.[36]

Around the same time, the American Museum obtained from Chicago's Field Museum the skull of Delia Akeley's record-breaking bull from the 1905–1906 expedition and put it on display next to Akeley's skeleton of Jumbo.[37]

In 1920, after the death of Theodore Roosevelt on January 6, 1919, the proposed African Hall was renamed the Roosevelt African Hall.[38] Akeley wrote in *In Brightest Africa*, "The thought that my greatest undertaking was to stand as a memorial to Theodore Roosevelt doubled my incentive. I am giving the best there is in me to make Roosevelt African Hall worthy of the name it bears."[39]

Gorilla Country

After finishing the elephant group, Akeley's focus turned to the African gorilla. The original plans for the 1909–1911 expedition had been to travel south to collect gorillas after the elephant hunting, but this project had been abandoned after the mauling Akeley received from the elephant attack and postponed further by World War I. The plan was resurrected in 1920, when Akeley persuaded Herbert E. and Mary Hastings Bradley, a wealthy couple he had known for years, to join him on a gorilla expedition. As Mrs. Bradley wrote of Akeley's passion for the undertaking: "The gorilla took possession of his imagination."[40]

Accompanying the Bradleys was their five-year old daughter, Alice, who grew up to lead a fascinating life. Among other things, she became a famous science-fiction author, writing under the male pseudonym James Tiptree Jr. Tiptree's secret identity was inadvertently revealed to be Alice Bradley Sheldon when her mother died.[41]

At the time of this expedition, scientific knowledge of gorilla behavior was based on ignorance and misinformation. The gorilla was believed to be a ferocious creature given to abducting women and crushing hunters' guns with its teeth. Akeley's intuition told him that the great apes had an undeserved bad reputation, and he was, as he put it, "prepared to find in him a decent and amiable creature."[42]

The party departed from Cape Town, South Africa, by train on September 3, 1921, and worked its way to the Belgian Congo by train and boat. Accompanied by a large team of native assistants, they then made their way by foot to gorilla country, a triangle of three volcanoes—Mount Mikeno, Mount Karisimbi, and Mount Visoke, all part of the Virunga Mountain Range—northeast of Lake Kivu in what is now the eastern edge of the Democratic Republic of the Congo.

On October 30, Akeley left the Bradleys at a Belgian post while he and a team of natives headed for the rain forests of Mount Mikeno to search for gorillas. After acquiring two females, an old male, and a young male, Akeley sent for the Bradleys. Several days later, on Mount Karisimbi, Herbert Bradley shot the great silverback male gorilla that dominates the museum's gorilla diorama and has become one of the institution's most iconic images.

The location portrayed in the diorama is the one where Bradley shot the gorilla, one that Akeley thought had the most beautiful view he had ever seen, with Mount Mikeno "at her best . . . sharply outlined against the blue of the tropical sky" with the vegetation's "warm greens and browns."[43] According to Mrs. Bradley, Akeley said wistfully, "I wish I could be buried here when I die."[44]

Throughout the expedition, Akeley did groundbreaking filming with the so-called Akeley camera, a movie camera he had invented for just this purpose, producing the first footage of gorillas in their native habitat.[45]

As for his intuitions about the gorilla's temperament, Akeley was proved right. He saw no signs of ferocity from the beasts, "even on just provocation."[46] After shooting them, he wrote in *In Brightest Africa*, he felt that he, rather than the gorilla, "was the savage and the aggressor."[47]

While on Mount Mikeno, Akeley's beliefs about the immense scientific importance of the study of the gorilla, along with his fear of their extinction, led him to the idea of turning the region into a gorilla sanctuary.[48] Almost immediately upon his return home he began trying to persuade the Belgian government, which controlled colonial Congo, to create such a refuge. The result was the establishment, on March 2, 1925, of Parc National Albert, encompassing Mount Mikeno, Mount

Karisimbi, and Mount Visoke and named for Belgium's King Albert.[49] It was here that Dian Fossey, the intrepid zoologist, primatologist, and anthropologist of *Gorillas in the Mist* fame, would later establish her research camp.

Once back at the museum, Akeley mounted the five gorillas he had brought home and began designing the gorilla exhibit, with the aim of making it as accurate as possible. This included correcting the creature's reputation from vicious savage to what he called "a great amiable creature in a setting of extraordinary beauty."[50]

Akeley also believed that every tree and blade of grass had to be a true and faithful copy of nature and that the painter of the background and the preparers of the artificial vegetation had to examine the actual spot to photograph, gather materials, and collect data.[51] Osborn approved an expedition for this purpose and to collect other specimens for the African Hall, on the condition that Akeley raise the money.

Roy Chapman Andrews, later to become director of the museum and a leader of expeditions to Central Asia, recalled frequent discussions about Akeley with Osborn during this period, including one in which Osborn said, "Akeley will kill himself before the project can come into completion." And he added, "To get New York City to build a new addition at this time is next to impossible. If only he would settle for one of the existing halls, we might get somewhere. Won't you talk to him and see what you can do?" But Akeley would settle for nothing less than a custom-built hall based on his models.[52]

During this period, Akeley wrote and lectured tirelessly to promote his vision, including publishing in 1923 his autobiographical *In Brightest Africa*. Its final chapter contained detailed designs for the African Hall.[53] However, it appears that Osborn managed to talk Akeley down from forty dioramas, as proposed in *In Brightest Africa*, to thirty-six.[54]

The Last Expedition

By 1925, Akeley had found three donors to pay for an expedition—George Eastman, cofounder of the Eastman Kodak Company; Daniel Pomeroy, a banker and museum trustee; and Colonel Daniel B. Wentz.[55] On January 30, 1926, Akeley departed for Africa with his second wife, Mary Jobe Akeley, who, like his first wife, was an experienced explorer and hunter in her own right. On their way to Africa, they stopped in Belgium to meet with King Albert to discuss the Parc National Albert sanctuary that Akeley inspired.

In the spring, the couple met the rest of their team in eastern Africa. This group included donors Eastman and Pomeroy (Wentz had died); some staff members of the museum, including the landscape artist William R. Leigh; and the filmmaking team of Martin and Osa Johnson, who had been on an extended expedition to Africa for Akeley and the museum since 1923.[56]

The team spent several grueling months in Uganda, Kenya, and Tanganyika (now Tanzania) collecting material for ten African Hall diorama groups.[57] In August, Akeley developed a high fever, became extremely weak from the exertion, and had to travel three hundred miles for treatment in Nairobi. His health had already been compromised by repeated injuries and by bouts of dysentery and malaria during previous expeditions.

By October 14, Akeley insisted that he was well enough to travel to where the gorillas had been collected in 1921, in the Parc National Albert sanctuary, the part of the expedition he was most anticipating. During the journey he became so weak that at times he had to be carried. By November 14, when the group reached the saddle between Mounts Mikeno and Karisimbi, he was bedridden, and he died three days later, on November 17, 1926. As he had often wished, Akeley was buried at the site he loved so much. The expedition team worked in twelve-hour shifts excavating a tomb in the lava rock. They then built a mahogany coffin and surrounded the grave with an eight-foot-high fence.

Despite this tragic turn of events, the expedition proceeded, with Mary Jobe Akeley taking charge, and the team spent the next six weeks gathering materials for the diorama group. Mrs. Akeley and the artist William Leigh located the spot on Mount Karisimbi where Bradley had shot the great silverback male gorilla, and Leigh did painting studies for the diorama's background. The team also photographed and collected samples of vegetation, soil, and rocks.[58]

The Akeley African Hall

Although Akeley had always assumed that the African Hall would be named after Theodore Roosevelt, in June 1927 the museum trustees decided to name the space in Akeley's honor: the Akeley Memorial Hall of African Mammals, or simply the Akeley African Hall.[59]

James Clark, Akeley's long-time protégé and associate, was put in charge of the preparation and installation of the space and its dioramas.

He took on this responsibility in 1927, shortly after returning from an expedition to Mongolia, in which he had been detained and tortured by bandits near the Russian border. His responsibilities included hiring a talented staff of artists and taxidermists and leading several expeditions to collect specimens. It also fell to Clark to get the architects to modify their plans for the east transept to accommodate Akeley's models, widening it and adjusting the placement of columns. In addition to creating the Akeley African Hall, Clark also led the creation of the museum's Hall of South Asiatic Mammals and Hall of North American Mammals.[60]

Mrs. Akeley assumed the role of advisor on the Akeley African Hall, working in an office at the museum surrounded by her husband's work.[61] She was also instrumental in getting the Parc National Albert sanctuary expanded tenfold in 1929,[62] wrote prolifically about the Akeleys' African adventures,[63] and returned to Africa on an expedition for the museum in 1935.[64]

Funding for the Akeley Wing was finally approved in 1929. The freeze on construction that had began in 1908 ended in 1922, with the museum filling in the southern portion of Manhattan Square. In 1929, money was approved for four new buildings to be built simultaneously: the Akeley Wing (the east transept), the Roosevelt Memorial (the Central Park West entrance pavilion), the Whitney Wing (the north wing on Central Park West), and the Power and Service building (in the northeast courtyard), with construction of all four projects to proceed simultaneously.[65]

While the final design of the African Hall was faithful to Akeley's original plans, some modifications were made. By 1931, the number of planned dioramas had dropped to twenty-eight. The rhino groups, originally planned for the corners of the central elephant group, became dioramas.[66] And in the spring of 1933, the African Hall committee decided to expand the elephant group from four specimens to eight and to send F. Trubee Davison to Africa to obtain them.[67] Davison had become president of the American Museum a few months earlier, in January 1933, after Osborn's retirement, and in this short time had already succeeded in obtaining funding for the museum's long-desired planetarium. Davison was accompanied by his wife, Dorothy, and their mission was to collect four medium-sized "Shamba" elephants—rogue elephants that killed natives and trampled property.

The expedition's most exciting moment occurred on August 3. By that date, Davison had gotten a young bull, his wife had gotten a larger bull, another team member had gotten a medium-sized cow, and the

search was on for one more cow. That day, the team had tracked a herd
for five hours and selected a suitable specimen. Davison downed the cow
while his wife stood behind him filming. Then a large bull started
charging the couple. Davison took a shot and was knocked backward
into his wife, and the two of them fell into thorn bushes. Two other
members of the party also fired, and the bull went down just eighteen
paces from where Davison had stood.[68]

The Akeley African Hall was dedicated on May 19, 1936, on what
would have been Akeley's seventy-second birthday.[69] When the space
opened, only ten of the planned twenty-eight dioramas had been completed. The final ones, the cheetah and chimpanzee dioramas on the
third-floor gallery, were not installed until 1942.[70]

Epilogue: In Akeley's Footsteps

This chapter ends, like Akeley's life, in Akeley's gorilla country.

In November 2010, Stephen C. Quinn, then a senior project manager
for the museum and the author of the book *Windows on Nature: The Great
Habitat Dioramas of the American Museum of Natural History*, retraced Akeley's steps on an expedition supported by the museum and several other
institutions. The mission was to document the changes to the region
since Akeley's visits in the 1920s.

Quinn visited the saddle between Mounts Mikeno and Karisimbi (in
Akeley's Parc National Albert, since renamed Virunga National Park),
where Akeley died and was buried, and shot footage of gorillas in their
native habitat. On November 28, he visited the site depicted in the
diorama, where Bradley shot the great silverback male, by hacking his
way through the forests of Mount Karisimbi, using Leigh's sketches and
painting as a guide. He then painted an updated image of the view,
which depicts a landscape profoundly transformed since Akeley's visits
nearly a century earlier, now heavily marred by refugee camps, radio
towers, and deforestation.[71]

7

The Evolution of the Dinosaur Exhibits

The American Museum of Natural History is probably best known for its dinosaur exhibits. The gigantic creatures that dominated Earth's surface hundreds of millions of years ago never fail to capture the public's imagination. For more than a century, the museum has been home to the world's most important collection of dinosaur fossils, a trove that traces its roots to the origins of modern paleontology.

Dinosaurs and their closest relatives lived throughout the Mesozoic Era, a time period subdivided into the Triassic Period (250 to 208 million years ago), the Jurassic Period (208 to 144 million years ago), and the Cretaceous Period (144 to 65 million years ago). The earliest dinosaurs appeared around 230 million years ago, during the Triassic Period, but the best-known species date to the Jurassic and Cretaceous Periods.

What distinguishes dinosaurs from other reptiles is their hip structure, posture, and locomotion, all of which are related. Dinosaurs had evolved hip structures that allowed their rear legs to extend straight down to the ground, resulting in a more erect posture compared to that of other reptiles, and a stride in which the legs swung vertically backward and forward.

There are two main groups of dinosaurs: ornithischian ("bird-hipped") and saurischian ("lizard-hipped"). The pelvises of ornithischian dinosaurs have backward-pointing pubic bones, like birds, whereas the pubic bones of saurischian dinosaurs point forward. Paleontologists have recently concluded that the modern-day bird evolved from dinosaurs—but from saurischian dinosaurs rather than from "bird-hipped" ornithischian dinosaurs.

The history of the museum's dinosaur halls can be traced from the origins of modern paleontology, through the growth of its buildings, to the current exhibits, by tracing the history of the six specimens shown in the accompanying table, which have historically formed the center-pieces of those halls.

The *Apatosaurus* ("deceptive lizard," formerly known as *Brontosaurus*, or "thunder lizard"), one of the largest animals ever to walk on land. It is a member of a subgroup of saurischian dinosaurs known as sauropods ("lizard-footed") and lived during the Jurassic era.	
The *Allosaurus* ("different lizard"), a member of a subgroup of saurischian dinosaurs known as carnosaurs ("flesh lizards"). Carnosaurs were the largest meat-eating animals ever to walk on land. The *Allosaurus* lived during the Jurassic era.	
The *Stegosaurus* ("covered lizard"), named for the prominent plates jutting from its back. It is a member of a subgroup of ornithischian dinosaurs known as thyreophorans ("shield carrier") and lived during the Jurassic era.	
The *Tyrannosaurus rex* ("king tyrant lizard"), one of the largest of the carnosaur subgroup of saurischian dinosaurs. It is one of the fiercest and best-known dinosaurs and lived during the Cretaceous era.	
The *Triceratops* ("three-horned face"), named for the three horns jutting from its face and characterized by the frill at the back of its skull. It is a member of a subgroup of ornithischian dinosaurs known as marginocephalians ("fringed head") and lived during the Cretaceous era.	
The *Anatotitan* ("titanic duck," formerly known as *Trachodon*, or "rough tooth"), a member of the family of duck-billed dinosaurs known as hadrosaurs ("large lizard"), which is a subgroup of ornithischian dinosaurs. It lived during the Cretaceous era.	

Modern Paleontology

In 1842, the British naturalist Richard Owen coined the term *dinosaur*, from the Greek for "terrible lizard." Although dinosaur fossils had been turning up for centuries, it was Owen who correctly interpreted their scientific significance, accurately asserting that the fossils were from an extinct group of large reptiles with an upright posture.

In 1858, one year before the publication of Darwin's *On the Origin of Species* and three years before the outbreak of the Civil War, the first nearly complete dinosaur skeleton was discovered in Haddonfield, New Jersey. Over the next several decades the new field of dinosaur paleontology emerged, and with it, one of the more dramatic episodes in scientific history. It involved the two leading figures in the field: Edward Drinker Cope, one of the youngest members of the Academy of Natural Sciences in Philadelphia, and Othniel Charles Marsh, a Yale professor. Their professional relationship began cordially, but it erupted into a bitter rivalry that ultimately destroyed their reputations, finances, and health.

Cope and Marsh both employed teams of men, and their hunts for dinosaur fossils took them on grueling multiyear expeditions, traveling by rail, stagecoach, and covered wagon to the American West, particularly to Colorado, Wyoming, Montana, and South Dakota, where unique geological conditions existed for preserving dinosaur remains. All the while, they spied on each other and sabotaged each other's efforts.

Collectively the two discovered hundreds of extinct species and tens of thousands of fossil specimens. According to a letter from Darwin, Marsh's work proved to be "the best support of the theory of evolution." And on January 12, 1890, the rivalry between the two men jumped from the domain of small scientific circles to mass public awareness when the *New York Herald* published a front-page article about their stormy relationship headlined "Scientists Wage Bitter Warfare."

Although the museum had featured fossils since its creation in 1869, still by 1891 the institution had no dinosaur specimens. That year, in the wake of the recent publicity over the feud between Cope and Marsh, the museum's president, Morris K. Jesup, decided that the time had come for the museum to get into the dinosaur game. He first tried to woo Marsh and his fossils away from Yale. After that effort failed, in May of that year Jesup hired a young paleontologist named Henry Fairfield Osborn, who had been mentored by Cope at Princeton, to establish and curate the museum's department of vertebrate paleontology.[1]

By 1897, Osborn had greatly expanded the museum's vertebrate fossil collection. But the institution still had no dinosaurs. So that year, Osborn began organizing dinosaur-hunting expeditions and hired a twenty-three-year-old fossil hunter named Barnum Brown. That summer, on an expedition to a region of Wyoming that Cope and Marsh had been exploring since the late 1870s, Osborn and Brown found what would become the museum's first dinosaur, a *Diplodocus*.[2]

Over the next several years, the fossil-hunting staff grew, and the region yielded tons of dinosaur bones. It was there, for example, in 1898, that Walter Granger, one of Osborn's paleontologists, found the museum's prized *Apatosaurus* specimen, which became the institution's first mounted dinosaur and remains one of its biggest attractions.[3] Brown would become a celebrity. He continued to be involved with the museum and hunted dinosaurs around the world until his death just days before his ninetieth birthday, ultimately collecting more than anyone else in history.

In 1899, Jesup purchased Cope's entire reptile and dinosaur collection for the museum from Cope's widow. (Cope had died in 1897. The museum had purchased his fossil mammal collection in 1895.)[4] This purchase, combined with the acquisitions from the museum's expeditions, gave the institution the world's most important dinosaur collection. (Incidentally, 1899 was also the year that Marsh died.)

1905—The Hall of Fossil Reptiles/Dinosaur Hall

The museum also finished construction of its Seventy-Seventh Street façade that same year, 1899. From the beginning, the museum's dinosaur's exhibits have always been located on the fourth floor. The first dinosaurs were displayed in the southeast corner pavilion as part of the Hall of Fossil Reptiles, later called Dinosaur Hall. (Today, the space is the home of the Hall of Primitive Mammals.) The *Apatosaurus* was unveiled there in February 1905. At the time, the creature was known by the name *Brontosaurus*.

The mount consisted primarily of the specimen found by Granger in 1898, although missing bits were filled in from various other sources. From the time of its discovery until its unveiling in 1905, a museum team worked full time unearthing, preparing, and mounting the *Apatosaurus*, inventing techniques as they went along. It was the largest fossil skeleton and the first dinosaur of its kind ever mounted. One thighbone weighs 570 pounds.[5] An article about the new *"Brontosaurus"* mount in the April 1905 issue of the *American Museum Journal* promised, "The preparation and mounting of entire skeletons of three other large and very extraordinary types (the Carnivorous, Duck-billed and Armored Dinosaurs) are well under way, and diligent search is being made for complete and mountable skeletons of other important kinds."[6]

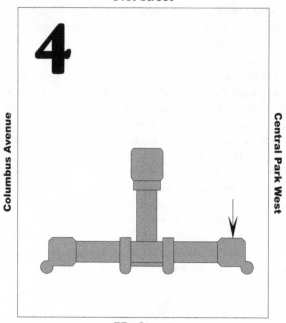

81st Street

4

Columbus Avenue

Central Park West

77th Street

Location of first dinosaur hall.

Apatosaurus, then Brontosaurus, the museum's first dinosaur mount, 1905.
Source: AMNH ID 5407.

The museum's *Allosaurus* was found by a member of Cope's crew in Wyoming in 1879 and was part of the Cope collection acquired by the museum in 1899. However, no one at the museum realized what they had until the boxes containing the skeleton were unpacked in 1903. The *Allosaurus* was a surprise find in one of the last boxes, whose opening had been put off because nothing of interest was expected to be found there. The preparation and mounting were completed and unveiled in January 1908. It was mounted over a partial *Apatosaurus* skeleton, as if feeding.[7]

Also in 1908, the museum unveiled the *Anatotitan* group. The museum had been lucky enough to have acquired two nearly complete skeletons—one from the Cope collection and found in 1892, and another found by Brown in 1906. The first one was put on display April 1908, and the second was added in October of that year.[8]

The first *Tyrannosaurus rex* ever discovered was found by Brown in Montana in 1902, and six years later, he found another superb specimen, with a complete skull, in the same region.[9] The museum team began experimenting with poses for mounting these two specimens together in a group. Because the bones were so large and heavy (the pelvis weighed two thousand pounds),[10] in order to experiment with different poses, the artists created scale models with flexible joints and incorporating every bone.[11]

In 1915, the specimen found by Brown in 1908 was completed and put on display in the Hall of Man, located in the fourth floor of the Seventy-Seventh Street entrance pavilion, because there was no room in Dinosaur Hall.[12] In late 1917 or early 1918, the *Tyrannosaurus rex* was moved to Dinosaur Hall,[13] and from 1918 to 1922, the museum guidebooks complained, "This hall is badly crowded owing to the delay in constructing a new wing."[14]

Although the plan was originally to form a group with both of the museum's *Tyrannosaurus rex*, the one found by Brown in 1902 was never added. It was sold in 1941 to the Carnegie Museum of Natural History in Pittsburgh, Pennsylvania. According to Brown, "We were afraid the Germans might bomb the American Museum in New York as a war measure, and we had hoped that at least one specimen would be preserved."[15]

Tyrannosaurus rex in the museum's first dinosaur hall, with
Apatosaurus and Allosaurus in background, 1921.
Source: AMNH ID 38713, American Museum of Natural History, Library.

1927—The Second Dinosaur Hall

In 1924, the long-delayed south wing on Central Park West was completed and became the new home of Dinosaur Hall, which opened in
March 1927.[16] The increased space allowed the addition of the *Triceratops*
mount, composed from a composite of specimens found in various locations in 1909 by Brown and others.[17] The *Stegosaurus*, found in 1901,[18]
was added in 1932.[19]

In the meantime, throughout the 1920s, tens of thousands of new
fossil specimens had been flooding in thanks to a series of expeditions to
Central Asia's uncharted Gobi Desert in Outer Mongolia, led by Roy

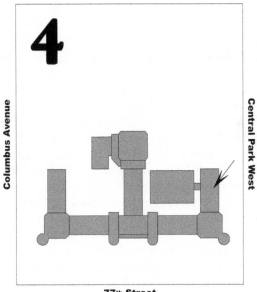

Location of second dinosaur hall.

Anatotitan in the museum's second dinosaur hall, with Allosaurus and Apatosaurus to left in background, July 1927.
Source: AMNH ID 311978, American Museum of Natural History, Library.

Chapman Andrews, with Walter Granger as chief paleontologist. Andrews had started working at the museum scrubbing floors in 1906, despite already being an experienced taxidermist, and went on to serve as the museum's director from 1935 to 1941 and become a prolific author.

The Central Asiatic Expeditions were among the museum's most famous and productive, and they involved many perilous adventures, which suited Andrews. As he explained in his 1935 book *This Business of Exploring*, "I was born to be an explorer. There never was any decision to make. I couldn't do anything else and be happy." He continued, "I have seen my whole camp swept from the face of the desert like a dry leaf by a whirling sandstorm. I have fought with Chinese bandits. But these things are all a part of the day's work."[20] Andrews is considered by many to be the real-life model for the movie character Indiana Jones.

Perhaps the most exciting finds took place in 1923 at the Flaming Cliffs of Shabarakh Usu. There, the team found an abundance of fossils of a new ornithischian ceratopsian dinosaur that they named *Protoceratops andrewsi*—*Protoceratops* because it was believed to be an early ceratopsian (horned face) dinosaur, and *andrewsi* after Andrews. But more stunningly, they found the first known dinosaur eggs, which they assumed to be *Protoceratops* eggs. And lying atop one of the groups of eggs was a new small saurischian dinosaur. They assumed the creature was preying on the eggs, so they named it *Oviraptor philoceratops*, which translates to "egg thief that loves ceratopsians."[21]

When the new Dinosaur Hall opened in 1927, new specimens from the Central Asiatic Expeditions were put on display in the recently vacated fourth floor of the southeast corner pavilion.[22]

1939—Jurassic and Cretaceous Halls

In 1934, the museum opened a new wing in the east transept, named the Akeley Wing, and the dinosaur exhibits spread into this space. With two large halls available, the dinosaur exhibits were subdivided chronologically into Jurassic Hall and Cretaceous Hall, organized as a walk through time. Jurassic Hall was located in the new space in the Akeley Wing, and the Jurassic dinosaurs *Apatasaurus*, *Allosaurus*, and *Stegosaurus* were moved there. The original Dinosaur Hall became Cretaceous Hall and housed the Cretaceous dinosaurs *Tyrannosaurus rex*, *Triceratops*, and *Anatotitan*. The two new halls, curated by Brown, opened in April 18, 1939.[23]

The fourth floors of the east transept and south wing on Central Park West have been dedicated to the dinosaur exhibits ever since.

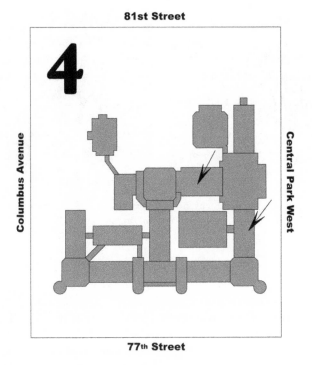

Locations of Jurassic/Brontosaur and Cretaceous/
Tyrannosaur Halls.

The 1950s—Brontosaur and Tyrannosaur Halls

In the 1950s, the two halls were renovated under the curator Edwin H.
Colbert. Jurassic Hall reopened on May 22, 1953, and was renamed
Brontosaur Hall (later referred to as the Hall of the Early Dinosaurs).
The main change involved placing the *Apatosaurus*, *Allosaurus*, and *Stegosaurus* on a large island in the center of the space.[24] Integrated into the
island was a series of dinosaur tracks excavated in Texas in 1938 by
Roland T. Bird, Brown's assistant.[25] In 1952, Colbert brought Bird out
of retirement to oversee the reassembly at the museum.[26] Originally, it
was thought that these were tracks of an *Apatosaurus* and an *Allosaurus*,
but that conclusion has recently come into doubt.[27]

Apatosaurus, Stegosaurus, and Allosaurus in
Brontosaur Hall, 1988.
Source: AMNH ID 3758.

Tyrannosaurus rex, Anatotitan, and Triceratops
in Tyrannosaur Hall, 1959.
Source: AMNH ID 884.

Cretaceous Hall reopened on July 1956 and was renamed Tyrannosaur Hall (later referred to as the Hall of the Late Dinosaurs). The main
change involved placing the *Tyrannosaurus rex*, *Triceratops*, and the *Anatotitan* group on a large island in the center of the space.[28]

1995—The Halls of Saurischian and Ornithischian Dinosaurs

In the 1990s, the two halls were renovated as part of a major $45 million
renovation of the entire fourth floor, which included the construction
of a new library and the restoration of the original architectural features
of the halls, for example, removing false ceilings to reveal the original
ceilings and uncovering the original columns and windows. As part of
the renovation, the two dinosaur halls were made part of a loop that
included the Hall of Vertebrate Origins in the south transept (Bickmore
Wing) and two Mammal Halls in the southeast corner pavilion and the
east wing on Seventy-Seventh Street.

The paleontologist Lowell Dingus directed the renovation. Roche,
Dinkeloo and Associates, a firm that had worked on the Metropolitan
Museum of Art, were the architects. The exhibit designer was Ralph
Appelbaum, whose firm specializes in museum exhibits and got its start

working on several temporary exhibits for the American Museum in the late 1970s and early 1980s. It was also working on the Motown Museum in Detroit, the Holocaust Museum in Washington, DC, and Chicago's Adler Planetarium at the time. The renovation began under the museum's president George Langdon and was completed under Ellen Futter, who took over the presidency in 1993.

In conjunction with the renovation, the museum installed a gigantic mount of a *Barosaurus* rearing up to protect its young from an *Allosaurus* in the Roosevelt Memorial Rotunda, and in June 1995, the two dinosaur halls reopened as the Hall of Saurischian Dinosaurs and the Hall of Ornithischian Dinosaurs, curated by Mark A. Norell and Eugene S. Gaffney.[29]

As part of the renovation, the exhibits were updated to reflect current scientific theory. In a major change, the exhibits were reorganized from a walk through time to a walk along a family tree reflecting evolutionary relationships, grouping animals based on shared characteristics. The system used to determine the evolutionary relationships of organisms, called *cladistics*, was developed in part at the museum.

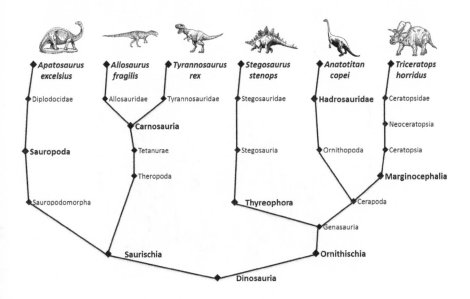

The cladistic relationships between the specimens discussed in this chapter.

Instead of being divided by chronological era into early (Jurassic) and late (Cretaceous), the dinosaur halls are now divided into the two main cladistic groups: saurischia and ornithischia. The Hall of Saurischian Dinosaurs replaced Jurassic Hall in the east transept, and the Hall of Ornithischian Dinosaurs replaced Cretaceous Hall in the south wing on Central Park West. Because of this change, the *Stegosaurus* and *Tyrannosaurus rex* had to be relocated.

Black paths on the floors of the halls lead a visitor along the trunk of the evolutionary tree. Circular branching points indicate important evolutionary developments. Today, all the fossil halls on the fourth floor, not just the dinosaur halls, have been reorganized in this fashion.[30]

The renovation was also used as an opportunity to update the *Apatosaurus* and *Tyrannosaurus rex* mounts. Scientists had realized that all these years the *Apatosaurus* mount actually bore a head from a different species. In addition to replacing the skull, vertebrae were added to the neck and tail, increasing the overall length from sixty-six to eighty-six feet. And

Location of Hall of Saurischian Dinosaurs and Hall of Ornithischian Dinosaurs.

	Hall of Saurischian Dinosaurs East transept	Hall of Ornithischian Dinosaurs South wing on Central Park West
Jurassic/Brontosaur Hall East transept	*Apatosaurus* *Allosaurus*	*Stegosaurus*
Cretaceous/Tyrannosaur Hall South wing on Central Park West	*Tyrannosaurus rex*	*Triceratops* *Anatotitan*

because scientists have concluded that the *Apatosaurus* did not drag its tail, the tail was suspended in a graceful whip-like position.[31]

Scientists had also sharply revised their ideas about the posture of *Tyrannosaurus rex* and modified the mount accordingly. Instead of the upright posture of the original mount, scientists now believe that a stalking stance, with the body tilted far forward, was more typical.[32]

Beginning in 1991, sixty years after the last Central Asiatic Expedition, museum scientists were invited back to Mongolia for a series of expeditions led by Michael Novacek, the museum's vice president and dean of science. And in 1993, seventy years after the discovery of the first dinosaur

Updated Apatosaurus mount in the Hall of Saurischian Dinosaurs.
Source: Wikimedia, author: ScottRobertAnselmo.

Updated Tyrannosaurus rex mount in the Hall of Ornithischian Dinosaurs.
Source: Wikimedia, author: J. M. Luijt.

eggs, the scientists discovered a rich, previously unexplored trove of fossils in a hilly region of the Gobi Desert known as Ukhaa Tolgod. Among other things, the site had an abundant supply of dinosaur eggs identical to the ones found in 1923, and Mark Norell discovered one that was broken open, exposing embryonic bones. Further examination revealed that the embryo was that of an *Oviraptor*, not a *Protoceratops*, as previously assumed. Furthermore, a few days later they found another group of eggs with an adult *Oviraptor* sitting on it in the posture of a brooding bird. Evidently the *Oviraptor* had been misnamed. That first specimen found in 1923 was probably the parent, not predator, of the eggs beneath it. This was the first evidence that dinosaurs and birds share similar nesting and brooding behavior. As Lowell Dingus explains in his 1996 book *Next of Kin*, "As a result, several of the labels that we had written for the fossilized eggs in the exhibition [which was then being put together] had to be quickly modified to reflect our newly discovered knowledge."[33]

So although the museum's famous dinosaur collection has its roots in the earliest years of dinosaur discovery, its exhibition has evolved to reflect the latest scientific theories—theories scientists at the museum helped shape.

8
The Years 1936 to 1999

When the building boom that had started during the Osborn presidency came to completion, the United States was enduring a gloomy depression that was followed by World War II. This led to decades of relative inactivity for construction at the museum. Between 1936, when the Theodore Roosevelt Memorial was completed, and 1999, several proposals were considered for completing the master plan, but none were implemented. Instead, construction was limited to filling in voids in the courtyard areas.[1] The period, nevertheless, was an active one for exhibit creation.

In 1942, the museum, in collaboration with Robert Moses and the Parks Department, hired the architect Aymar Embury to remodel the museum, with the architect Eliel Saarinen consulting. Embury's plans called for filling out Manhattan Square with façades along Columbus Avenue and Eighty-First Street. They also called for stripping the detail from all the façades except the Roosevelt Memorial and recladding them. The plans, which had the approval of the museum's board of trustees, were publically released in 1943 but never acted on.[2]

In 1973, the city and the museum hired the architecture firm William F. Pedersen and Associates to propose a plan to guide future building. The plan, released in 1975, closely followed Vaux and Mould's original master plan, but it too wasn't acted on. The firm also designed the Hall of Gems that opened in 1976 and, around the same time, renovated the auditorium in the central pavilion.[3]

In the mid-1980s, the museum once again was considering building a new wing along Columbus Avenue. According to Thomas A. Lesser, who at the time was the museum's manager for development, "Spurred on by the possibility of the Museum of the American Indian's Hyde Collection being moved to the museum, we began discussing a new wing on Columbus Avenue. The collection ended up going to the Smithsonian and the project was dropped."[4]

In the meantime, in 1967, the New York City Landmarks Preservation Commission designated the museum a landmark, finding that the museum was

> an interesting complex of buildings, incorporating outstanding examples of Romanesque Revival and Roman Classic architecture of the late nineteenth and twentieth centuries, blended into a unified composition of great distinction and individuality befitting this museum and that it ranks as one of the great institutions in the world, a tremendous asset to the cultural life of the city and to the country.[5]

In 1975, the commission designated the Memorial Hall of the Theodore Roosevelt Memorial building an interior landmark, finding it

> provides an impressive main entrance to the American Museum of Natural History, that it is one of the City's most monumental interior spaces, that it is distinguished by a high barrel-vaulted ceiling which lends grandeur to the space, that it was designed by the noted architect John Russell Pope, who made expressive use of the rich materials and fine classical detail, that it is a fitting monument to Theodore Roosevelt as a political leader and naturalist, that it is a fitting symbol of a period which witnessed the evolution of the United States as a world power, and that Memorial Hall is an important and well integrated part of the American Museum of Natural History.[6]

In 1976, the museum was added to the National Register of Historic Places.[7] Since receiving these designations, the museum is required to get approval for any new construction from the New York City Landmarks Preservation Commission.

Interestingly, as the museum's building projects wound down after the Osborn era, so did other construction in the museum's neighborhood. The last buildings built on Central Park West between Sixty-First and Ninety-Sixth streets were finished in the 1930s, including the four iconic Art Deco twin-towered apartment buildings the Century, the

Majestic, the San Remo, and the Eldorado. In 1982, the district was added to the National Register of Historic Places,[8] and in 1990, the New York City Landmarks Preservation Commission designated it a historic district.[9]

Although no new major sections were added to the museum during this period, some structures were built to fill in voids in the courtyard areas, including:

Building 1A, constructed in 1955 and named for being adjacent to the museum's first building. In 1971, this section was remodeled and opened to the public for temporary exhibits as Gallery 77.[10]

The ten-story Frick building, home to the vertebrate paleontology department, containing mass fossil storage, completed in 1973.[11]

The Perkin Wing, an extension to the Hayden Planetarium, completed in 1974.[12]

The Research Library, completed in 1992 in conjunction with the remodeled dinosaur halls.

Interstitial sections added between 1936 and 1999:
(a) Building 1A/Gallery 77 (1955, 1971), (b) Frick Building (1973), (c) Perkin Wing (1974), (d) Research Library (1992), (e) C. V. Starr Natural Science Building (1999).

The eight-story C. V. Starr Natural Science Building, completed
in 1999, with the first three stories containing a new museum
shop, coinciding with the opening of the Rose Center.[13]

In addition, this period was an active one for exhibit creation.
The Hall of North American Mammals opened in 1942 in the first
floor of the east transept, with the final dioramas completed in 1954.
Completed under the direction of James L. Clark and Albert E. Butler,
the hall was the culmination of twenty years of expeditions and planning, and it contains the museum's iconic Alaska Brown Bear diorama.[14]
The museum's famous ninety-four-foot, 21,000-pound blue whale
model suspended from the ceiling of the Hall of Ocean Life was completed in 1969. (The museum had had a seventy-six-foot model of a blue
whale on display since 1907 in the Mammals Hall on the third floor of
the east wing on Seventy-Seventh Street. The Mammals Hall and whale
were removed around 1969.)[15] In 2003, the hall reopened as the Milstein
Hall of Ocean Life after being closed for eighteen months to undergo
major upgrades, including a modernization of the blue whale, based on
recent scientific discoveries.[16]
On May 18, 1971, the Hall of Peoples of the Pacific on the fourth floor
of the south wing on Columbus Avenue was dedicated by Margaret
Mead, the hall's creator, who had worked at the museum since 1926 after
studying under Franz Boas at Columbia University. The hall was the
culmination of almost half a century of her pioneering studies in the field
and laboratory.[17] Five years later, the hall was closed to accommodate
museum construction. Mead worked at the museum until her death in
1978, and in 1984, the hall reopened as the Margaret Mead Hall of Pacific
Peoples on the third floor of the south wing on Columbus Avenue.[18]
The Morgan Memorial Hall of Gems and the Harry Frank Guggenheim Hall of Minerals opened in 1976 on the first floor of the south
wing on Columbus Avenue. The hall features many valuable gems
donated by J. P. Morgan at the turn of the century, which were previously on display on the fourth floor of the west wing on Seventy-Seventh
Street. The design by the architecture firm William F. Pedersen and
Associates was described by Paul Goldberger, the architecture critic for
the *New York Times*, as "a lively, dynamic space, alive with level changes,
curves, ramps, and steps . . . covered in a rich, earth-tone carpeting,
creating a soft and sensual mood that calls to mind the backroom of an
expensive jeweler's."[19]
The Hall of Biodiversity opened in 1998 on the first floor of the
south wing on Central Park West. According to the museum's president

Ellen Futter, it was "the museum's first truly interdisciplinary hall." Curated by Niles Eldredge, the hall was designed by Ralph Appelbaum Associates and Polshek Partnership, the firms that also collaborated on the design of the Rose Center for Earth and Space. The hall includes a hundred-foot-long diorama of the Dzanga-Sangha rain forest in the Central African Republic and the Spectrum of Life Wall, with models and specimens of 1,500 species, including microbes, plants, insects, and large animals, organized to show their evolutionary relationships.[20]

And, as covered in Chapter 7, the museum's famed dinosaur halls received major renovations in the 1950s and 1990s.

PART II
The Heavens in the Attic

Colin Davey and Thomas A. Lesser

9
From the Beginning of Time to October 2, 1935

On the evening of October 2, 1935, a Wednesday, the "first-night" audience at the American Museum's Hayden Planetarium was treated to what the *New York Times* described as "an awe-inspiring spectacle of artificial stars in a man-made heaven going through their celestial paces at the bidding of man . . . a make-believe world where, like the Olympians of old, they were masters of space and time . . . like seeing the splendors of the universe for the first time." The article continued: "There was a composite 'Ah!' from the invisible audience, which at once became silent again in the presence of the majesty beheld . . . as though every one present had entered a sort of space-ship, making a journey among the stars at inconceivable speed."[1]

The planetarium opened to the public the next day, presenting eight shows, each filled to capacity.[2] On the following Saturday, lines for each show were a half-block long, stretching up the circular drive in front of the planetarium to Eighty-First Street and over Central Park West. An extra show had to be added to meet the demand.[3]

This opening was the result of many forces and events—cosmological, scientific, economic, and political.

Early Astronomy and Astronomical Models

The story of the Hayden Planetarium starts with the story of the universe. The universe as we now know it consists of billions of galaxies, each made up of billions of stars. Our current understanding suggests that it began about 13.8 billion years ago, in an event known as the Big Bang. At least one of those galaxies (the Milky Way) has a star (the Sun) with a planet orbiting it (Earth) where intelligent life evolved (*Homo sapiens sapiens*, more commonly known as people or earthlings).

The earthlings attempted to understand the universe, and that understanding evolved over time. This study became known as astronomy. Originally, it was thought that Earth was flat because that is how it appeared to our unaided senses. But it has been known that Earth was round since at least the time of Pythagoras (600 BC).

By the fourth century BC, most educated Greeks believed that Earth was a sphere at the center of a spherical heaven. This became known as the geocentric model of the cosmos and is sometimes called the Ptolemaic model, named after Claudius Ptolemaeus, who standardized the details of the model in the second century AD.

The geocentric model fit the observed behavior of the stars, which appeared to move as if attached to the inside of a rigid celestial sphere that rotated around a fixed axis, with Earth at the center. The Sun, Moon, and five "wandering stars," or "planets," also appeared to move around the celestial sphere, but each had an individual motion independent of the fixed stars. Their paths were hard to explain using the geocentric model.

In 1543, Nicolaus Copernicus published a heliocentric model in which the Sun, rather than Earth, was positioned at the center of the universe, with Earth and the other planets orbiting the Sun. This model more simply explained the peculiar paths taken by the planets through the sky. The Copernican model did not become widely accepted until the 1700s, after the contributions of Kepler, Galileo, and Newton.

Throughout this time, mankind developed an evolving series of technologies for modeling the universe. Geocentric models consisted of globes representing the celestial sphere, with stars and constellations on the surface. The best-preserved and scientifically most significant celestial globe of ancient times is the Farnese Atlas, in the National Museum at Naples, dating from the first century BC. The viewer would gaze on the constellations from the outside, seeing them reversed from the view of an observer on Earth within the sphere.[4]

Starting around 1650, hollow globes large enough to admit a small audience were developed to simulate the view from Earth. These globes had the stars affixed to them and could rotate, illustrating the movement of the stars in the night sky. The last historical example of these hollow globes was the Atwood Celestial Sphere, unveiled in 1913 at the Museum of the Chicago Academy of Science.[5]

In the late 1600s, after general acceptance of the Copernican model, there started appearing mechanical models, based on clockwork mechanisms, of planets orbiting the Sun. These devices became known as orreries, after Charles Boyle, the fourth Earl of Orrery, who commissioned one of the earliest models in the early 1700s. They would also become known as Copernican planetariums.[6]

By the time of the Hayden Planetarium's opening night, several major astronomical discoveries had recently been made. In the early 1920s, it was concluded that the Milky Way, previously considered synonymous with the entire universe, was just one of many galaxies. Closer to home, in 1930, Pluto was discovered by Clyde Tombaugh. (Ironically, the life of Pluto as a planet roughly spanned the life of the original planetarium. The planetarium existed from 1935 to 1997. Pluto, discovered in 1930, was demoted to "dwarf planet" by the International Astronomical Union in 2006.)

Early Astronomy at the American Museum

The American Museum's earliest foray into the field of astronomy began in 1904. That year, the thirty-four-ton Ahnighito meteorite that Robert Peary had brought back from Greenland in 1897—and had been stored at the Brooklyn Navy Yard since then—finally arrived at the museum, pulled by thirty-five horses. The museum had no place to put it, so it was parked on a platform outside the Seventy-Seventh Street entrance.[7]

Also that year, work was underway renovating the foyer of the Seventy-Seventh Street entrance, about which the museum's 1903 *Annual Report* stated, "it is hoped that an attractive entrance hall will soon take the place of the present uninviting approach."[8] The resulting space, which reopened in 1906, was designed with an astronomical theme for displaying the museum's meteorite collection. As Richard Leonard Tobin, who led the renovation of the hall one hundred years later, described it: "The bronze inlaid Sun at the center of the gallery was surrounded by bronze zodiac inlays. Radiating out from this circle were inlaid stone mosaic stars of ever diminishing size to the perimeter of the Gallery's walls which formed an ellipse." The inlaid sun and mosaic stars remain to this day, although the bronze zodiac inlays were removed in 1974.[9]

Tobin continues, "At the perimeter of this ellipse were placed the meteorites in some fixed heavenly gravitational dance about the Sun." The museum had assembled eleven meteorites into an exhibit circling the space. These included the Ahnighito, finally finding a home inside the museum, along with the Dog and the Woman, the two other meteorites Peary had brought back from Greenland. Because of the Ahnighito's mass, the renovation required special concrete pylons to support it.

Also included was the Willamette meteorite, which the museum had acquired earlier that year from Oregon. At 15.5 tons, the Willamette was the largest meteorite ever discovered in the United States.

In keeping with the astronomical theme, when the hall opened, it included a model of the solar system. As the *New York Times* described the hall:

> The Solar System is represented in the foyer, the Sun a small round light in the centre, with the Earth, proportionate in size, at a relative distance on the one side and with Venus and Mercury on the other. More distant planets extend into the adjoining halls. The one most distant of all [at the time, believed to be Neptune], if placed in its relative position from the tiny museum Sun, would have to be hung at the further side of Central Park. With this miniature Solar System overhead and the signs of the Zodiac in the floor of the foyer, the meteorites or fallen stars are thought to be appropriately placed in a circle around the walls.[10]

Astronomy at the museum got a major boost when Henry Fairfield Osborn succeeded Morris Jessup as the museum's president in 1908. Osborn immediately began pushing to add astronomy to the museum's

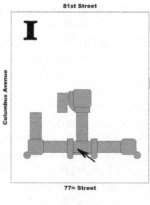

Cape York meteorites on display in the foyer of the Seventy-Seventh Street entrance pavilion in 1907. The Ahnighito is on the left, the Woman on the right, and the Dog to the left of the Woman. November 27, 1907.

Source: AMNH ID 31792, American Museum of Natural History, Library.

mission. By the end of his first year, the model of the solar system in the foyer was upgraded, and a second astronomy exhibit, an astronomical clock, was installed on the second floor of the Seventy-Seventh Street entrance pavilion. The latter consisted of a four-foot-wide model of Earth that spun on its axis every twenty-four hours and followed a twenty-eight-foot-wide orbit around the Sun, which was represented by a powerful lamp. The exhibit illustrated the causes of day and night, the differences of local time, the succession of the seasons, and the reason for the existence of leap years.[11]

In the museum's *Annual Report* for 1908, the first of Osborn's presidency, he proposed further developing astronomy at the museum, encouraged by the success of the two exhibits. He elaborated further in his 1910 special report, *History, Plan, and Scope of the American Museum of Natural History*. "In the pure sciences," he wrote, "astronomy has never found its way into any natural history museum until the present admirable beginning made in this institution, to the instruction and delight of thousands of visitors. It is obvious from the laws of the unity of nature, taught by Humboldt and Darwin, that all causes are ultimately

Astronomical clock on the second floor of the Seventy-Seventh Street entrance pavilion, December 1, 1908.
Source: AMNH ID 32182, American Museum of Natural History, Library.

astronomic and physical."[12] Yet by 1913, both of the museum's astronomy exhibits were gone. How and why did they disappear?

In the 1908 *Annual Report*, Osborn had expressed an interest in having a hall devoted to astronomy and had articulated his plan more fully in *History, Plan, and Scope*. The plan called for building a new five-story rotunda to replace the auditorium that existed at the center of the museum site. The first two floors of the new rotunda would be devoted to astronomy. The second floor of the rotunda would be occupied "by an elaboration of the planetary system which is now placed in the foyer." Of the foyer, Osborn wrote, "It will be appropriate to devote the foyer, after the removal of the meteorites and the planetary system, entirely to memorials of the trustees, of prominent members of the scientific staff, and of men distinguished in the history of American science."[13] Three years later, the 1911 *Annual Report* stated: "These changes and the improvement of the foyer will call for the withdrawal for the time being of the astronomical exhibit, for which more ample provision will be made in projected sections of the building."[14]

The foyer's solar system model was removed by early 1913.[15] "There have been, naturally, a few inquiries for the astronomical exhibit that has been necessarily withdrawn, pending the providing of future quarters in the Astronomical Hall," the museum's *Annual Report* for 1912 stated, "but the slight educational loss occasioned by the withdrawal of this is more than compensated for by the greatly enhanced appearance of Memorial Hall [the foyer] and the adjoining rooms."[16]

The plan called for the construction of six new units over the next twelve years. At this rate, the rotunda with its astronomy exhibits would have been finished by approximately 1916. The plan was based on the assumption that construction would proceed at least as briskly as it had in recent decades. Between 1890 and 1908, the institution had expanded steadily, quintupling in size. During that time the entire façade along Seventy-Seventh Street was built and the south wing on Columbus Avenue finished. However, the planned construction was not to be. As the 1913 *Annual Report* stated: "In view of the present financial condition of the City, the Board of Estimate and Apportionment has suspended all appropriation for building."[17] Osborn's plans for the new astronomy department and exhibits had stalled, and given the city's finances, there would be no new buildings until the mid-1920s.

By July 1913, even the astronomical clock was gone. The 1913 *General Guide to the Exhibition Halls* said of the clock's former site: "This hall illustrates a phase of Museum progress, the temporary disorder that precedes an ultimate change for the better. At present the hall contains a mixed assemblage of animals brought hither from other halls in process of re-arrangement; later it is hoped that it will contain a series of groups of birds from various parts of the world."[18] It ultimately did become the Birds of the World Hall, which exists to this day, but not for several decades.

The Astronomic Hall

In 1916, Osborn began campaigning for support for the centrally located Astronomic Hall from the newly formed Carnegie Corporation. The campaign gathered steam in the 1920s as museum building started picking up. And after the death in 1919 of Andrew Carnegie, Osborn proposed erecting the hall as a memorial to him.[19] By the early 1920s, plans for the Astronomic Hall had grown to encompass the entire five-story central pavilion. Osborn argued, "It is evident that astronomy will be the central feature of our plan because all the processes of Earth's history and all the processes of life center around original astronomic causes."[20] In making his case to the Carnegie Foundation for funding, Osborn predicted that the Astronomic Hall would "not only be a unique monument to Mr. Andrew Carnegie but will exert a profound influence on the life and thought of the entire United States, as our Department of Paleontology is now doing."[21]

In 1923, Osborn formed an advisory committee on astronomy, chaired by William Wallace Campbell of the Lick Observatory in California, consisting of George Ellery Hale of the Mount Wilson Observatory; Henry Norris Russell, professor of astronomy at Princeton; and Clyde Fisher as the associate curator in charge.[22] The following year the museum formed an astronomy department led by Fisher,[23] and the committee began working with the architects Trowbridge & Livingston on designs for the Astronomic Hall.[24]

Fisher had begun working in the museum's education department after receiving his doctorate in botany from John Hopkins University in 1913 at the age of thirty-five; he eventually became the museum's curator of visual instruction. By the time Fisher began working at the museum, he already had a reputation as a polymath, with accomplishments in the fields of geology, zoology, paleontology, and astronomy, among others. He also was a seasoned educator with years of experience at numerous grade schools and colleges, having begun teaching science even before starting his own college education, and he loved sharing his passion for science with children. He was also a prolific traveler, and during a 1927 expedition to North Dakota, Fisher was adopted into the Sioux Indian tribe. Several years later, he would marry Te Ata, the famous Chickasaw Indian actress and storyteller.[25]

One of Fisher's first acts as the head of the astronomy department was to create an Astronomical Room, which he referred to as a "good beginning." Harkening back to the museum's earlier astronomical exhibits, Fisher referred to "a large orrery or planetarium, which was dismantled some twelve or fifteen years ago," adding, "The fact that this exhibit is still asked for by visitors should be considered in plans for future equipment."[26]

In April 1925, Howard Russell Butler joined the team working on the design of the Astronomic Hall.[27] Butler was a Renaissance man with degrees in physics from Princeton and law from Columbia University, and he had previously worked for Andrew Carnegie in several roles, including painting thirteen portraits of Carnegie and serving as an architectural advisor for his Fifth Avenue mansion (now the Cooper-Hewitt National Design Museum). He was also a renowned painter of astronomical subjects.[28] When Fisher installed the Astronomical Room, it contained two paintings by Butler, one of an eclipse and one of an aurora borealis.[29]

But even as the campaign for the Astronomic Hall was picking up, events were taking place thousands of miles away that would revolutionize the way astronomy would be taught at museums.

The Zeiss Projection Planetarium

The father of the modern planetarium was Oskar von Miller, the founder and director of the Deutsches Museum (German National Museum), an innovative museum of science and technology established in 1906 in Munich. According to the 2005 book *Theaters of Time and Space: American Planetaria, 1930–1970* by Jordan Marché: "As early as 1905, Miller sought to procure two mechanical devices for the museum's astronomical department. The first was a Copernican (heliocentric) planetarium, while the second demonstrated apparent movements of sky objects from a Ptolemaic (geocentric) perspective."[30]

In 1913, von Miller commissioned Carl Zeiss Optical Works, a firm located in Jena, Germany, to build room-sized models of both types of planetariums. The Copernican planetarium proved to be fairly straightforward. For the geocentric planetarium, the scientists began by thinking in terms of a hollow sphere similar to the Atwood Celestial Sphere.

Their efforts were interrupted by World War I.[31] But ultimately, the Zeiss engineers Walther Bauersfeld and Werner Straubel, along with von Miller, devised a breakthrough solution. Rather than having a large movable dome with the heavenly bodies affixed to it, they proposed projecting the heavenly bodies onto the dome with a moveable projector. A large staff of scientists, engineers, and others spent five years developing the invention, which was unveiled at the Zeiss factory in August 1923.[32]

That same year, the Deutsches Museum's planetarium was built with a dome on the roof and a ceiling-mounted Copernican planetarium in the lobby below the dome. The planetarium opened on May 7, 1925.[33] It proved an instant sensation. By September, two lecturers were giving nine demonstrations daily. And at the Zeiss factory, up to twelve demonstrations were being given every day, with standing-room crowds of up to six hundred people.[34]

One week after the opening of the Deutsches Museum's planetarium, the American Museum decided to send Fisher to investigate.[35] In September, Fisher visited the Zeiss factory and the Deutsches Museum, and upon his return, he enthusiastically recommended a Zeiss planetarium for the American Museum's Astronomic Hall. As he wrote later in *Natural History*, the museum's magazine, "Judging from the experience at Jena and at Munich, I believe it will attract more people to the museum than anything we have ever had here. When it becomes more widely known, it is sure to come to America. May the first one come to the American Museum of Natural History!"[36] But just as Fisher was returning to New York, the Carnegie Corporation decided not to fund the Astronomic Hall. Despite this setback, Osborn, Fisher, and their colleagues continued to press for the hall, hoping to attract other funders.[37]

On March 24, 1926, the museum unveiled a new astronomical exhibit called the Pro-Astronomic Hall, located on the first floor of the west corridor of the Seventy-Seventh Street entrance pavilion. Its cornerstone was a spectacular set of three paintings of solar eclipses by Howard Russell Butler that the museum had commissioned the previous year, arranged as a twenty-four-foot-wide triptych.[38] On display at the entrance of the new hall were architectural drawings for the Astronomic Hall developed by Butler and the architects.

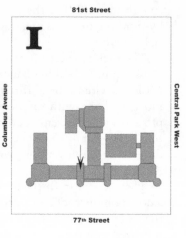

Entrance to the Pro-Astronomic Hall. Note the display of the Astronomic Hall design proposed for the central pavilion, 1926.
Source: AMNH ID 311771.

The July/August 1926 issue of *Natural History* was dedicated to the subject of astronomy and included three articles promoting the plans for the Astronomic Hall. "Use of Models in an Astronomical Museum," by Henry Norris Russell, described how to make museum astronomy exhibits clearer and more interesting. "The New Projection Planetarium," by Clyde Fisher, described his 1925 trip to Germany and advocated for the acquisition of a Zeiss projection planetarium for the Astronomic Hall. And "An Ideal Astronomic Hall," by Butler, described plans for the Astronomic Hall developed by Butler and the architects and included the drawings that were on display at the entrance of the Pro-Astronomic Hall. In his article, Butler quipped: "Had the Museum built its hall ten years ago, provision for this unique device [the Zeiss planetarium] would not have been made. . . . So I congratulate the Museum on not having been too hasty."

In 1927, on the advice he received from a German observatory director on his 1925 trip, Fisher founded the Amateur Astronomers Association in an effort to gauge and drum up interest in a planetarium. The association began holding twice-monthly meetings that spring. The *AMNH Annual Report* for 1927 crowed, "The enthusiastic interest shown in this society is a significant indication of the widespread and growing interest in the subject of Astronomy."[39] The group is active to this day.

Yet there was still no money for the project. In March 1928, discouraged by this lack of success, Fisher suggested installing a Zeiss planetarium in a temporary dome somewhere on the museum grounds, in order to, as he put it, "have any chance at all of securing the first planetarium in America."[40] Museum officials promptly selected a site in the northeast courtyard for this undertaking and began trying to raise funds.[41] But in June, newspapers reported that Chicago would have America's first planetarium, the Adler Planetarium, which opened in 1930. For several more years, museum officials would nurse the idea of building a centrally located five-story Astronomic Hall after building a temporary standalone planetarium, before the idea faded.[42]

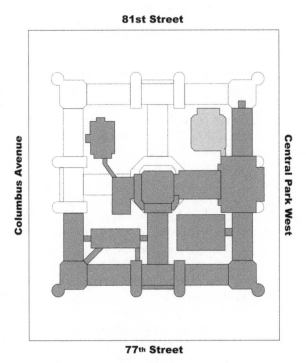

Planetarium location in northeast courtyard.

Hard Times, the New Deal, and the Planetarium Authority

Just when it seemed that things couldn't get worse, the stock market crash culminating on Black Tuesday, October 26, 1929, triggered the Great Depression. In the next two years, unemployment in the United States soared from 2.5 million to thirteen million. By December 1930, the Bank of the United States, one of the nation's largest financial institutions, had gone bankrupt. Stocks had fallen to less than a tenth of their 1929 values. On a single frigid day in January 1931, 85,000 New Yorkers waited in breadlines. Shantytowns for the homeless sprouted up around the country, including in Central Park, just across the street from the museum.[43]

On January 10, 1933, Osborn resigned from the museum's presidency, and his successor, Frederick Trubee Davison, was inaugurated.[44] Davison came from a wealthy banking family. His father, Henry Pomeroy Davison, had been senior partner at the J. P. Morgan & Co. bank. At Yale, Davison had been an aviation pioneer and a Skull and Bones member. He had been a member of the New York State Assembly from 1922 to 1926 and a museum trustee since 1923.

At the time of Davison's inauguration, he was serving as assistant secretary of war for aviation under President Hoover and could only assume his duties at the museum part-time until the newly elected president, Franklin Delano Roosevelt, was sworn in on March 4, 1933. Roosevelt's inauguration took place on a Saturday, and one of his first acts in office was to declare a "bank holiday," shutting down all American banks as of the following Monday, in an effort to halt a month-long run on them.[45] Davison's first acts after assuming full-time leadership of the museum included closing exhibition halls in rotation, ten at a time, and discharging staff because of the Depression.[46]

Ironically, only under these harsh conditions did political forces at all levels of government come together to create a mechanism for funding the long-desired planetarium: a Planetarium Authority.

When Davison was inaugurated the museum's president, president-elect Roosevelt had just finished a four-year stint as governor of New York State, to be replaced by Herbert Lehman. Lehman's first challenge was to ease the hardships of the Depression on his state, and one strategy was to attract federal money for public works projects, which in turn would stimulate employment and the economy. By February 2, Lehman had established the State Emergency Public Works Commission to evaluate projects for submission to the Reconstruction Finance Corporation and appointed Robert Moses as its chairman.[47]

The Reconstruction Finance Corporation had been formed in January 1932 by the Hoover administration and Congress to stimulate the economy. Through legislation approved on July 21, 1932, the agency was authorized to make loans for public works projects that could generate enough revenue to pay back the costs of construction.[48] Less than a month later, on August 17, Marcus A. Heyman, a New York City businessman, suggested to Osborn that the museum try to secure a loan from the agency for the desired planetarium.[49] There's no evidence that Osborn followed up on this idea.

Robert Moses is legendary as the controversial and powerful public official who transformed the New York metropolitan area from the 1920s through the 1960s by overseeing the construction of the region's most important roads, bridges, parks, and beaches, as well as the United Nations building and Lincoln Center, among other major projects. But despite several comprehensive books about Moses and his career, little attention has been paid to his role with the Hayden Planetarium.[50]

At the time he was appointed to the Public Works Commission, Moses was a forty-four-year-old powerhouse who had spent the previous nine years transforming the face of Long Island while simultaneously holding several offices in state government. Starting with his position on the Public Works Commission, Moses's career began to focus more on New York City. When Moses assumed the chairmanship of the commission, he understood that Roosevelt favored a new type of entity for carrying out public works projects: the public authority, a public-private entity established to conduct public business.

In 1931, while Roosevelt was governor, the Port Authority of New York and New Jersey had completed the George Washington Bridge on time and under budget. The agency, founded in 1921 to coordinate transportation infrastructure projects between New York and New Jersey, was the first major modern American public authority. At the dedication ceremony for the bridge in 1931, Roosevelt praised the agency as a "model for government agencies throughout the land." That same year, he also established the New York Power Authority.[51]

Weeks before Roosevelt's inauguration, Moses had already begun to shape his first authorities, including the Triborough Bridge Authority. According to Moses's biographer Robert Caro, when Moses came to the public authority, it was in its infancy. As Caro noted, "He raised this institution to a maturity in which it became the force through which he shaped New York and its suburbs in the image he personally conceived."[52] Moses would ultimately create and head many such authorities during his long career.

Roosevelt's first term in office was characterized by the New Deal, a set of programs and agencies created to lift the nation out of the Depression. A major mechanism used was financing public construction and engineering projects in order to stimulate the economy. The first hundred days of Roosevelt's presidency were notable for the remarkable vigor with which he put these projects in motion, expanding and streamlining the Reconstruction Finance Corporation and using it as the primary agency for financing them.[53]

As Moses anticipated, Roosevelt also favored the creation of public authorities as a mechanism for building public works projects. In April 1933, during his second month in office, Roosevelt proposed to Congress "legislation to create a Tennessee Valley Authority, a corporation clothed with the power of government but possessed of the flexibility and initiative of a private enterprise," which would build dams and provide electricity to the residents of the Tennessee Valley.[54] On May 18, Congress passed the Tennessee Valley Authority Act,[55] and in 1934 Roosevelt's administration wrote personal letters, along with sample legislation, to the governors of all forty-eight states encouraging them to establish such entities for their public works projects.[56]

In March 1933, as Davison was taking over the reins of the museum, he came up with the idea of creating a Planetarium Authority for the purpose of borrowing money from the Reconstruction Finance Corporation.[57] It was the first month of the Roosevelt administration, and Moses was just beginning to set up his earliest authorities. Over the next two months, Davison accumulated the support of Governor Lehman, Mayor John Patrick O'Brien, the State Senate and Assembly, trustees of the museum, the city's Board of Estimate, and Moses's State Emergency Public Works Commission.[58]

On June 5, 1933, Moses presented to the federal government a package of funding requests for public works that included the planetarium, the Triborough Bridge, and, on behalf of the Port Authority, the Thirty-Eighth Street Tunnel (later named the Lincoln Tunnel). Simultaneously, he asked Governor Lehman to call a special session of the legislature to clear away any obstacles to closing the deal.[59]

As Moses recalled in his 1970 autobiography *Public Works: A Dangerous Trade*:

> I was the chairman of the commission appointed by Governor
> Lehman to present projects to the RFC. I asked [former] Governor

[Al] Smith to speak for us. Jesse Jones, head of the RFC, liked the Governor and wangled the planetarium loan. He told Al Smith confidentially that one member of the RFC voted for the planetarium thinking it was a cafeteria.[60]

On June 26, the agency approved a loan of $650,000 to build the planetarium.[61] And as the loan was taking shape, museum officials were hashing out the planetarium's basic specifications. The final plan called for a two-story structure atop a basement. The first floor would have a central ceiling-mounted Copernican planetarium. The second floor would house a central projection planetarium, crowned by a dome seventy-five feet in diameter. On each floor, surrounding the central planetarium, would be corridors where exhibits would be displayed.[62] Although not America's first planetarium, it would be the only one in the world to duplicate the Deutsches Museum's model, combining a Copernican planetarium with a geocentric projection planetarium.

On June 15, ten days after Moses submitted the funding request to Washington and eleven days before the loan was approved, Davison departed on a four-month expedition to Africa to obtain elephants for the museum's new Akeley Hall of African Mammals.

Charles Hayden

By October 11, 1933, when Davison returned home, his hard-won plans for the planetarium were starting to unravel. That day, George Sherwood, the museum director under Davison, drafted a letter to Carl Zeiss, Inc., saying that the Zeiss projector, "being a foreign product," no part of the loan of the Reconstruction Finance Corporation may be used "for the purchase of the planetarium instrument proper." A negotiation over price ensued. "It is quite impossible for my firm to reduce the price of the instrument for the Zeiss planetarium," replied Franz Fieseler of Carl Zeiss, Inc., on October 31.[63] But also upon Davison's return from Africa, as he tells it, "My brother Harry met me at Quarantine and said that Charles Hayden, the investment banker, was interested in the planetarium. . . . Well, the next day [Theodore Roosevelt's son] Kermit Roosevelt, one of our trustees, got on the phone and told me the same thing about Charlie Hayden."[64]

Hayden was an American financier and philanthropist, and this communication led to Davison's meeting him at the Hayden, Stone & Co. office. According to Davison's account of the meeting, Hayden swiveled his chair so that his back was facing Davison and said, "The greatest spiritual thing in my life has been the Adler Planetarium in Chicago. You're all set on the building, but I'm sorry that you have to use museum funds for the instrument. I'll give ten thousand dollars if you get fourteen others to put up the rest."[65] Hayden had seen the newly opened Adler Planetarium the previous summer while visiting Chicago's World's Fair.[66] Davison recalled, "I went to the trustees and said, 'I think if we name the planetarium after him, he'll give the whole hundred and fifty thousand.'"[67]

On November 15, Davison returned to Hayden with the proposition. The meeting lasted about five minutes.[68] In a letter dated November 17, 1933, Davison described the meeting to John D. Rockefeller III, saying that Hayden "has given us $150,000 outright to purchase a Zeiss and Copernican planetarium. I made the suggestion to him and said that I had no doubt that the Board of Trustees would be glad to name the planetarium 'Hayden Planetarium.' Under those conditions he accepted immediately."[69] On January 4, 1934, Davison publically announced Hayden's donation and the decision to name the planetarium after him.[70]

This later led Moses to say at a dinner thrown by Hayden celebrating the opening of the planetarium, while Hayden was still on the dais, "Charlie, never in the history of philanthropy has anyone earned immortality so cheaply."[71] This insult reflected that the namesakes of the other American planetariums (Chicago's Adler, Philadelphia's Fels, and Los Angeles's Griffith) had footed the entire bill rather than just paying for the equipment.[72] But it may also have reflected Moses's feelings that his own efforts in securing funding for the planetarium had not been sufficiently recognized. "I have no objection to striking bargains with philanthropists in return for their immortality," he wrote in *Public Works*, "but I like the government to get something like its money's worth. I was the chairman of the commission appointed by Governor Lehman to present projects to the RFC . . . and wangled the planetarium loan."[73]

With the announcement of Hayden's donation came drawings of the façade by Trowbridge & Livingstone: a two-story brick building in the Art Deco/Art Moderne style, with six Grecian columns, an entrance marquee, and vertical stairwell windows. The plans included batteries of concealed floodlights that would dramatically light up the dome at night.

Construction

Detailed design specifications were distributed to qualified construction companies on April 23, 1934, with bids due by May 11, 3:00. On May

11, the White Construction Company, Inc., was selected as the lowest bidder.[74]

The groundbreaking ceremony took place on May 28, with Hayden turning over the first shovelfull of earth. The grand opening was scheduled for the summer of 1935.[75] But once the excavation got underway, unanticipated problems were encountered in building the foundation. Because the planetarium site had been a lake before Manhattan Square was tamed to become the home of the museum, special procedures were necessary to lay the foundation, causing the opening to be delayed by several months.[76]

In October and November 1934, as the contractors were struggling with the excavation, Moses ran against Herbert Lehman for governor under the Republican Party, recruited by Davison, who also managed his campaign. In this, Moses's only attempt at elected office, Moses lost by a landslide.[77]

The construction of the dome also presented special challenges. It actually consisted of two domes: an outer structural dome eighty-one feet in diameter and an inner projection dome seventy-five feet in diameter, and suspended from the structural dome. The structural dome, with walls only about three inches thick, was made of reinforced concrete and derived its strength from its shape rather than from trusses or other support mechanisms. It had to support not only itself but also the projection dome, which weighed fifteen tons.

A dome package was available for purchase from Zeiss, but the terms of the loan from the Reconstruction Finance Corporation disallowed foreign products. So after consultation with several thin-shell dome experts, the designers developed a plan. The cement for the structural dome was blown into place with an Akeley cement gun, a device invented by Carl Akeley, the museum's multitalented African explorer and exhibit designer.[78]

The Copernican planetarium was designed and built by J. W. Fecker Company, a Pittsburgh-based telescope manufacturer. The Zeiss projector arrived in thirty-one boxes by boat from Germany in January 1935,[79] and the work involved in setting it up began in July and continued for two months.[80]

Also in July, the fifteen-ton Willamette meteorite and the three Cape York meteorites, including the thirty-four-ton Ahnighito, were moved a half-mile from the foyer of the Seventy-Seventh Street entrance to the planetarium. Museum officials considered this one of the most difficult engineering feats in years. Building special supports into the foundation for the meteorites presented an additional engineering challenge.[81]

Hayden Planetarium, L: Under construction. October 31, 1934; R: Complete, August 1, 1939.
Source: L: AMNH ID 337392. R: Gottscho-Schleisner Collection, Library of Congress.

Besides the Copernican and projection planetariums and the meteorites, the attractions also included the collection that had been on display in the Pro-Astronomic Hall, arranged in the corridors that surrounded the planetarium theaters on both floors.

Epilogue: Frenemies

Although Moses and Davison were allies on the quest to build the planetarium as well as during Moses's campaign for governor, the two clashed at both the beginning and end of their careers. In 1922, Moses was an aide to Governor Al Smith, just learning to acquire and wield power, and he was starting to envision a massive system of roadways, beaches, and parks throughout Long Island. Davison was beginning his first term in the New York State Assembly, representing the elites of Long Island's North Shore, including the Morgans, Vanderbilts, and Carnegies, who were opposed to Moses's plans.

In 1924, Moses recruited the naïve young Davison to introduce bills, written by Moses, establishing the State Council of Parks and the Long Island State Park Commission. The bills were riddled with deceptively innocuous language concealing the overwhelming powers conferred on these new bureaucracies. The moment the governor signed the bills, Moses pounced and proceeded to shape Long Island according to his vision, including the creation of Jones Beach. "I felt awful, of course," Davison later recalled to Robert Caro. Moses "had the power under the law I had introduced. There was nothing else for me to do but to admit . . . that I just hadn't studied it thoroughly before I introduced it."[82]

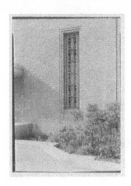

Images of the Hayden Planetarium from the Gottscho-Schleisner Collection, August 1, 1939.
Source: Gottscho-Schleisner Collection, Library of Congress.

Moses's final crusade once again brought the two into conflict: an attempt to build a bridge crossing the Long Island Sound, allowing direct travel from Long Island to the mainland, bypassing New York City. On June 20, 1973, Governor Nelson Rockefeller announced his decision to discontinue plans for its construction.[83] Yet even in 1977, when Moses was eighty-eight, he told an interviewer, "I'm not beaten yet on the Sound Crossing."[84] Davison took an active role opposing the bridge, whose Long Island side would be located near his home, and he even trained his dog to bark whenever he said "Robert Moses."[85] This round went to Davison. The Sound Crossing was never built.

10
Robert Moses and the Norman Bel Geddes Report

Despite the Hayden Planetarium's auspicious grand opening,[1] by 1941, with the nation still reeling from the Depression, paid attendance had been consistently disappointing. This was a problem because the loan that Robert Moses had wrangled for the planetarium from the Reconstruction Finance Corporation in 1933 was based on the assumption that the planetarium would be able to pay back the money through admission fees. These had been only about two-thirds of what was anticipated by the loan documents,[2] which also stated that if the Planetarium Authority defaulted on payments, the entire debt could be declared due.[3]

The planetarium received some relief from the Charles Hayden Foundation, which had been established after Hayden's death in 1937. Between 1938 and 1939, the foundation donated over $100,000 to the planetarium for operating expenses and for interest and principal payments to the Reconstruction Finance Corporation.[4] In an attempt to generate public interest, the planetarium put on an exhibit at the 1939 World's Fair called the Theatre of Time and Space. But attendance continued to lag.[5] By 1941, negotiations involving the planetarium, Moses, and the Reconstruction Finance Corporation had become, according to Moses, "involved and unsatisfactory."[6] Moses by this time had become a very powerful man.

Moses's Rise to Power

On January 1, 1934, Fiorello La Guardia was inaugurated mayor of New York. Within the first few weeks of his administration, La Guardia and Moses pushed a bill through Albany, designed by and for Moses, that consolidated the five borough park departments into a single agency under a single parks commissioner. The law allowed the commissioner to hold other unsalaried city and state offices to coordinate city, state, and metropolitan parks, parkways, and highway systems. Moses, of course, was appointed to the post, and reorganization began immediately.[7]

As commissioner of parks, Moses became an ex-officio member of the board of the American Museum.[8] And, on February 2, La Guardia appointed Moses chief executive officer and secretary of the Moses-created Triborough Bridge Authority. The bridge opened on July 11, 1936, and facilitated travel between New York City, upstate New York, Long Island, and Connecticut and smoothed access to the Long Island parks Moses had opened. (That same summer, among other things, Moses also opened ten pools in the city.) That year, the Triborough Bridge Authority was renamed the Triborough Bridge and Tunnel Authority. Moses was named the authority's chairman, and the agency would become the base of his empire.

According to Anthony Flint, the author of *Wrestling with Moses*, by 1936, between his roles as chairman of the Triborough Bridge and Tunnel Authority, city parks commissioner, president of the Long Island State Park Commission, chairman of the state's Council of Parks, and other offices (including membership on the executive committee of the Planetarium Authority), Moses "controlled virtually every batch of concrete poured, every shovel in the ground, and every land transaction linked to the development of roads and parks in and around New York City."[9]

Moses to Hayden Planetarium:
Get Rid of Debt or Close Shop

Five years later, in a report presented to La Guardia on March 3, 1941, Moses launched a broadside on the city's museum system. No institution was off limits. The report took swipes at the Metropolitan Museum of Art, the New-York Historical Society, the Museum of the City of New York, the New York Botanical Garden, the Museum of Modern Art, the American Museum of Natural History, and others.[10] The day of its release, the report was extensively quoted in a long front-page article in the *New York Times* under the headline "Museums Too Musty for Moses." The article began, "A thorough overhauling of the museums that occupy city park property . . . is recommended by Park Commissioner Robert Moses."

Museums fell under the jurisdiction of the Parks Commission because, as Moses explained in his report, "The word 'museums' is used in the broad sense to cover institutions which occupy city park property, on whose governing board the head of the Park Department serves as an ex officio member." Signaling his intentions, he continued, "Up to recently it has been the more or less accepted principle that the city's ex officio representatives on these boards were not expected to attend museum meetings, but if they did, were supposed to be seen and not heard." The report did not mince words about the planetarium's disappointing attendance, stating, "The Hayden Planetarium has to get rid of its bonded debt or close shop."[11] However, Moses, ready now to be heard as well as seen, was not lacking in ideas for preventing the latter outcome.

Norman Bel Geddes

On June 4, 1941, Moses laid out his plans in a letter to A. Perry Osborn, the museum's vice president and the son of Henry Fairfield Osborn. The letter included options for refinancing the debt, which included gifts from the Charles Hayden Foundation and having the Reconstruction Finance Corporation write off some or all of the debt. The letter also offered suggestions for increasing attendance by livening up the show.[12] To this end, in October, Moses proposed that the museum hire the theatrical and industrial designer Norman Bel Geddes to study the planetarium and make recommendations for increasing its popularity.

Moses and Bel Geddes had been friends since the 1939 World's Fair in Flushing Meadows Park, Queens, for which Bel Geddes had designed General Motors' Futurama pavilion. Moses's contribution to the fair included building the park from the dumping ground that was portrayed in F. Scott Fitzgerald's *The Great Gatsby* as the "valley of ashes." He also built the roads that led to it, which were integrated into his Triborough Bridge network.

By coincidence, Bel Geddes and his wife had seen a show at the Hayden Planetarium on the topic of Mars just days before Moses's recommendation, after which he sent a letter to Roy Chapman Andrews, now the director of the museum, strongly criticizing the show ("static and dull . . . drivel . . . nothing imaginative or convincing").[13]

Moses offered Bel Geddes the job in an October 14 letter:

> At its dedication I said that Charlie Hayden had purchased immortality very cheaply. . . . Immortality appears to have been too strong a word. As the matter stands, it is not unlikely that the Planetarium will have to shut its doors or get a large contribution from some other millionaire in return for substituting his name for that of Hayden. Before this contingency arises, I have told the members of the planetarium board that I believe a real effort should be made to reorganize the planetarium so as to make it really attractive, and I suggested that you were the man to make the recommendations. To my astonishment, I heard this morning that you had already written them a letter on this subject.[14]

The following month, the museum formally hired Norman Bel Geddes & Company, Inc., to prepare an initial report.[15]

Bel Geddes and a team of six worked on the report through early January 1942, reading popular astronomy books recommended by the planetarium staff, seeing the show, getting behind-the-scenes tours, learning the capabilities of the Zeiss projector, inspecting blueprints of the planetarium building, viewing the planetarium's film presentation from the 1939 World's Fair, and surveying other planetariums and their shows.[16] Bel Geddes's team presented a draft of the report to Moses and the museum on January 6 for feedback ("Eliminate the word[s] 'uninspiring' and 'mauseleum'"), and for Moses to add an introduction.[17] Later that month, the final *Preliminary Report to the Hayden Planetarium Authority* was distributed to the museum trustees, the Hayden Foundation, and the Reconstruction Finance Corporation.[18]

Bel Geddes's Recommendations

What Bel Geddes recommended was a major overhaul of the planetarium. The report contained many suggestions for making the planetarium experience more theatrical, dramatic, and controlled. But most radical were his recommendations regarding the Sky Theater. Bel Geddes wanted to modify the Sky Theater so that the spectacle would take place not just on the dome above the audience but also downward and straight ahead. To accommodate this, the seating would be modified from the existing concentric circles on the floor to bleacher-style seats at one end of the theater.

Bel Geddes also wanted to create the illusion of space travel. For this purpose, the Zeiss projector was too limited: It could only provide views of the sky as seen from Earth. The report called for the integration of other media, such as film, sound effects, lighting, and most notably large-scale three-dimensional animated models of heavenly bodies—the Sun, planets, and comets—that could be made to soar through the auditorium from hidden pits on hidden tracks. The narration would be prerecorded rather than provided by a live lecturer.

To accommodate these changes, the planetarium building would have to undergo major alterations. The report offered four different plans. The first, the one favored by Moses, was the most radical redesign. The final one required only minor alterations and no major structural changes.[19]

Responses

Since Bel Geddes's report was preliminary and based on just seven weeks of study, the next step was to create three-dimensional models to flesh out the details. Moses was anxious to begin work on the model making, but the Charles Hayden Foundation and the Reconstruction Finance Corporation were reluctant to throw more money at the planetarium, given the financial uncertainty caused by the recent December 7, 1941, attack on Pearl Harbor by the Japanese, signaling America's entry into World War II.[20]

Since the funds weren't available to fund more work by Bel Geddes, the museum tried negotiating to have its own staff make the models based on his ideas. To this end, they sent their heavy hitter, James L. Clark, to talk to Bel Geddes about this possibility. But Bel Geddes protested that there were still many details to work out and that his creative process required him to be actively involved in the model making.[21]

On June 1, 1942, Wayne Faunce, acting director of the museum, wrote to Bel Geddes to say that the proposal for the next steps would be taken up by the museum's trustees at its next meeting. Ultimately, no further action was taken on the report. According to Moses, the document "horrified the staff, was resented by most of the trustees, and was promptly buried. Norman's ideas were too explosive, novel, unconventional, and unmathematical."[22]

Resolution

The planetarium's financial situation was eased in 1948, as Moses recalled, after he "happened to meet Morton McCartney, chief of the Self-liquidating Division of the Reconstruction Finance Corporation, in the Oak Room at the Plaza, and over a couple of tall ones . . . hatched a scheme." Of the $570,000 the planetarium owed the Reconstruction Finance Corporation, the agency would write off $145,000, the Charles Hayden Foundation would contribute $200,000, and the museum would buy the remaining debt of $225,000. As a result, rather than owing the Reconstruction Finance Corporation $570,000, the planetarium owed the museum a manageable $225,000. This solution matched Moses's refinancing suggestions from his June 4, 1941, letter to A. Perry Osborn.

Moses: "And so in the end Charlie Hayden paid vicariously for his immortality."[23] It should be noted that the Charles Hayden Foundation contributed over $13,500,000 to the museum and planetarium between 1938 and 2012 for, among other things, new Zeiss projectors for the planetarium in 1960 and 1969 and the construction of the Hayden Planetarium's new incarnation at the Rose Center for Earth and Space.[24]

Epilogue: Clinging to Unwelcome Ideas

One evening in the late 1960s, after spending the day interviewing Moses, who was nearly eighty years old, Robert Caro came to a key realization about his subject. Although Moses had been able to build nearly everything he wanted, he obsessed not about the things he had succeeded in building but about those he hadn't. Earlier that day, the two were discussing a highway that Moses had envisioned in the 1920s that would link Robert Moses State Park to other Long Island roads and parks that he had created. At one point, Moses suddenly grabbed Caro by the arm and demanded, "Can't you *see* there ought to be a road there?" Caro: "Suddenly you forgot the paunch and the liver spots. All you could see were those eyes. . . . To this day, I can feel the grip of those fingers."[25]

Similarly, Moses could not let go of Bel Geddes's recommendations for the planetarium. In November 1949, Moses wrote a two-part series for the *New York Times Sunday Magazine*, once again taking on the city's museums. "Several years ago," he wrote, "I succeeded in getting Norman

Bel Geddes employed to make a report on the planetarium. Some of the changes Mr. Bel Geddes advocated were no doubt revolutionary and shocked the pedestrian minds who were operating the planetarium." He continued: "In any event, the entire stimulating Norman Bel Geddes program . . . was rejected, with something like derision." His withering conclusion: "What remains at the planetarium is a worthy, educational, second-rate show in a community which is entitled to first-rate things."[26]

In an October 4, 1955, letter to Bel Geddes, he wrote: "The proposals you made in that fine report are as exciting, worthwhile and desirable now as they were fourteen years ago when I heartily endorsed them . . . and I join you in the hope of seeing them some day carried out. You may be sure that I shall be happy to ask the Planetarium Authority to reconsider the report whenever the time seems opportune."

On January 29, 1960, reopening ceremonies were held at the Hayden Planetarium. The planetarium had shut down for twenty-six days to replace the original twenty-five-year-old Zeiss projector, which was worn out and obsolete. Moses was among the speakers, and yet again he returned to the subject of the Bel Geddes proposal. "This now famous branch of the American Museum of Natural History has itself had a remarkable natural history," Moses said:

> This is a post-war baby, a by-product of World War I, born of Charles Hayden and the Reconstruction Finance Corporation. . . . Our incubator was a public authority, a quaint device condemned by some of the purists of political science but, like the "ad hoc" agencies of the United Nations, a very effective way of getting things done. . . . Norman Bel Geddes at my suggestion some years ago offered a brilliant plan which shocked the professors and the trustees of the museum. I still believe his plan had marvelous dramatic possibilities and that it should be exhumed and reconsidered. You see I still cling to temporarily unwelcome ideas.[27]

And at the age of eighty-one Moses once again reiterated his support for Bel Geddes's proposal in his 1970 autobiography *Public Works: A Dangerous Trade.*[28]

11

The Golden Age of Spaceflight and the Hayden Planetarium

Having survived its difficult early years, the Hayden Planetarium was about to experience a reversal of fortunes with the dawning of the Space Age. The planetarium played a key role in the era's beginnings and in turn thrived as a result of the phenomenon it helped start.

By 1950, visionary rocket scientists had convincingly shown through their writings and demonstrations that space travel was technologically feasible. Yet thoughts of artificial satellites and manned flight to the Moon and Mars were mostly limited to these scientists and science-fiction buffs. A 1949 Gallup poll revealed that only 15 percent of Americans believed that man would reach the Moon in the next fifty years.[1] Nonetheless, by 1961, newly elected president John F. Kennedy committed the nation to landing on the Moon before the decade was out, and by 1969 it would succeed.

In order to bridge the gap between feasibility and reality, it was necessary to make space travel seem real in the imaginations of the American public, leading to support by the taxpayers for massive investment by the government in the nation's space program. The Hayden Planetarium played a pivotal role in igniting this process. During these years, the planetarium enjoyed a heyday. Attendance soared, and the institution's most iconic exhibits were created, exhibits that made space travel seem real in the minds of the public and that remained among the planetarium's most popular until its original building closed in 1997.

The Pre-1950 Visionaries

Three men—Konstantin Tsiolkovsky of Russia, Robert H. Goddard of America, and Hermann Oberth of Germany—all born in the mid- to late nineteenth century, are considered the fathers of rocketry and astronautics. They explored how rockets could be used for space travel and worked out many of the necessary equations and principles, including the use of liquid fuel and multistage rockets.

In 1925, the second edition of Oberth's 1923 book, *The Rocket into Interplanetary Space*, inspired two gifted young German men to dedicate their lives to space travel: a nineteen-year-old university science student named Willy Ley and the thirteen-year-old Wernher von Braun. Oberth, Ley, and von Braun were early members of the German Spaceflight Society (Verein für Raumschiffahrt), which was founded in 1927. In May 1930, Ley introduced von Braun to Oberth,[2] and in 1931, the society began successful experimentation with rockets. But two years later, the organization was forced to disband.

In the meantime, the German military had taken an interest in rocketry and had recruited von Braun to head its research team. Von Braun ultimately led the development of the V-2 rockets that the Nazis used to pummel London and other Allied targets during World War II. Fate would deal Ley a different hand. By the end of 1934, the German rocket program became enveloped in secrecy, and private individuals, including Ley, were forbidden from working on or writing about rockets.[3] Ley fled to the United States in 1935 as the Nazis were rising to power, and there he continued to work ceaselessly to promote his visions of space travel.

In 1945, when the war ended, von Braun and his team surrendered to the Americans and began working on military rocket programs for the US Army, and in 1946, von Braun reunited with his old friend Willy Ley, visiting Ley at his home in the New York City borough of Queens.[4]

Under the Nazis, von Braun had been unable to devote his talents to his childhood dreams of artificial satellites, space stations, and trips to the Moon and Mars. At one point, he was arrested by his Nazi employers for two weeks for diverting attention from weapons development to space travel. But after his defection to America, he was able to work on scientific as well as military projects, and he was freer to discuss his dreams of space travel with whoever would listen. But as of 1950, he hadn't yet found a platform that received the mass public attention he desired.

Another early space-travel visionary was the American artist Chesley Bonestell, who pursued an early interest in astronomy before developing a career in architectural art. In the 1940s, Bonestell combined his artistic skill with his interest in astronomy, developing a uniquely realistic style of space art. His work was published in numerous national magazines, beginning with a series of stunning paintings of Saturn viewed from several of its moons, published by *Life* in 1944.

The Space Age would eventually unfold largely as envisioned by Ley and von Braun by 1949. But, as the Gallup poll of that year showed, Americans were not yet ready to accept that reality.

Enter the Hayden Planetarium

On a trip to New York, Bonestell met Gordon A. Atwater, the chairman of the Hayden Planetarium from 1945 to 1951. Atwater suggested that Bonestell consider publishing his paintings in book form with accompanying text, leading Bonestell to ask Atwater if he would be interested in doing the writing. Atwater declined, but he suggested Willy Ley for the job and later came up with the title of the book. *The Conquest of Space* by Ley and Bonestell was published in 1949.[5]

Since just after its opening, through the 1940s, the Hayden Planetarium had been suffering from disappointing attendance figures. According to Atwater, until 1950, "all Hayden programs were centered around the work of astronomers. . . . People were staying away in droves on this sort of fare." At that point, he added, "we embarked on a whole new philosophy in selecting the shows we produced." The emphasis shifted toward making space travel seem real.

After *The Conquest of Space* had been published, the planetarium featured a special show simulating a spaceship journey to the Moon based on Bonestell's artwork. The first thing visitors saw as they entered the building was a reservations desk taking bookings for the first trip. "We were mobbed as people scrambled to sign up for the first space flight," Atwater later recalled, adding that the show "turned out to be our greatest triumph."[6]

During the early 1950s, the planetarium continued to solicit reservations for interplanetary space travel by handing out applications at Sky Theater shows and placing coupons in newspaper and magazine ads around the world.[7] In keeping with the theme of making space travel seem real, in February 1951, the planetarium installed an exhibit called Your Weight on Other Worlds. The exhibit consisted of five Toledo scales showing a person's weight on the Moon, Mars, Venus, Jupiter, and the Sun and was accompanied by four of Bonestell's paintings from *The Conquest of Space*.[8] Your Weight on Other Worlds remained one of the planetarium's most popular exhibits until the original planetarium building closed in 1997.

According to the museum's *Annual Report for 1950*, "Paid attendance during 1950–1951 was substantially increased over the previous years, from 322,129 to 355,643 admissions."[9]

First Annual Symposium on Space Travel

One day in the spring of 1951, Willy Ley suggested over lunch to Robert R. Coles, then chairman of the planetarium, that Americans organize a conference in astronautics, modeled after a successful conference held in Paris the previous year. Coles replied without hesitation, "Go ahead, the planetarium is yours."[10]

The two men proceeded to organize the First Annual Symposium on Space Travel, held on October 12 of that year, featuring papers on space travel by leading American scientists and engineers.[11] This conference arguably was the first of a chain of events that led to the Space Age and a renaissance for the Hayden Planetarium and American planetariums in general. "The time is now ripe to make the public realize that the problem of space travel is to be regarded as a serious branch of science and technology," Ley explained in his letter to potential speakers. "Invitations will be sent to institutions of learning, to professional societies and research groups, and also to the science editors of metropolitan newspapers and magazines."[12]

At the conference Coles presented an imaginary trip to Mars, making use of the current planetarium sky show, based on *The Conquest of Space*. Willy Ley then spoke on the topic "Thirty Years of Space Research." He began by reviewing progress and accomplishments in rocket science from 1921 to the present, adding, "The obvious question is what will come next." He then presented his vision for using two-stage rockets to create artificial satellites. At first these satellites would be unmanned. But they would evolve into manned space stations that could serve as research laboratories and fuel-supply depots for spaceships bound for the Moon or other planets.

Ley was followed by Robert P. Haviland, an engineer at General Electric, who spoke on "engineering and application of the satellite vehicle"; Dr. Fred L. Whipple, the chairman of Harvard's astronomy department, who spoke on "the empty atmosphere and 'empty' space"; Dr. Heinz Haber of the US Air Force, who spoke on space medicine; and Oscar Schachter, a UN aide and law professor, who discussed the legal aspects of space travel.[13]

The symposium was attended by three hundred authorities in astronomy, aviation, engineering, medicine, geophysics, electronics, and international law.[14] The event was also notable for who was not present: Wernher von Braun.[15] According to Whipple, "at that time, von Braun was sort of in the doghouse, for some people did not want a German engineer sending up our first satellite."[16]

The symposium received considerable press attention. The next day, under the headline "Platforms in the Sky Now Seen Feasible," the *New York Times* described the conference in an article that began, "Buck Rogers and Captain Video would have felt right at home yesterday with a group of fascinated scientists who listened to speculations on the future of interplanetary space travel."[17]

The event was so successful that plans were immediately made for a second conference to be held in October of the following year.[18] Most important, however, the symposium was attended by two reporters from *Collier's*. The weekly publication, which had a circulation of 3.1 million, was one of the top ten magazines in the United States at a time when millions of Americans received most of their information about current events through such periodicals.[19]

San Antonio Symposium

Gordon Manning, the managing editor of *Collier's*, was among those intrigued by descriptions of the symposium. So, when a short time later, he spotted a brief article in the *New York Journal-American* about a forthcoming space conference in Texas,[20] he decided to send Cornelius Ryan, an associate editor, and Chesley Bonestell, the space artist. As a result, Ryan and Bonestell found themselves at the Air Force's Symposium on the Physics and Medicine of the Upper Atmosphere, held in San Antonio from November 6 to 9, 1951.

At this conference, the momentum that the cause of space travel had recently acquired at the Hayden Planetarium would snowball, thanks to the presence of Wernher von Braun, who had been invited to attend the conference but had not been asked to speak, because his American handlers still kept him on a tight leash.[21]

Ryan reportedly arrived at the conference skeptical and uninformed about the concept of space travel, and he had trouble following the highly technical discussions. At one point, according to his wife,

he was sitting in a room where this rather striking blue-eyed blond German was at the blackboard, chalking all sorts of mathematical equations. Suddenly, there was a sort of collective gasp around the room; there seemed to be a tremendous amount of excitement in the air. Connie [as she called her husband] happened to be seated next to Chesley Bonestell, whom he knew, and Chesley was as excited as everyone else. Connie asked Chesley: "What's going on here?" Chesley replied: "Dr. von Braun has just shown us a way to go into space!"[22]

Von Braun himself relates:

Leaving one of the sessions and stepping to the bar of the hotel . . . I made the acquaintance of a good-looking Irishman who, gazing at the crystal highball between his hands, was sunk in a brown study. "They've sent me down here to find out what serious scientists think about the possibilities of flight into outer space," he growled. "But I don't know what these people are talking about. All I could find out so far is that lots of people get up there to the rostrum and cover a blackboard with mysterious signs." I volunteered to help.[23]

Whipple, who had been one of the speakers at the symposium at the Hayden Planetarium, was also at the San Antonio conference, where he too met von Braun for the first time. "I was delighted to meet him," Whipple recalled, "because I felt that he would be the man who was going to put us into space."[24] Whipple described an evening when he, von Braun, and Joseph Kaplan, a professor of upper atmospheric physics at the UCLA and one of the symposium's organizers, cornered Ryan in the dining room. Long into the night, over cocktails, dinner, and after-dinner cocktails, "The three of us worked hard at proselytizing Ryan," Whipple recalled. "That evening he appeared to be highly skeptical. Von Braun," he pointed out, was "certainly one of the best salesmen of the twentieth century. Additionally, Kaplan carried the aura of wisdom and the expertise of the archetypal learned professor, while I had learned by then to sound very convincing."[25] As a result, according to Ryan's wife, "He was absolutely convinced. He came back trying to figure out how to get Collier's interested in space stations, spaceships, and flights to the Moon."[26]

"Man Will Conquer Space Soon"

After the San Antonio conference, von Braun followed up by sending Ryan and Bonestell samples of his writing about space. Collier's, in turn, scheduled a December 11 meeting at its offices that included the scientists von Braun, Heinz Haber, Willy Ley, and Fred Whipple, along with the artists Bonestell, Fred Freeman, and Rolf Klep.

Over the next few months, this team, along with Joseph Kaplan and Oscar Schacter, worked together on a special issue of *Collier's*. Von Braun worked closely with the artists, sending them design drawings and then critiquing their drafts. Ley spent days at the *Collier's* offices working with Ryan and the staff to make sure that the concepts described were accessible to the average reader.

On March 22, 1952, the issue was released, with the cover blaring "Man Will Conquer Space Soon. Top Scientists Tell How in 15 Startling Pages." The issue included articles by Haber, Ley, Whipple, Kaplan, Schachter, and von Braun, and was lavishly illustrated by Bonestell, Freeman, and Klep. The opening editorial, titled "What Are We Waiting For?" urged prompt action and, with the nation gripped by the Cold War with the Soviet Union, discussed the potential uses of space for war and/or peace in the Atomic Age. "*Collier's* became interested in this whole program last October," the editorial explained, "when members of our editorial staff attended the First Annual Symposium on Space Travel, held at New York's Hayden Planetarium."

The issue's centerpiece was a long article by von Braun detailing how three-stage rockets could launch astronauts and supply ships into orbit for the purpose of building a permanent space station. Among the many benefits of the space station was that it would make it easy to send men on a five-day round trip that would sweep past the far side of the Moon. Additional articles addressed such issues as the effects of zero gravity, artificial gravity, climate control, cooking and eating in space, the ability to make improved astronomical observations and scan the entire Earth's surface from space, and the legal aspects of claiming territory in space.

The publication of the issue was accompanied by what von Braun described as "by far the greatest public advertising campaign for spaceflight and the artificial satellite . . . the world has ever seen." He appeared on radio and all the national television networks. *Collier's* sent press kits to senators, congressmen, and other influential people and even distributed window displays to shops along New York's prestigious Fifth Avenue.[27]

The August 1952, issue of *Popular Science* contained an article titled "The Line Forms Here for Trip to Moon." The topic was the Hayden Planetarium's ad campaign soliciting reservations for interplanetary travel. According to the article, 24,000 people had signed up, with one applicant saying, "This chance to put our names on file for future space flight gives me the feeling that interplanetary travel is just over the horizon." Included in the article was a picture of the planetarium's new Weight on Other Worlds exhibit.[28]

In September, Viking Press, which had published Ley and Bonestell's *Conquest of Space*, published *Across the Space Frontier*, a book based on expanded versions of the articles from the special issue of *Collier's*. The following month, *Collier's* published a two-part series explaining how man could reach the Moon, describing the first mission, which would be six weeks long, in realistic detail.

Second Symposium on Space Travel

In the midst of all this, the Hayden Planetarium's Second Symposium on Space Travel took place on October 13, 1952. Not surprisingly, von Braun was on the speaker list for this one, and at the heart of the event was a debate between him and Milton Rosen, the leader of the Viking rocket project at the Naval Research Laboratory. At issue was the question of whether the scenario von Braun had presented in *Collier's* was too bold and speculative, with Rosen suggesting a more conservative approach in a paper titled "A Down-to-Earth View of Space Flight."[29]

In advance of the symposium, von Braun, Ley, Rosen, and the planetarium staff discussed whether it would be wise to expose this rift in the spaceflight community. Von Braun welcomed the debate, saying, "If he agrees with us, it won't attract any attention at all." Von Braun prevailed, and the debate garnered headlines.[30] The symposium also included talks by Ley, Coles, Haber, and Whipple.

Space Fever

By this time, space fever had struck the public. This could be seen, for example, in the proliferation of space-travel-themed toys and children's books, including *Rocket Away!*, by Frances Frost, published in early 1953. *Rocket Away!*, with a foreword by Coles, tells the story of a family outing to the Hayden Planetarium and an imaginary trip to the Moon, ending with the children filling out an interplanetary-tour reservation form. By this time, according to Coles's foreword, 25,000 people had signed up for the planetarium's interplanetary tours.[31]

It was during this period, from 1952 to 1953, that the Hayden Planetarium's iconic black-light murals were developed. The east, west, and south corridors on the first floor were filled with gigantic fluorescent murals of astronomical objects as they might appear from a spaceship or the surface of an alien world. The murals remained in place until the original planetarium building closed in 1997.

All of this activity boosted the planetarium's attendance figures, which increased steadily through the early 1950s. Annual attendance exceeded half a million for the first time in the fiscal year of 1952 and did so again in 1953.[32]

Collier's, with the help of Ley, von Braun, Bonestell, and others, kept the momentum going with five more issues published between February 28, 1953, and April 4, 1954.[33] The final issue proposed a plan for putting men on Mars. In October 1953, Viking Press published *Conquest of the Moon*, based on articles from *Collier's* October 1952 issue.

On June 30, 1955, the planetarium, then under the leadership of Joseph M. Chamberlain, opened Viking Rocket Hall on the second floor of the planetarium's south corridor. The exhibition's centerpiece was an actual Viking 10 rocket, donated by its manufacturer, the Martin Company, with cutaway windows for examining the rocket's interior. The project leader for the rocket, developed for exploring Earth's upper atmosphere, had been Milton Rosen, who had debated von Braun at the Hayden Planetarium's second symposium. At the exhibit's opening, the Martin Company gave away copies of *The Viking Rocket Story* by Rosen, which had been published the previous month.[34]

In July, the White House announced plans to launch an Earth-orbiting satellite during the forthcoming International Geophysical Year, a massive study of Earth that had been established in 1952 and was scheduled to run from July 1957 through December 1958. The goal was to promote international cooperation, and eventually sixty-seven countries became involved.

Rosen proposed a satellite based on an enlarged Viking rocket. Von Braun's proposed a satellite called Project Orbiter that was based on the rockets he had been working on for the US Army. Rosen's proposal was selected in September, and the project was named Vanguard, with Rosen as the technical director.[35]

All this activity affected the public perception of the feasibility of space travel. In 1955, a Gallup poll asked the same question it had in 1949, this time revealing that 38 percent of Americans believed that man would reach the Moon in fifty years, compared to 15 percent six years earlier.[36]

As for the planetarium's financial situation, on October 4, 1955, Robert Moses wrote to Norman Bel Geddes: "Annual attendance has been increasing steadily. The Planetarium Authority is able to pay 4½% interest on the face value of its bonds which are now held by the American Museum of Natural History, and still show a surplus which can be used for rehabilitation and improvements."[37]

After the publication of the final issue of the *Collier's* series, von Braun, Ley, and their colleagues were in need of a new vehicle for promoting space travel. At the same time, Walt Disney was building Disneyland, which opened in the summer of 1955, and was developing a tie-in television show for ABC-TV. Disney recruited von Braun and Ley to create three episodes based on the *Collier's* themes, resulting in *Man in Space* (airing March 9, 1955), *Man and the Moon* (December 28, 1955), and *Mars and Beyond* (December 4, 1957).[38]

Sputnik: Things Just Got Real

On October 4, 1957, two months before the final episode of the Disney trilogy aired, the Space Age began when the Soviet Union launched *Sputnik 1*, the first manmade satellite, into an orbit around the Earth— the Cold War equivalent of Pearl Harbor. The Soviets followed up on November 3 with *Sputnik 2*, containing a dog named Laika, the first animal launched into orbit.

The United States responded by attempting its first satellite launch on December 6, atop Rosen's Vanguard rocket. However, after a few seconds, the rocket fell back to the launch pad and exploded. The country then turned to von Braun, who had been developing the Jupiter rocket, evolved from the German's V-2 rocket, for the US Army. On January 31, 1958, the Jupiter rocket was used to launch America's first satellite, *Explorer 1*, four months after the first *Sputnik*. On March 17, America launched its second satellite aboard a Vanguard rocket.[39]

Stimulated by the satellite launches, Hayden Planetarium attendance spiked to a record high of 618,000 for the fiscal year of 1957.[40]

On July 29, 1958, President Dwight D. Eisenhower signed into law the act creating the National Aeronautics and Space Administration (NASA), which opened for business on October 1, 1958. And in 1959, a Gallup poll revealed that 52 percent of Americans believed that man would reach the Moon within the next twenty years.[41]

The 1960s

The Russians put the first man in space, Yuri Gagarin, on April 12, 1961. On May 5, the United States sent up Alan Shepard as part of

Project Mercury, atop a rocket that von Braun had worked on. This was followed on May 25 by President Kennedy's famous speech before Congress, where he said, "I believe that this nation should commit itself to achieving the goal, before this decade is out, of landing a man on the Moon and returning him safely to the Earth." Project Mercury led to Project Gemini, which in turn led to Project Apollo. On July 20, 1969, the Apollo 11 mission landed the first men on the Moon.

Von Braun was the chief architect and director for the Saturn V rocket (the successor to his Jupiter rocket) that powered the lunar program. Ultimately, von Braun was able to make his teenage dreams of artificial satellites and men on the Moon come true. Willy Ley, who was serving as an advisor to NASA, died of a heart attack on June 24, 1969, as he was preparing to leave his home in Queens for the launch at Cape Kennedy, Florida. A crater on the far side of the Moon was named for him a year later.[42]

And as the public's obsession with the space race surged, so did the fortunes of planetariums in general and the Hayden Planetarium in particular. Between 1963 and 1969, the number of planetariums in the United States grew from fewer than eighty to nearly one thousand.[43] During this period, the Hayden Planetarium upgraded its Zeiss projector twice. In January 1960, the original Model II was upgraded to a Model IV, replaced for the first time since the planetarium's opening in 1935. And in September 1969, it was upgraded to a Model VI. In 1964, the innovative Astronomia exhibit, sponsored by IBM, was installed on the planetarium's second-floor south corridor. Between 1967 and 1972 the planetarium held several exhibitions of Chesley Bonestell's paintings.[44]

Not surprisingly, the 1960s was a great decade for the planetarium's attendance figures. Throughout the decade, the planetarium's average annual attendance was greater than 605,000, and the fiscal year ending July 1, 1969, the month of the Moon landing, was the best year ever, with 655,360 visitors.[45] In July 1969, every show was sold out.[46]

On December 7, 1972, Apollo 17, the final Apollo mission, featuring the final manned Moon landing, blasted off.

12

A Visit to the Original Hayden Planetarium

A visit to the original Hayden Planetarium was structured around the Sky Theater show under the dome on the second floor, which would be preceded by the opening act in the Copernican Hall of the Sun on the first floor. Before the opening act, you would typically view the exhibits in the first-floor corridors, and after the Sky Theater show you would view the exhibits in the second-floor corridors.

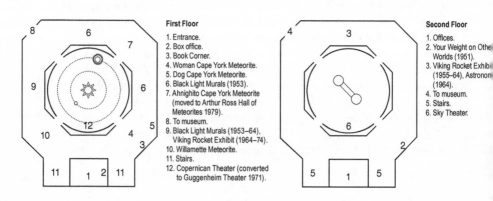

First Floor

1. Entrance.
2. Box office.
3. Book Corner.
4. Woman Cape York Meteorite.
5. Dog Cape York Meteorite.
6. Black Light Murals (1953).
7. Ahnighito Cape York Meteorite (moved to Arthur Ross Hall of Meteorites 1979).
8. To museum.
9. Black Light Murals (1953–64), Viking Rocket Exhibit (1964–74).
10. Willamette Meteorite.
11. Stairs.
12. Copernican Theater (converted to Guggenheim Theater 1971).

Second Floor

1. Offices.
2. Your Weight on Other Worlds (1951).
3. Viking Rocket Exhibit (1955–64), Astronomy (1964).
4. To museum.
5. Stairs.
6. Sky Theater.

Hayden Planetarium floor plan, first and second floors.

Meteorites

When the planetarium first opened, the corridor exhibits consisted largely of items that previously had been on display in the museum's Pro-Astronomic Hall. In addition, the first floor contained the museum's meteorite collection, including the Willamette meteorite, the Cape York meteorites, and other meteorites that previously had been located in the foyer of the Seventy-Seventh Street entrance pavilion. The Willamette meteorite was located in the northeast corner, the Ahnighito was in the southwest corner, and the Dog and Woman were in the northwest corner.

The Black Light Murals

On February 10, 1953, a major new permanent exhibit opened at the planetarium: the Black Light Murals, encompassing the east, south, and west corridors of the first floor, including the corner housing the Ahnighito Meteorite. In 1956, the meteorite was placed on a Toledo scale, and its weight was determined for the first time. (In 1979, the

Ahnighito Meteorite in the southwest corner of the first floor of the Hayden Planetarium, June 1936.
Source: AMNH ID 314968, American Museum of Natural History, Library.

Ahnighito Meteorite in the southwest corner of the first floor of the
Hayden Planetarium, 1956, now mounted on a Toledo scale and
surrounded by black-light murals. To left, a mural of the Ahnighito
crashing on Earth.
Source: AMNH ID 324502, American Museum of Natural History, Library.

Ahnighito was moved from the planetarium to the Arthur Ross Hall of
Meteorites.)

The *New York Times* described these murals as "a brilliant and awe-
inspiring spectacle, the 'heavens' at the Planetarium cover 4,000 square
feet of wall on the building's first floor. They present a picture that has
never been painted before, a three-dimensional cosmos achieved
through the use of fluorescent painting and black, or ultra-violet ray
lighting techniques."[1] According to the museum's 1953 *General Guide*,
these murals showed "in vivid detail such subjects as sunspot activity,
the Aurora Borealis, solar prominences, eclipses of the Sun and the
Moon, galactic nebulae and our neighboring worlds, the planets."[2] And
as Joseph M. Guerry, designer of the murals, described the installation,
"The black-light technique gives the illusion of deep space and a three-
dimensional effect that makes some of the stars seem to go back a million
miles. One is not conscious of the painted walls, and, instead, the planets
appear to be hanging in space."[3]

The overall effect was that of incredibly realistic, life-sized astronomical images as you might see them from the cockpit of a spaceship or standing on the surface of an alien world. The lunar landscape mural was thirty-four feet wide by 13.5 feet tall.

The murals were officially unveiled on February 9, 1953, and *Sky and Telescope* described how they were created in its May 1953 issue's cover story: "The process involved, in many cases, the projection of observatory photographs onto the wall surfaces" so the artists could paint directly on the images. The luminous paint "was originally used for theatrical costumes" but was "attaining ever-widening applications for exhibit purposes."

Thomas Voter working on the aurora borealis black-light mural, 1953.
Source: AMNH ID 322418, American Museum of Natural History, Library.

Guerry, the designer of the murals, described the experience as "like painting with fire." According to Thomas Voter, the museum artist in charge of the project, "the 'old master' technique was followed, rather than the techniques of modern commercial work." The article continued, "To make even more realistic the mural of the aurora, a moving ultraviolet light, hidden from view, sweeps slowly over the wall to create the illusion of the shimmering blue-green curtains of the northern lights."[4]

The original set of fourteen murals, moving from east to west, depicted sunspots, solar prominences, the aurora borealis, a total solar eclipse, Mars, the Whirlpool Nebula, Morehouse's comet, the Great Nebula in Andromeda, the Leonid meteor shower of November 1833, Saturn and its rings, a lunar eclipse, a globular star cluster, the Horsehead Nebula in Orion, and the Great Nebula in Orion.[5]

According to the museum's 1952 *Annual Report*, "Further murals will be added under our overall plan for the modernization of the Planetarium's permanent exhibits."[6] In late 1954, three more murals were created: Jupiter viewed from the surface of its moon Io; a lunar landscape, with the Earth visible on the horizon; and the Ahnighito meteorite crashing into Earth. These murals opened to the public on February 1, 1955.[7]

In 1964, the Astronomia exhibition was installed on the second floor, causing the Viking rocket exhibit to be moved to the east corridor on the first floor. As a result, the area devoted to the black-light murals was reduced to three thousand square feet, encompassing just the planetarium's south and west corridors, requiring a reduction in the number of murals.[8] (In 1974, the Viking rocket was donated to the Smithsonian Institution's National Air and Space Museum.)[9]

The murals were frequently updated to reflect the most current astronomical information. This included, most notably, an alteration to the lunar-landscape mural in December 1968, after the revelations of the NASA spacecrafts of the 1960s, and the Saturn mural in the late 1980s, after discoveries from the missions of the Voyager spacecrafts.[10]

The Copernican Hall of the Sun

About fifteen minutes before the Sky Theater show was scheduled to begin, there would be an opening act in the Copernican Hall of the Sun, which would consist of a short taped or live lecture related to the topic of the current Sky Theater show.[11] The Copernican Hall of the Sun was

Black-light murals: Jupiter seen from Io, Solar eclipse, Morehouse's comet, Mars, Andromeda Nebula, Saturn, Lunar landscape, Whirlpool Nebula.
Sources: Andromeda Nebula: AMNH ID 322409; Saturn: AMNH ID 328; Whirlpool Nebula: AMNH ID 331.

Lunar-landscape black-light mural, 1969.
Source: AMNH ID 334276.

a Copernican planetarium consisting of a ceiling-mounted orrery (animated model of the solar system based on clock mechanisms) forty feet in diameter.

Suspended from the ceiling at the center of the hall was a large luminous globe representing the Sun. Six planets orbited the Sun on circular tracks. Uranus, Neptune, and Pluto were not represented given their enormous distances from the Sun. At the model's scale, the outermost three planets would far exceed the forty-foot diameter.

Children admiring the lunar-landscape black-light mural, March 1969.
Source: AMNH ID 334037.

Each planet rotated on its axis, and Earth's moon, Mars's two moons, and five moons each for Jupiter and Saturn orbited their respective planets. The constellations of the zodiac were painted on the circular walls surrounding the room. These features allowed the following phenomena to be understood: day and night, seasons, eclipses, phases of the Moon, and the movements through the constellations of the zodiac of the Sun, Moon, and planets.

The bodies moved at correct relative speeds, sped up so that an orbit of Earth around the Sun, representing a year, took place in twelve minutes. At this rate it took Saturn, the slowest planet, six hours to finish an orbit, giving it the appearance of motionlessness.[12]

In the center of the floor was a reproduction of the Aztec Calendar Stone.

In the late 1950s, the Copernican planetarium was upgraded and repaired. Each planet was painted with fluorescent colors and had a black–light fixture added such that the black light came from the same direction as the light from the Sun. This enhanced the phenomenon of

Copernican planetarium, 1935. Note the Willamette meteorite, seen through doorway.

Source: Wurts Bros./Museum of the City of New York. X2010.7.2.6437.

Copernican planetarium, soon after the 1960 upgrade. Note the permanent chairs. *Source*: AMNH ID 946.

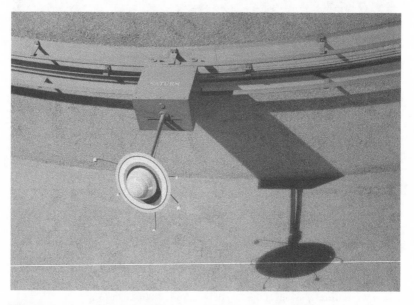

The Copernican planetarium's Saturn model, October 10, 1935. *Source*: Wurts Bros./Museum of the City of New York. X2010.7.1.12438.

The planets of the Copernican planetarium, January 1940.
Source: AMNH ID 292430.

day and night. Also, permanent chairs were installed (previously, folding chairs had been used), and extensive repair was done to the system's gear system, which had had no major repairs since 1935.[13]

In 1971, the space was converted to an eleven-screen theater in the round and named the Guggenheim Space Theater, after the Daniel and Florence Guggenheim Foundation, which donated the money for the project. For the first few years, the theater was troubled by equipment failures. Over time, the ceiling orrery, which was no longer the main focus of the space, fell into disrepair.[14]

The Sky Theater

After the opening act in the Copernican planetarium (or, later, the Guggenheim Space Theater), you would proceed up the stairs to the Sky Theater for the main show. According to Thomas Lesser, "at one time the lecturer, sometimes dressed in a tuxedo, would then lead the

The Zeiss projector in the Sky
Theater.
Source: AMNH ID 962.

audience up the east stairway and into the Sky Theater where the same
lecturer would then present the Sky Show."

In the center of the room was a contraption consisting of a tube
approximately seven feet long, with globes approximately 2.5 feet in
diameter on either end, giving it the appearance of a large dumbbell.
Supported by spindly legs, it was also reminiscent of a gigantic insect.
This device, the Zeiss projector, was responsible for producing star-
tlingly realistic views of the night sky as well as other astronomical
phenomena on the overhead dome, which was seventy-five feet in
diameter. One globe was responsible for projecting the stars of the
northern hemisphere, and the other was responsible for the southern.

Fitted with numerous motors, the device was capable of rotating
independently on three axes. Rotation on one axis allowed the presentation of the sky as it would appear from any point on Earth. Rotation
on another axis simulated the rotation of Earth, showing the sky as it
would appear at any time during the day. Rotation on a third axis
simulated the slow precessional wobbling of Earth's axis, allowing viewing of the sky as it would appear thousands of years in the past or future,
when, for example, Polaris would no longer be the pole star. Separate
projectors with independent movement were responsible for projecting
the planets and Moon.

When the planetarium opened, the projection of the night sky and
some nine thousand stars was awe inspiring, and it was sufficient for the
shows to be something as simple as "The Stars of October" or "The

Stars of April." You would see a presentation on what stars, constellations, and other astronomical objects were visible that month. But almost immediately, the staff began adding technologies to increase the available effects and the range of astronomical topics that could be presented.

A small sample of the sky-show topics, which averaged about nine per year, included: "The End of the World," "Rocket to the Moon," "4,000 Years of Astronomy," "Exploring the Milky Way," "The Expanding Universe," "Astronomy in the News," and "Universe of Atoms." Every December there would be a Christmas special that proposed a scientific explanation for the Star of Bethlehem. Each show would typically begin with a presentation on the night sky for that month.

Planetarium technicians were constantly conceiving, designing, and building ever more sophisticated special-effects projectors. The presenter's console was also frequently upgraded to give improved control over the equipment.

By late 1958, the original Zeiss Model II projector, which had been in daily use since 1935, had become obsolete and was showing significant signs of wear. In October of that year, the planetarium's chairman, Joseph Chamberlain, traveled to Oberkochen, West Germany, to negotiate an upgrade to a Model IV with Walther Bauersfeld, who had invented the Zeiss projector in 1923 and who would die one year later. The new model produced more realistic images of the sky and was mechanically smoother and faster. In January 1959, the Charles Hayden Foundation agreed to pay for the upgrade.[15]

Along with the projector upgrade, the room's chairs were replaced, and the cardboard silhouette of the Manhattan skyline that had been affixed to the dome's horizon since 1935 was replaced with fourteen horizon projectors, allowing the horizon to be shown for any location on or off Earth.[16]

The new projector was unveiled on January 29, 1960, with talks by Chamberlain, museum president Alexander M. White, Robert Moses, and Mayor Robert Wagner, followed by the new sky show, called "New Skies for New York," presented by Thomas Nicholson, who would later become chairman of the planetarium and, later still, director of the museum.[17]

From the planetarium's opening through the late 1960s, the shows were presented by a live lecturer who would use a flashlight-like pointer to guide the audience's attention to the area of interest on the dome. In the late 1960s, another technological advance took place with the introduction of taped shows. In September 1969, the projector was upgraded to a Model VI, once again paid for by the Charles Hayden Foundation.

The new projector was unveiled on October 3, 1969, with the show "Adventure of a Lightbeam."[18]

Over the years, the shows became increasingly difficult to produce because of the increasing complexity of the artwork, special-effects projectors, and other elements. As a result, the number of shows per year gradually decreased from twelve when the planetarium first opened to three in the late 1970s.

On October 1, 1982, Thomas Lesser pushed a button—and for the first time, the Sky Show ran automatically. In what was at the time the world's largest computer-controlled multimedia system, two computers controlled audiotape decks, movie projectors, fifty-two slide projectors, and up to 150 special effects. However, manual control was still required for controlling the Zeiss projector. Lesser had led the yearlong automation project, which had begun after seven years of discussion.[19]

From the first show at the planetarium to the last, the purpose was the same—to inspire people with the amazing wonders of the universe and perhaps to slip in some educational information about astronomy.

Astronomia

After the Sky Show, you would typically view the corridor exhibits on the second floor. After its opening on June 29, 1964, the second-floor corridor exhibits were dominated by Astronomia, an innovative exhibition hall donated by IBM, located in the south corridor and southwest corner. Its bright and colorful interactive exhibits were a major and startling departure from what had typically been the planetarium's exhibitions up until that time.

Astronomia's opening ceremonies took place on June 29, 1964, and they were attended by educators and scientists, including the celebrated science and science-fiction writer Isaac Asimov.[20] According to the museum's 1963 *Annual Report*, the exhibit was "the most important to appear in the Planetarium corridors since the opening of Viking Hall in 1955."[21]

Astronomia, however, was not the first exhibition donated to the Hayden Planetarium by IBM. On September 13, 1958, Computers in Astronomy, also provided by IBM, opened on the first floor, just inside the main entrance. It used animated models, light boxes, and film strips to depict the orbits and motions of celestial objects, air navigation by the stars, nuclear fusion, the birth and death of stars, and other astronomical subjects.[22]

The style of Astronomia was highly influenced by the style of Mathematica: A World of Numbers . . . and Beyond, an exhibition that first

Entrance to Astronomia, south corridor, 1964.
Source: Courtesy of Gordon Ashby.

appeared at the California Museum of Science and Industry in March 1961. Mathematica, also donated by IBM, was designed by the famous California design team of Charles and Ray Eames.[23] Gordon Ashby, the designer of Astronomia, began his career as a designer of museum exhibits when he worked with the Eames team on a version of Mathematica for the IBM pavilion at the 1964 World's Fair in Queens, and he began work on Astronomia shortly thereafter.[24]

Like Mathematica, Astronomia was located in a carpeted, brightly lit space with white walls. Both exhibitions used historical timelines and hands-on exhibits to make abstract concepts understandable to nonscientists.

According to Ashby, the exhibit was designed to calm and slow down children who might be coming in off the subway "wired, yelling and screaming." The carpets, for example, dampened the noise and evoked a private living room. Stewart Brand, who went on to create the *Whole Earth Catalog*, did research and writing for Astronomia.

The room in the southwest corner contained two freestanding, hands-on mechanical exhibits that aimed to present, as Ashby put it, "abstract concepts so regular people could understand," namely the gravity well and the parallax machine.

Astronomia, southwest corner, gravity well on left, parallax machine on right.
Source: Courtesy of Gordon Ashby.

In the gravity well, or celestial-mechanics machine, steel balls rolled into a hyperbolic funnel, in which they circled around until they eventually fell into a center hole. This exhibit was a visual demonstration of Kepler's laws describing the motions of planets around the Sun.

The parallax machine demonstrated the illusory nature of the constellations, which appear from Earth as if the stars are lying on the surface of a dome that makes up the night sky. Inside the box were grain-of-wheat light bulbs representing stars, arranged in three dimensions, modeling the stars in the constellation Orion. On one side of the box was a "telescope" through which a person could see Orion as it appears from Earth. It was possible to move the telescope back and forth and see the stars of Orion shift against the background stars. On the side of the box, to the right, was a window through which a person could see the relative positions of the stars and see that the stars that form Orion are, in fact, not all on the same plane.

When Astronomia first opened, the south corridor portrayed five centuries of astronomy, with a diorama for each century, from the Renaissance in the 1400s to the Industrial Revolution in the 1800s. The

Astronomia, Five Centuries of Astronomy, 1500 diorama.
Source: Courtesy of Gordon Ashby.

dioramas contained more than fifty antique objects never before exhibited in New York, including seventeenth-century telescopes, early navigation implements, and ancient manuscripts. Many of these were borrowed from the Adler Planetarium, the Harvard College Observatory, the Smithsonian Institution, and the Library of Congress.

In 1968, the hall was completely remodeled.[25] Objects borrowed for the original version of the exhibition were returned, new exhibits were added, and the style became influenced by the psychedelic aesthetic of the late 1960s. In 1974, when the planetarium's Perkin Wing was completed, Astronomia was expanded to include the planetarium's southeast corner, where display cases were added containing full-scale replicas of astronomical-based devices such as clocks and telescopes. The display

Entrance to Astronomia, south corridor, 1968.
Source: Courtesy of Gordon Ashby.

included a replica of Galileo's telescope, which was arranged so a person could look through it and see the Moon as Galileo saw it.[26]

Your Weight on Other Worlds

After leaving Astronomia, on your way to the stairs, you would pass by Your Weight on Other Worlds, an exhibit that opened in the northwest corner of the second floor in February 1951. Your Weight on Other Worlds consisted of five scales from the Toledo Scale Company showing the visitor's weight on the Moon, Mars, the Sun, Venus, and Jupiter.[27] This was accomplished by labeling the readout dial differently for each scale. Despite its simplicity, many visitors found this exhibit to be among the planetarium's most memorable.

When the exhibit first opened, it was accompanied by images by Chesley Bonestell of the Moon, Mars, Venus, and Jupiter from the book *The Conquest of Space*. The exhibit was extensively modernized in 1961 and upgraded again in 1969.[28]

Your Weight on Other Worlds, initial version, c. 1951. Note the Chesley Bonestell images above the scales.
Source: AMNH ID 321.

Your Weight on Other Worlds, 1969 version.
Source: AMNH ID 334305.

13

The Rose Center for Earth and Space

The Golden Age of Spaceflight ended with the Apollo program. As the program drew to a close in 1972, the public's interest in space-flight waned, as did the Hayden Planetarium's attendance figures, along with those of planetariums in general.

To supplement the income from astronomical programs, planetariums began offering psychedelic rock-music laser shows under the brand name Laserium, using the recently invented laser to present spectacles that combined color and music. The name Laserium combined the words laser and planetarium, and the technique had been devised by Ivan Dryer, who created the company Laser Images, Inc. The first Laserium show took place at the Griffith Observatory planetarium in Los Angeles in November 1973, and the Hayden Planetarium began featuring Laserium shows in October 1974.[1]

An article in the *New York Times* on January 4, 1991, foreshadowed what was to come. The article bemoaned that "though it is one of the best-known shrines in the city, for many residents who are casting about for a few hours of diversion, the Hayden Planetarium might as well not be there." The article quoted William A. Gutsch Jr., the planetarium's chairman since 1982, saying, "Yes, it is still valid to teach people to learn their way around the naked-eye sky. But it's also our job to teach people what we know about the known universe: questions like why stars explode, why planets form around stars, and what is the structure of the galaxy."[2]

According to Dennis Davidson, who had been the Hayden Planetarium's astronomical artist since 1987 and went on to become the Rose Center's manager for science visualization, "By 1990–1991 the planetarium was getting serious attention from [museum president George D.] Langdon and senior staff. George Awad's Power of Ten model of the universe was a catalyst for this."

In the spring of 1992, in an effort to reinvigorate and modernize the planetarium's exhibit halls, Gutsch convened a Planetarium Visiting Committee to recommend some options. The committee was chaired by the Princeton astrophysicist J. Richard Gott, reporting to Langdon, and included James S. Sweitzer, then assistant director and astronomer for Chicago's Adler Planetarium, who was also at the time doing astrophysical research in Antarctica.[3]

In December 1992, Langdon announced that he would be stepping down when he completed his five-year term. According to William T. Golden, chairman of the museum's board of trustees, "He brought us out of the Middle Ages, and now wants to move on to something else."[4]

Even as the museum was evaluating the committee's recommendations, the institution tried to increase attendance by, as the *New York Times* described the effort, transforming the planetarium into a shrine to the phenomenally popular television series *Star Trek*. The combined *Star Trek*–themed exhibit and Sky Show began on July 1, 1993, using the show as a vehicle to teach the public about the various types of stars and how they evolved. The exhibit closed in March 1994, and the Sky Show ended that June.[5] Despite the museum's hopes, the *Star Trek* material failed to boost attendance.

A few months earlier, in November 1993, as the *Star Trek* exhibit and Sky Show were limping along, Ellen Futter became the first female president of the museum, replacing Langdon.[6]

Having grown up in Long Island and with family in New York City, Futter visited the museum regularly as a child, often with her grandmother. "I fell in love with nature and the dioramas on these visits. I specifically recall my older brother having a birthday party in the planetarium and finding it magical when the lights went down and the stars came up!" she recalls. Regarding other childhood influences, she recalls, "At the same time, as a youngster I was a sort of amateur naturalist and collector—shells, rocks, and butterflies, and I still actively collect shells today. I was also of the generation when we started the space race. I recall being very inspired by President John F. Kennedy saying, 'we choose to go to the Moon, not because it is easy, but because it is hard.'"[7]

Futter graduated from Columbia Law School in 1974, and in 1980, after a stint at a Wall Street law firm, she took the position of acting president of Barnard College, her undergraduate alma mater. The following year, at the age of thirty-one, she was named permanent president, becoming the youngest president of a major American college, a post she held until leaving to join the museum.[8]

According to Golden, "For many years the attitude at the museum was if the money came, it came, and if it didn't, it didn't. But now that we have decided to modernize our exhibits and provide more nourishment for our scientific and educational departments, we know this is going to take resources. Ellen Futter's intelligence, managerial skill, fund-raising ability and inexhaustible energy suit her for the job."

Aware of being one of the few nonscientist museum presidents, she said, "I, as an educator and nonscientist, may be particularly effective in helping to translate issues so that lay people can grasp and take delight in them."[9] Note how this echoes Morris K. Jesup, who said, "I am a plain, unscientific business man. I want the exhibits to be labeled so that I can understand them, and then I shall feel sure that others can understand."

In early 1994, shortly after Futter's arrival, the museum formed a committee to review proposals from architects and exhibition designers for reimagining the planetarium. At first, the committee looked at proposals limited to revitalizing the exhibits in the existing planetarium building and possibly modifying the building. The committee included Sweitzer and Neil deGrasse Tyson, then in his mid-thirties, who at the time was completing postdoctoral research at Princeton University.[10]

Tyson had decided on a career in astrophysics at the age of nine, after his first visit to the Hayden Planetarium in the late 1960s. It was his first encounter with the night sky, having grown up in the Bronx, where, on a good night, only a handful of stars are visible.

During junior high and high school, he took at least half a dozen courses at the planetarium, including two with Fred Hess, whose rich voice Tyson remembers as having a godlike quality and whose style as a lecturer would influence his own. Tyson also took courses from Mark Chartrand III, the planetarium's chairman from 1974 to 1980, including, at the age of fifteen, a class called "Astronomy Roundup," which covered the physics and mathematics of relativity, black holes, quasars, and the Big Bang.[11]

Around this time, on a cloudless night in the Mojave Desert at an astronomy camp, he saw the night sky away from the city for the first time. He found himself thinking, "It reminds me of the Hayden

Planetarium." Apparently, he had been suspecting that the night sky shown at the planetarium was a hoax.[12] Tyson also remembered being deeply moved by the planetarium's Astronomia exhibit, which he found "beautiful, and bright, and interesting, and modern."[13]

After graduating from Bronx High School of Science, Tyson earned a bachelor's degree in physics from Harvard, a master's degree in astronomy from the University of Texas in Austin, and a doctoral degree in astrophysics from Columbia University before beginning his postdoctoral research at Princeton in July 1991. In July 1994, after finishing his postdoctoral research, he was hired by the Hayden Planetarium as a staff scientist, along with a joint appointment to Princeton as a visiting research scientist and lecturer.

By this point, the architects James S. Polshek and Todd Schliemann of the architecture firm Polshek Partnership had joined the project, and several ideas had been proposed for improving the planetarium. One from Polshek called for extending the existing planetarium dome into a complete sphere, with the sphere protruding about eight feet below the basement floor.[14] But the plan presented several problems, among them the fact that the complete sphere would not be visible, other than the fact that some of the rooms would have awkwardly rounded walls. And so the idea was shelved.[15]

As the committee was struggling with designs based around preserving or at most modifying the existing building, the museum trustee Richard Gilder suggested the idea of completely replacing the building, thereby giving the designers a blank slate.[16] (According to Davidson, the idea had been floated years earlier by Gutsch in informal planning sessions.)[17] Gilder provided ongoing inspiration and encouragement for the project and would go on to become the single largest donor in the museum's history.

This led Polshek to revisit the idea of a sphere, this time proposing that it be placed in a transparent enclosure, at first with the equator at ground level. This evolved into the idea of elevating the sphere within the enclosure. Numerous ideas were considered for supporting the sphere, including suspending it from the ceiling, cantilevering it from the walls, and supporting it on a pedestal. (Tyson: "It looked like a golf ball on a tee.")[18] Ultimately, the designers proposed placing the sphere on a tripod, with the beams arranged so as to be barely visible. The final plan called for a sphere that would rise twelve feet higher than the planetarium's original dome and would appear to float in a monumental glass cube on the footprint of the original planetarium.[19] The building's entrance would echo the museum's 1892 wide-arched Seventy-Seventh Street entrance.

In early 1994, as the architectural issues were starting to be hammered out, the museum began considering proposals from numerous exhibit-design firms. By fall of 1994, Ralph Appelbaum and his firm were selected for the job. Appelbaum had recently helped renovate the museum's dinosaur halls and had also worked with Sweitzer on a design for the Adler Planetarium. Applebaum joined the team as it began considering elevating the sphere.[20] According to *Natural History*, "Throughout the planning, Tyson, Polshek, and Appelbaum have worked so interdependently that it is often hard to tell who thought of what."[21]

The plan that was ultimately developed included six elements:

> Models of the planets suspended throughout the cube;
>
> The Space Theater, a Zeiss projection planetarium, housed in the sphere's upper half, featuring a Zeiss Model IX projector;
>
> The Big Bang Theater, housed in the sphere's lower half and presenting an animated multimedia show portraying the Big Bang;
>
> The Hall of the Universe, on the lowest level beneath the sphere, with separate zones for planets, stars, galaxies, and the universe. Included in the Planets Zone would be two favorites from the original planetarium: a modernized version of Your Weight on Other Worlds and the Willamette Meteorite;
>
> The Scales of the Universe walkway, located on a balcony overlooking the sphere and the Hall of the Universe, which would illustrate the range of sizes in the universe from subatomic particles to galaxies; and
>
> The Cosmic Pathway, a ramp that would spiral around the sphere from the exit of the Big Bang Theater down to the Hall of the Universe, with images and diagrams illustrating the cosmic timeline from the Big Bang to the present.

After the decision was made to replace the original planetarium, the project evolved into a larger plan that would enhance the museum in several ways: It would smooth out the undeveloped appearance of the museum's north side along Eighty-First Street by incorporating the new planetarium into a unified structure that would include a terrace concealing a new multilevel parking structure and a new, long-desired entrance on Columbus Avenue. The plan also came to encompass the addition of a new earth sciences hall connected to the planetarium via the first floor of the Whitney Wing (the north wing on Central Park West). Thus visitors could proceed from the study of the universe, stars, and planets to the study of our specific planet, Earth, as originally envisioned by Henry Fairfield Osborn in his 1910 report *History, Plan, and Scope*. This became known as the North Side Project.

The design was announced in January 1995,[22] and the following November the plan was unanimously approved by the New York City Landmarks Preservation Commission, approval required because the museum was an official city landmark. With the approval, Futter announced that half the estimated cost of the project, $60 million, had been raised. This included $20 million from an anonymous donor, $33 million from the city, $5 million from another anonymous donor, and $2 million from the Charles Hayden Foundation.[23]

That year, Tyson became the planetarium's acting director, and in May 1996, he became the first Frederick P. Rose Director of the Hayden Planetarium, a position created by Frederick Phineas Rose, a museum trustee since 1990 and chairman of the real estate firm Rose Associates.[24] In November 1996, Rose and his wife Sandra revealed that they were the donors of the anonymous $20 million gift and that the new planetarium would be named the Frederick Phineas and Sandra Priest Rose Center for Earth and Space.[25]

In the meantime, new innovations were afoot. The museum's scientific-visualization team, funded by NASA and led by Davidson, Sweitzer (who had become a museum employee in 1996), and Carter Emmart, pioneered the next generation of digital planetarium technology for the Space Theater—the Digital Galaxy, which has since expanded to become the Digital Universe. Emmart was recruited by Davidson and Sweitzer in 1998, becoming the museum's director for astrovisualization. Davidson had become acquainted with Emmart and his work through the International Association of Astronomical Artists.[26]

The system maintains a massive computer model of the universe, constructed from data from NASA and the European Space Agency, which is continuously updated as new information becomes available. With this system, the presenter can navigate around the universe using a graphical computer interface, as seven video projectors distributed around the room combine to form a single image on the dome, derived from the digital model.

The Zeiss projector and the Digital Universe were intended to compliment each other: The Zeiss projector creates the more realistic experience of the full glory of the night sky on a glare-free cloudless night (the only experience for many city residents whose night sky is obscured by light pollution and haze), whereas the Digital Universe lets the audience roam around the rest of the known universe.[27]

On January 5, 1997, the original Hayden Planetarium closed its doors forever.[28]

The plan for the Rose Center did not arrive without controversy. It was opposed by members of neighborhood organizations who feared that construction would bring traffic, noise, pollution, and disruption to the neighborhood. Additional opposition came from old-school planetarium enthusiasts and people nostalgic about the planetarium they remembered from their childhood.[29]

On January 17, just days after the planetarium closed, two neighborhood groups filed a lawsuit in Manhattan's state supreme court in a last-ditch effort to halt the project. The suit was dismissed five weeks later.[30] Demolition began in March, and construction proceeded over the next three years.

The final price tag for the Rose Center and the North Side Project was $210 million, with $20 million coming from the Roses and the lion's share from the city and state.[31] Many other donors and institutions contributed. Elements of the project named for major contributors included:

> The Hayden Planetarium: the Space Theater housed in the top half of the sphere (funded by the Charles Hayden Foundation);
> The Lewis B. and Dorothy Cullman Hall of the Universe: the portion of the planetarium under the sphere containing astronomical exhibits;
> The Harriet and Robert Heilbrunn Cosmic Pathway: the ramp spiraling around the sphere with images and diagrams that illustrate the cosmic timeline;
> The David S. and Ruth L. Gottesman Hall of Planet Earth: the new earth sciences hall;
> The Arthur Ross Terrace: the outdoor space to the west of the planetarium covering the multilevel parking structure; and
> The Judy and Josh Weston Pavilion: the Columbus Avenue entrance.

The Gottesman Hall of Planet Earth opened on June 12, 1999. The space included many innovative multimedia exhibits as well as materials collected over the previous four years during twenty-eight expeditions,

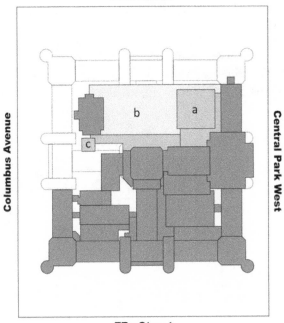

81st Street

Columbus Avenue

Central Park West

77th Street

The Rose Center and Northside Project: (a) Rose Center
for Earth and Space (2000), (b) Aruthur Ross Terrace
(2000), (c) Judy and Josh Weston Pavilion (2001).

The Hayden Planetarium and the Rose Center.
Sources: (*left*) Gottscho-Schleisner Collection, Library of Congress; (*right*) Carol M. Highsmith Archive,
Library of Congress.

including a black smoker—a type of underwater vent that emits heated water and is teeming with strange life—retrieved from the bottom of the Pacific Ocean by a robotic vehicle.[32]

In September 1999, just months before the opening of the Rose Center, Frederick Rose died at the age of seventy-five, consulting on the construction site until the end.[33] The center's grand opening took place on February 19, 2000.

Epilogue
The Gilder Center for Science, Education, and Innovation

On December 11, 2014, after an early draft of this book was complete, the museum announced that its board had authorized the creation of a major new section of the institution: The Gilder Center for Science, Education, and Innovation, with the goal of completing the new building by 2019 or 2020, around the time of the museum's 150th anniversary in 2019.

The unanticipated advent of the Gilder Center is a fitting conclusion to this story—the story of a master plan devised 150 years ago and the generations-long struggle to fulfill its aims as the times and architectural styles changed. Despite frustrating obstacles and decades-long periods of inactivity, the growth of the museum progressed. Yet in 2014, as I completed that early draft, the story seemed unresolved.

Despite tremendous progress over the decades in expanding the museum, several key aspects of the master plan had not been realized. These included sufficient space for the collections, a major presence on Columbus Avenue with a central entrance, and connections between the museum's southwest and northwest sections so visitors could move through the museum by way of looping paths.

Indeed, much of the museum's west side had something of an unfinished appearance, in part because of the utility buildings there, which were closed to the public. In the meantime, the west side of Theodore Roosevelt Park had become an important neighborhood amenity.

And the early draft of this book asked if, when, and how these issues would be resolved.

The December 2014 announcement revealed that Jeanne Gang, a recipient of the 2011 MacArthur "Genius Grant," had been selected to design the center. Ralph Appelbaum, whose firm had designed the exhibits in the museum's Rose Center for Earth and Space, the fourth-floor fossil halls, and the Hall of Biodiversity, would design the exhibitions.

The center's namesake was Richard Gilder, a stockbroker-turned-philanthropist who donated $50 million to the project. This donation, added to earlier contributions of $75 million, made him the single largest donor in the museum's history. Gilder was instrumental in the creation of the Rose Center as well as of the Richard Gilder Graduate School, which began at the museum in 2008.

On November 4, 2015, the museum announced early designs for the project, with the museum's president, Ellen Futter, explaining:

> The Gilder Center embraces the museum's integrated mission and growing role in scientific research and education and its enhanced capacity to make its extensive resources even more fully accessible to the public. It will connect scientific facilities and collections to innovative exhibition and learning spaces featuring the latest digital and technological tools. Jeanne Gang's thrilling design facilitates a new kind of fluid, cross-disciplinary journey through the natural world while respecting the museum's park setting.[1]

The new center would add about two hundred thousand square feet for collections, exhibits, and education spaces—while being built almost entirely within the footprint and envelope of the existing museum, limiting its encroachment into park and air space.

It would accomplish this by filling in the largely unoccupied space bounded by the south wing on Columbus Avenue, the southwest courtyard's School Service Building, the northwest courtyard's Power and Service Building, and the central auditorium, connecting to those buildings and approximately matching their heights. The low-rise buildings in the space would be demolished: the Power House and Boiler House in the west transept area, which was completed in 1904; and the Judy and Josh Weston Pavilion, which was added during the Northside Project in 2001.

The new building would include an entrance on Columbus Avenue and Seventy-Ninth Street leading to a central exhibition hall with well-organized north-south and east-west connections to the museum's existing buildings, allowing visitors to circulate by way of loops,

consistent with the perimeter and east-to-west and north-to-south circulation proposed by the original master plan, improving flow by elim-
inating dead ends and bottlenecks. As well as establishing connections
between the buildings, it would also allow visitors to reinforce intellec-
tual connections by easily traversing integrated science, exhibition, and
educational-program areas.

Employing a contemporary architectural language with a futuristic
undulating, curving design, the new building would continue the
museum's tradition of creating new structures using the architectural
language of the time—Gothic Revival for the initial Bickmore wing,
Romanesque Revival for the Seventy-Seventh Street façade, Roman
Revival for the Theodore Roosevelt Memorial, Art Deco for the original Hayden Planetarium, and contemporary for the Rose Center. In
addition, the landscape design team of Reed Hilderbrand would work
with the Parks Department on the portion of the park surrounding the
new center.

The result is a design that fulfills the aims of the master plan while
respecting the park space that had evolved in the western portion of
Theodore Roosevelt Park.

Plans for new exhibits included an insectarium, a live butterfly con-
servatory, an Invisible Worlds Theater that would provide an immersive
experience of scientific imaging, and a multistory Collections Core—a
glass-walled space for housing a substantial share of the museum's collection of specimens and artifacts previously not on display.

An important objective of the Gilder Center is to extend substantially
the museum's role in enriching formal science education for children of
all ages and to provide professional development for teachers, important
functions of the museum since its earliest days. To that end, the center
would include many next-generation classrooms.

On October 11, 2016, the city's Landmarks Preservation Commission unanimously approved the project. And on December 4, 2017, the
Parks Department approved the project, following a lengthy environmental review process that began in March 2016 and culminated in a
"Final Environmental Impact Statement" issued by the Parks Department on November 15, 2017.

On October 16, 2017, the museum announced that as part of the
lead-up to the opening of the Gilder Center, it would do a complete
redesign of the popular Morgan Memorial Hall of Gems and Harry
Frank Guggenheim Hall of Minerals, which had formed a dead end
in the first floor of the south wing on Columbus Avenue. The newly

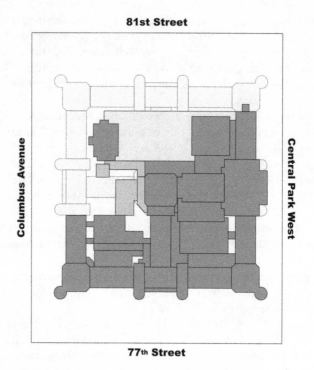

81st Street

Columbus Avenue

Central Park West

77th Street

Buildings to be demolished for Gilder Center.

designed halls would feature a dramatic link to the Gilder Center on the north side via a stunning Crystalline Pass and would be named the Mignone Halls of Gems and Minerals, for Roberto and Allison Mignone, longstanding museum supporters and volunteers. Construction on the new halls began with the closure of the previous halls on October 26.[2]

On April 25, 2018, the Landmarks Preservation Commission and Parks Department approved design refinements. Preparatory activities for construction took place from April to September 2018, including relocating shrubbery, plantings, and trees; installing trailers; moving the time capsule designed by Santiago Calatrava for the *New York Times*; fencing off the construction site; and demolition inside the building.

The plan to schedule a major addition to the museum, including a central entrance on Columbus Avenue, to mark a major anniversary

81st Street

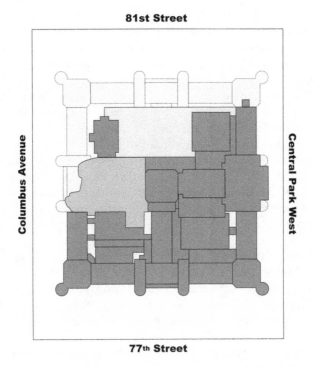

Guilder Center layout.

echoes Henry Fairfield Osborn's attempt to do the same a century earlier.

By 2020, the time of the Gilder Center's scheduled opening, Ellen Futter's tenure at the museum as its president will be twenty-seven years, second only to Morris K. Jesup's twenty-eight. With the additions of the Rose Center and the Gilder Center on her watch, she will join Jesup and Henry Fairfield Osborn as the museum presidents with the greatest impacts on the institution's physical structure.

Stop the Presses!

After the final copy editing of this book was complete, news regarding the Gilder Center was breaking, with the future of the project becoming ambiguous.

On October 2, 2018, Community United to Protect Theodore Roosevelt Park, a neighborhood group that had opposed the Gilder Center project since 2016, took the museum to the New York State Supreme Court, Judge Lynn R. Kotler presiding, in an attempt to stop the project.

Community United's lawyer, Michael S. Hiller, argued that the project would result in the loss of public park space and that the construction would risk the unearthing of toxic chemicals. The city and museum argued that the contaminants present were typical of urban construction sites and could be handled using standard techniques. They also noted the project's review process, which had lasted approximately two years and included extensive public consultation. But perhaps more critical to the eventual outcome, both sides disagreed on interpretations of city and state law and the 1878 lease agreement between the museum and the city.

On Friday, October 26, as the parties were waiting for Judge Kotler's decision, Hiller returned before the judge to present a motion for a restraining order to keep the museum from continuing construction while the judge's decision was still pending. The following Monday, Kotler ordered a halt in construction and tree removal until the next court date, on December 11.

The museum appealed the restraining order, and on November 2, a state appeals court kept the order in place, forbidding work that impinges on the park space but allowing the museum to do interior work and limited exterior work. Both sides declared victory.[3]

Postscript

On December 10, 2018, as this book was being prepared for final type-setting, Judge Kotler made a ruling, requiring one final update to this Epilogue. My editor allowed it, saying "To the degree possible, please keep the changes to a minimum. I need this back within a day." Kotler ruled in favor of the museum, allowing the Gilder Center project to proceed, dismissing the lawsuit, and lifting the restraining order. The project is now expected to be complete in 2021. Hiller indicated that Community United was considering an appeal.[4]

Acknowledgments

This book would not have been possible without the efforts of numerous individuals whom I would like to take this opportunity to thank. (The names in these paragraphs have been sorted alphabetically.)

The book would have never happened if I hadn't met Thomas A. Lesser while casually searching the Internet for information on the Hayden Planetarium. The idea for writing a book came after about two months and a hundred e-mails exchanged, including his sharing many items from his archives.

The following individuals provided key support for the project in numerous ways during its fragile formative period: space historian and author Andrew Chaikin; Jordan D. Marché II, author of *Theaters of Time and Space: American Planetaria, 1930–1970*; John Pazmino, founder of NYSkies Astronomy Inc.; Joe Rao, meteorologist and Hayden Planetarium lecturer; Hayden planetarium lecturer and veteran astronomy instructor Sam Storch; Neil deGrasse Tyson; and Claudio Veliz, architect and astronomer. Marché provided detailed comments on numerous drafts and shared his doctoral research on the history of planetariums in America, Storch provided detailed comments on numerous drafts, and Tyson provided several pleasurable visits/interviews and sustained valuable support throughout.

The following expert sources contributed to this book by, among other things, answering questions and/or careful reading of chapters: Ralph Appelbaum, who with his design firm collaborated on the renovation of the museum's dinosaur exhibits in the 1990s, the Rose Center for Earth and Space, and the Gilder Center; Gordon Ashby, designer of the original Hayden Planetarium's Astronomia exhibit, who also supplied photos; Joseph Chamberlain, who worked in various positions at the planetarium and museum from 1951 to 1967, including as chairman of the planetarium from 1956 to 1964, and his wife, Paula; Dennis Davidson, former astronomical artist and manager for science visualization at the Hayden Planetarium and Rose Center; Ward Dennis of Higgins Quasebarth & Partners; Lowell Dingus, the paleontologist who directed the renovation of the museum's dinosaur exhibits in the 1990s and author of *Next of Kin: Great Fossils at the American Museum of Natural History*; Anthony Flint, author of *Wrestling with Moses: How Jane Jacobs Took on New York's Master Builder and Transformed the American City*; Ellen Futter, the current president of the American Museum of Natural History; Sandra Kitt, planetarium librarian from 1974 to 2003; Kenneth Merin, president and CEO of the Charles Hayden Foundation; Sara Cedar Miller, official historian of the Central Park Conservancy and author of *Central Park: An American Masterpiece*; Stephen C. Quinn, former senior project manager for the museum and author of *Windows on Nature: The Great Habitat Dioramas of the American Museum of Natural History*; Melvin H. Schuetz, author of *A Chesley Bonestell Space Art Chronology*; James Sweitzer, who played several key roles in the transition from the original Hayden Planetarium to the Rose Center for Earth and Space; and Richard Leonard Tobin, who led the 2006 renovation of the museum's Seventy-Seventh Street entrance hall.

This book was also made possible by staff members of the museum: Betina Cochran, my initial contact person at the museum; Jennifer Kane, information and licensing manager; Eugenia Levenson, senior director of editorial and content, who took over as my contact person after Betina left the museum and who provided detailed comments on the manuscript; Mai Reitmeyer, the museum's research librarian, who unlocked the museum's trove of archives on my numerous visits; and Elizabeth Stachow, executive assistant to Neil deGrasse Tyson.

Obviously critical to this book's existence is Fordham University Press, which saw its potential during its embryonic stage and allowed it to reach that potential. At the Press I thank its director, Fred Nachbaur; editors Will Cerbone, Kem Crimmins, Rob Fellman, Eric Newman, and Constance Rosenblum; Kate O'Brien-Nicholson and Katie Sweeney Parmiter from Marketing; Mark Lerner, Design and Production Manager; the board of directors; and anonymous reviewers #1 and #2.

I'd also like to thank friends and family who provided valuable comments on early versions of some chapters: Robert Atkins, Steven Baker, Steven H. Jaffe, Stephanie Johnson, Ralph Stein, Lisa Swallow, and Ellen Williams.

I would also like to thank David Goldman for sharing his research on Benjamin Waterhouse Hawkins; Oscar Gregory for Robert Peary archive research assistance; Katherine Kirkpatrick for sharing her Robert Peary research, reviewing early drafts of chapters, and sage advice on navigating the pitfalls of the publishing world; Jay Pasachoff, for sharing his research on Howard Russell Butler; and Terra Williams, for valuable assistance.

Special thanks to Kermit Roosevelt III, whose great-great-grandfather's statue fronts the museum, for writing the Foreword.

Finally, I'd like to thank my parents for introducing me to the museum as a child, along with their emphasis on science and education, and my wife, Dawn Davey, who provided invaluable encouragement and support throughout this project.

Notes

1. Manhattan Square

1. Stern, Mellins, and Fishman, *New York 1880*, 9.
2. Bickmore, "Autobiography," 2:29.
3. Preston, *Dinosaurs in the Attic*, 18.
4. Bickmore, "Autobiography," 2:30. This quote continues: "except the 'Dacotah,' a fine apartment hotel at the corner of Central Park West and Seventy-second Street." This part of Bickmore's 1908 memory of his visit was incorrect, since the construction of the Dakota did not begin until 1880.
5. White, *New York: A Physical History*, 89.
6. Bickmore, "Autobiography," 2:28; *Curator*, "Theodore Roosevelt Park," 162.
7. William C. Bryant, "A New Public Park," *New York Evening Post*, July 3, 1844.
8. Goldberger, *City Observed*, 187.
9. Heckscher, *Creating Central Park*, 15.
10. Foord, *Life and Public Services*, 49.
11. Rubbinaccio, *New York's Father*, 35–42.
12. Foord, *Life and Public Services*, 34–40; Mazaraki, "Public Career of Andrew Haswell Green," 20–23.
13. Mazaraki, "Public Career of Andrew Haswell Green," 26.
14. Mazaraki, "Public Career of Andrew Haswell Green," 30–31.
15. "At the meeting of June 9th [1857] Mr. Green was nominated for the office of treasurer, and was declared unanimously elected at the succeeding meeting." Foord, *Life and Public Services*, 51. "A year after the organization of the commission [i.e., 1858] Mr. Green was made its president." Foord, *Life and Public Services*, 53. In the second annual report of the Board of the

Commissioners of Central Park [BCCP] (January 1859), Green is listed as both president and treasurer.

16. Heckscher, *Creating Central Park*, 20–24.

17. Foord, *Life and Public Services*, 53; Mazaraki, "Public Career of Andrew Haswell Green," 72. Starting with the third annual report of the BCCP (January 1860), Green is listed as comptroller only.

18. *AMNH Annual Report for 1930*, 3–5.

19. Heckscher, *Creating Central Park*, 15.

20. First annual BCCP report, 1857, 174.

21. Rosenzweig and Blackmar, *Park and the People*, 111.

22. "1858 Central Park Architect Report," Plan 25, 23, Plan 29, 78, Plan 32, 30, 39, https://www.nycgovparks.org/news/reports/archive#ar.

23. The Greensward Plan was Plan 33. Rosenzweig and Blackmar, *Park and the People*, 117; Description of a Plan for the Improvement of the Central Park, "Greensward" (1858, 1868), 22, https://books.google.com/books?id =QQ8DAAAAYAAJ&dq=greensward+plan. This source is the original Greensward Plan, republished in 1868 with additional annotations.

24. Fourth annual BCCP report, 1861, 57.

25. Third annual BCCP report, 1860, 11–13.

26. Paraphrased from *AMNH Annual Report for 1930*, 4.

27. Third annual BCCP report, 1860, 44.

28. "Introducing the Modern Zoo," Zoological Society of London, https://www.zsl.org/education/introducing-the-modern-zoo; "Philadelphia Zoological Gardens," *Encyclopedia Britannica*, https://www.britannica.com/ place/Philadelphia-Zoological-Gardens; NYC Parks, "History of Zoos in Parks," https://www.nycgovparks.org/about/history/zoos; Lenny Flank, "Philadelphia Zoo: America's First Zoo," *Hidden History*, September 8, 2015, https://lflank.wordpress.com/2015/09/08/philadelphia-zoo-americas-first -zoo; Lenny Flank, "Central Park Zoo: America's First Zoo," *Hidden History*, September 9, 2015, https://lflank.wordpress.com/2015/09/09/central-park -zoo-americas-first-zoo.

29. Heckscher, *The Metropolitan Museum of Art*, 10.

30. Rosenzweig and Blackmar, *Park and the People*, 343; Heckscher, *Metropolitan Museum of Art*, 10.

31. Rosenzweig and Blackmar, *Park and the People*, 343. The legislation date and language are from the eighth annual BCCP report, 1865, 65–66. The tenth annual BCCP report, 1867, contains Olmsted and Vaux's design proposal (42, 149–152) and other details concerning the zoo.

32. First annual report of the BCDPP, 1871, 217–218.

33. Rosenzweig and Blackmar, *Park and the People*, 343.

34. Heckscher, *Creating Central Park*, 65; Kelby, *New-York Historical Society*, 53.

35. Fifth annual BCCP report, 1862, 22–23.

36. Heckscher, *Creating Central Park*, 65; "Laws Respecting the Central Park and Other Works under the Control of the Department of Public Parks," 1870, 32–33, https://books.google.com/books?id=GEYAAAAAYAA J&dq=Laws+Respecting+the+Central+Park+and+Other+Works+under+ the+Control+of+the+Department+of+Public+Parks.

37. Besides the issue of encroaching on the park with buildings, discussed in the section on the zoo, issues included the risk of floods: "In consequence of the low ground and the proximity of the reservoir near the Arsenal Building, the Society urged a change to higher ground in the Park." Kelby, *New-York Historical Society*, 55.

38. Heckscher, *Creating Central Park*, 66.

39. Greensward Plan (see note 23), 29. In a plan that preceded the Greensward plan (the 1856 Viele plan), it was designated for a parade ground. Heckscher, *Creating Central Park*, 66.

40. Rosenzweig and Blackmar, *Park and the People*, 343.

41. Twelfth annual BCCP report, 1869, 47–48.

42. Heckscher, *Creating Central Park*, 66; Kelby, *New-York Historical Society*, 55.

43. Thirteenth annual BCCP report, 1870, 27.

44. Heckscher, *Creating Central Park*, 66; "Laws Respecting the Central Park and Other Works under the Control of the Department of Public Parks," 1870, 98.

45. Thirteenth annual BCCP, 1870, 81; Heckscher, *Creating Central Park*, 66.

46. When the opening took place, the building wasn't yet finished. Vail, *Knickerbocker Birthday*, 165, 173–74, 192.

47. Hawkins, "Report of Progress," 1:179, 180; "Natural History Popularized," *New York Times*, March 17, 1868; "Mr. Waterhouse Hawkins Lectures on Natural History," *New York Times*, March 25, 1868, "Unity of Plan in the Animal Kingdom—Lecture by Mr. Waterhouse Hawkins," *New York Times*, March 27, 1868; "Natural History," *New York Times*, April 22, 1868; "Lecture on Natural History by Mr. Waterhouse Hawkins," *New York Times*, April 23, 1868; "Natural History," *New York Times*, April 25, 1868; "Mr. Waterhouse Hawkins' Lectures—The Monkey in His Relation to Man," *New York Times*, April 29, 1868.

48. Twelfth annual BCCP report, 1869, 132–34.

49. Colbert and Beneker, "The Paleozoic Museum in Central Park," 141; Hoag Levins, "First Dinosaur Skeleton Ever Mounted for Public Display," http://www.levins.com/mount.shtml.

50. Hawkins, "Report of Progress," 1:182.

51. Bickmore, "Autobiography," 1:48–139.

52. Bickmore, "Autobiography," 2:3; Osborn, *History, Plan, and Scope*, 13.

53. Bickmore, "Autobiography," 2:32; Osborn, *History, Plan, and Scope*, 13.

54. Bickmore, "Autobiography," 2:1.

55. Bickmore, "Autobiography," 2:3–4.

56. "Burning of Barnum's Museum," *New York Times*, March 3, 1868.

57. "A Museum without Humbug," *New York Times*, March 18, 1868.

58. Bickmore, "Autobiography," 2:5–6.

59. Osborn, *History, Plan, and Scope*, 21.

60. Bickmore, "Autobiography," 2:8.

61. Bickmore, "Autobiography," 2:24.

62. Bickmore, "Autobiography," 2:9.

63. Choate, "Reminiscences of a Founder of the American Museum," 286.

64. Bickmore, "Autobiography," 2:9.

65. Ackerman, *Boss Tweed*, 17–19.

66. Ackerman, *Boss Tweed*, 37, 57–58.

67. Certainly between February 26, when the charter was approved by the Trustees, and April 6, when the bill was signed into law. Bickmore's description of the period between the meeting with Tweed and the signing of the bill into law gives the impression of a few days to a week.

68. Bickmore, "Autobiography," 2:10–11.

69. Bickmore, "Autobiography," 2:11–12.

70. Howe, *History of the Metropolitan Museum of Art*, 99–125.

71. Vail, *Knickerbocker Birthday*, 119.

72. Hawkins, "Report of Progress," 1:183; Park Commission documents, April 30, 1871, 3–4, https://www.nycgovparks.org/news/reports/archive #Minutes.

73. Thirteenth annual BCCP report, 1870, 29, 81; Colbert and Beneker, "The Paleozoic Museum in Central Park," 147.

74. Colbert and Beneker, "The Paleozoic Museum in Central Park," 144.

75. Bickmore, "Autobiography," 2:21–22.

76. Hawkins, "Report of Progress," 1:183.

77. Ackerman, *Boss Tweed*, 71–72; Mazaraki, "Public Career of Andrew Haswell Green," 116–17.

78. "Albany," *New York Times*, April 5, 1870.

79. Rosenzweig and Blackmar, *Park and the People*, 263; BCDPP minutes, May 3, 1870.

80. Mazaraki, "Public Career of Andrew Haswell Green," 117–19.

81. First annual BCDPP report, 1871, 3.

82. "The Public Parks," *New York Times*, May 25, 1870; BCDPP minutes, May 24, May 31, and September 13, 1870; Bickmore, "Autobiography," 2:23.

83. Bickmore, "Autobiography," 2:25.

84. Bickmore, "Autobiography," 2:26; "The Central Park Captives," *New York Times*, April 28, 1871.

85. Bickmore, "Autobiography," 2:26.

86. Howe, *History of the Metropolitan Museum of Art*, 139. The "representative of the Museum of Natural History" was Bickmore ("Autobiography," 2:27).

87. First annual BCDPP report, 1871, 217–18, 273–78; BCDPP minutes, December 6, 1870, December 13, 1870.

88. *AMNH Annual Report of 1871*, 13.

89. "The Great Fire," *New York Times*, May 23, 1866; "Disastrous Fire," *New York Times*, July 14, 1865; "Burning of Barnum's Museum," *New York Times*, March 3, 1868.

90. Hawkins, "Report of Progress," 1:184–185.

91. BCDPP minutes, December 6, 1870, December 13, 1870.

92. First annual BCDPP report, 1870, 18–20. Actually, the sight lines were considered in the design. "The building has been sunk ten feet into the ground, so that it may not be a prominent feature in the landscape when seen from the interior of the Park, and the roof is designed for the same, reason, with a somewhat flat pitch." Olmsted & Vaux to Sweeny, June 6, 1870, Park Commission documents, April 30, 1871.

93. "Meeting of the Lyceum of Natural History—Prof. Waterhouse Hawkins' Report on the Paleozoic Museum at Central Park," *New York Times*, March 7, 1871; Hawkins, "Report of Progress," 1:179–188.

94. "The Central Park Museum—Destruction of Mr. Hawkins' Restorations," *New York Times*, February 16, 1872.

95. Ackerman, *Boss Tweed*, 160–167; "Two Thieves," *New York Times*, July 19, 1871.

96. Ackerman, *Boss Tweed*, 213–19; Foord, *Life and Public Services*, 96–101.

97. Ackerman, *Boss Tweed*, 175.

98. Ackerman, *Boss Tweed*, 224.

99. Ackerman, *Boss Tweed*, 225.

100. Ackerman, *Boss Tweed*, 250.

101. Ackerman, *Boss Tweed*, 254–56, 405n31–32.

102. Ackerman, *Boss Tweed*, 254.

103. Third annual BCDPP report, 1875, iii–iv.

104. "The West Side," *New York Times*, February 4, 1872; "The West Side," *New York Times*, February 5, 1872.

105. Osborn, *History, Plan, and Scope*, 23–24.

106. Howe, *History of the Metropolitan Museum of Art*, 152; Osborn, *History, Plan and Scope*, 23–24.

107. Foord, *Life and Public Services*, 207; Howe, *History of the Metropolitan Museum of Art*, 152; Osborn, *History, Plan and Scope*, 23–24; BCDPP minutes, March 20, 1872.

108. Ackerman, *Boss Tweed*, 351.

109. Ackerman, *Boss Tweed*, 330.

110. Ackerman, *Boss Tweed*, 350–51.

111. BCDPP minutes, March 20, 1872; July 17, 1872; April 15, 1874; May 6, 1874, and March 29, 1876; "Prof. Hawkins' Appeal," *New York Times*, April 20, 1874; Peck, "Art of Bones," 28; Colbert and Beneker, "The Paleozoic Museum in Central Park," 149. Goldman, "Paleontology and Politics," https://www.copyrightexpired.com/hawkins/nyc/Benjamin_Waterhouse_Hawkins.html.

112. Peck, "Art of Bones," 28–29; Goldman, "Paleontology and Politics."

2. The Master Plan and the Bickmore Wing

1. BCDPP minutes, June 12, 1872.

2. Bickmore, "Autobiography," 2:31–32.

3. Bickmore, "Autobiography," 2:32–33; Stern, Mellins, and Fishman, *New York 1880*, 182–83.

4. Bickmore, "Autobiography," 2:33.

5. BCDPP minutes, August 7, 1872; "The Park Commissioners," *New York Times*, August 8, 1872.

6. Preston, *Dinosaurs in the Attic*, 19; Hellman, *Bankers, Bones, and Beetles*, 28.

7. *Scribner's Monthly*, "An American Museum of Art," August 1871, 412; *AMNH Annual Report for 1872*, 6; Third annual BCDPP report, 1875, 56.

8. Bickmore, "Autobiography," 2:35–38; Hellman, *Bankers, Bones, and Beetles*, 23–25; Preston, *Dinosaurs in the Attic*, 19–20; Kennedy, "Philanthropy and Science," 63–64; "Museum of Natural History," *New York Times*, May 30, 1874; "The New Museum of Natural History," *New York Times*, June 2, 1874; "Natural History Museum," *New York Times*, June 3, 1874.

9. "Natural History Museum," *New York Times*, June 3, 1874.

10. Preston, *Dinosaurs in the Attic*, 19.

11. Hellman, *Bankers, Bones, and Beetles*, 28.

12. *AMNH Annual Report for 1874*, 34–50.

13. "At the conclusion of these ceremonies, the Trustees gave to General Grant, the silver trowel, properly engraved, which he had used in laying our cornerstone, as a suitable souvenir of this memorable occasion." Bickmore, "Autobiography," 2:38. An image of the trowel can be seen at the website of the Smithsonian Institute's National Museum for American History: https://americanhistory.si.edu/presidency/2b4.html. Yet according to Hellman (*Bankers, Bones, and Beetles*, 25), the trowel was stolen: "'After the laying of the cornerstone,' the man who brought it over from Tiffany's later reported, 'General Grant left the trowel on the cornerstone, and when it occurred to Professor Bickmore to look for it, it had disappeared, probably forever.'"

14. Bickmore, "Autobiography," 2:46–49; Hellman, *Bankers, Bones, and Beetles*, 27–28; Preston, *Dinosaurs in the Attic*, 20; "Natural History Museum," *New York Times*, December 20, 1877; "The Museum of Natural History,"

New York Times, December 22, 1877; "New-York's New Museum," *New York Times*, December 23, 1877.

15. *AMNH Annual Report for 1878*, 43–54.

16. "New-York's New Museum," *New York Times*, December 23, 1877.

17. Hellman, *Bankers, Bones, and Beetles*, 26.

18. Murray Schumach, "Museum Finds Its 1874 Cornerstone," *New York Times*, November 22, 1968; "Natural History Museum," *New York Times*, June 3, 1874.

19. *AMNH Annual Report for 1968*, 38, 42.

3. The Jesup Years (1881–1908) and the Seventy-Seventh Street Façade

1. Bickmore, "Autobiography," 2:50.

2. Kennedy, "Philanthropy and Science," 72.

3. Bickmore, "Autobiography," 2:50–51.

4. "The Manhattan Company," *New York Times*, June 10, 1879.

5. Osborn, History, Plan, and Scope, 146.

6. Brown, *Morris Ketchum Jesup*, 151; Hellman, Bankers, Bones, and Beetles, 28–29.

7. Kennedy, "Philanthropy and Science," 79–80.

8. Kennedy, "Philanthropy and Science," 66; Bickmore, "Autobiography," 2:41–44.

9. Kennedy, "Philanthropy and Science," 73.

10. Kennedy, "Philanthropy and Science," 76.

11. Kennedy, "Philanthropy and Science," 79; Brown, *Morris Ketchum Jesup*, 137.

12. Hellman, Bankers, Bones, and Beetles, 32–33.

13. Preston, Dinosaurs in the Attic, 22–23.

14. Kennedy, "Philanthropy and Science," 79–80.

15. Kennedy, "Philanthropy and Science," 83.

16. "In and About the City," *New York Times*, December 30, 1886.

17. Rosenzweig and Blackmar, Park and the People, 360.

18. "In and About the City," *New York Times*, December 30, 1886.

19. Howe, History of the Metropolitan Museum of Art, 238; Kennedy, "Philanthropy and Science," 105; "In and About the City," *New York Times*, December 30, 1886; "A Policy of Inaction," *New York Times*, January 21, 1887.

20. "Methodist Legislation," *New York Times*, April 3, 1886.

21. The Museums in the Park: Should They Be Open on Sunday?

22. "Museums of Art and Sciences," *New York Times*, April 10, 1881.

23. N.B.G., "Open the Museum, and Perhaps the Saloons Will Do a Lighter Sunday Trade," letter to the editor, *New York Times*, March 7, 1890.

24. "In and About the City," *New York Times*, December 30, 1886; "Many Public Bequests," *New York Times*, January 6, 1892.

25. Rosenzweig and Blackmar, Park and the People, 255–56, 309–11.

26. Rosenzweig and Blackmar, Park and the People, 359.

27. Kennedy, "Philanthropy and Science," 90.

28. BCDPP minutes, April 20, 1881.

29. Kennedy, "Philanthropy and Science," 89.

30. Kennedy, "Philanthropy and Science," 90.

31. "Still Undecided," *New York Times*, April 26, 1885; "City and Suburban News," *New York Times*, May 19, 1885.

32. "The Museums on Sundays," *New York Times*, November 18, 1885; "Free Sunday Museums," *New York Times*, November 22, 1885; "They Want the Museums Opened," *New York Times*, November 29, 1885; "The Museums on Sunday," *New York Times*, December 18, 1885; "Sunday Opening of Museums," *New York Times*, December 27, 1885; "Sunday Should Be a Holiday," *New York Times*, January 3, 1886; "The Museums on Sunday," *New York Times*, January 3, 1886; "Open Museums on Sunday," *New York Times*, January 17, 1886; "Not Ready to Decide," *New York Times*, February 9, 1886; "Open Museums on Sunday," *New York Times*, March 10, 1886.

33. "Will the Trustees Yield," *New York Times*, January 1, 1887.

34. Kennedy, "Philanthropy and Science," 104.

35. "Not Ready to Decide," *New York Times*, February 9, 1886.

36. "A Policy of Inaction," *New York Times*, January 21, 1887.

37. Howe, History of the Metropolitan Museum of Art, 242; "Evenings for the People," *New York Times*, December 27, 1888; "Sunday Opening Deferred," *New York Times*, December 28, 1888; "Museum of Natural History," *New York Times*, December 30, 1888; and "The Museum Open Sundays," *New York Times*, January 3, 1889.

38. "Will the Trustees Yield," *New York Times*, January 1, 1887; "A Policy of Inaction," *New York Times*, January 21, 1887; "The Albany Lawmakers," *New York Times*, February 10, 1887; "The Wise Men at Albany," *New York Times*, February 12, 1887; and "The State Legislature," *New York Times*, March 1, 1887.

39. "The New Museum Building," *New York Times*, March 29, 1888.

40. "Enlarging the Museum," *New York Times*, September 5, 1888.

41. "Plans Seriously Criticised," *New York Times*, March 8, 1888; "A Forgotten Architect of the Gilded Age," 23.

42. The American Architect and Building News 26, no. 709 (July 27, 1889): 37, plate; Stern, Mellins, and Fishman, New York 1880, 186.

43. Curran, "A Forgotten Architect of the Gilded Age," 23.

44. BCDPP minutes, July 26, 1881, and September 7, 1881.

45. Stern, Mellins, and Fishman, New York 1880, 31–34; Schuyler, "The Romanesque Revival in New York," 7–38.

46. "Monster Girders," *New York Times*, May 17, 1889.

47. "The Museum of Natural History," *New-York Daily Tribune*, January 17, 1889; "For the Natural History Museum," *New-York Daily Tribune*, February 8, 1889; "Open the Museum on Sundays," *New York Times*, May 28, 1889; "The Museum's New Wing," *New York Times*, May 29, 1889; "Must Be Open Sundays," *New York Times*, May 30, 1889; "City Officers at Odds," *New York Times*, December 12, 1889.

48. "To Open the Museum Sundays," *New York Times*, March 20, 1891; "Sunday Opening of the Museum," *New York Times*, April 19, 1891; "To Open the Museum Sundays," *New York Times*, March 20, 1891; "Sunday Opening of the Museum," *New York Times*, April 19, 1891; "The Masses Will Speak," *New York Times*, May 6, 1891; "Victory Is Won at Last," *New York Times*, May 19, 1891; "The Sunday Opening," *New York Times*, May 19, 1891; "The Museums on Sundays," *New York Times*, August 7, 1892; Howe, *History of the Metropolitan Museum of Art*, 243–46.

49. "Only a Question of Time," *New York Times*, May 20, 1891.

50. "The Museums on Sundays," *New York Times*, August 7, 1892; Rosenzweig and Blackmar, Park and the People, 363.

51. Brown, *Morris Ketchum Jesup*, 177.

52. "In and About the City," *New York Times*, November 3, 1892.

53. Kennedy, "Philanthropy and Science," 106–8.

54. Higgins & Quasebarth, *Planetarium & North Side Project*, 15.

55. Higgins & Quasebarth, *Planetarium & North Side Project*, 16; Higgins Quasebarth and Partners, *Richard Gilder Center*, 10.

56. "The Toilet of a Meteorite," *New York Times*, May 18, 1906. Tobin, "Deconstructing James Lord Brown," 2, 57–58; *AMNH Annual Report for 1903*, 11.

57. Osborn, *History, Plan, and Scope*, 37.

58. Brown, *Morris Ketchum Jesup*, 160–61.

59. Preston, *Dinosaurs in the Attic*, 23.

60. Brown, *Morris Ketchum Jesup*, 157–58.

61. Brown, *Morris Ketchum Jesup*, 153.

62. Preston, *Dinosaurs in the Attic*, 168; Quinn, *Windows on Nature*, 15, 16, 166; Brown, *Morris Ketchum Jesup*, 172, 173; Kennedy, "Philanthropy and Science," 98–100; McWilliams, "Frank M. Chapman," 664; Osborn, *History, Plan, and Scope*, 34.

63. Sherwood, *Free Education*, 7–9; Bickmore, "Autobiography," 2:51–139; Brown, *Morris Ketchum Jesup*, 174, 180–81; Kennedy, "Philanthropy and Science," 84–86, 152–53; Osborn, *History, Plan, and Scope*, 114–17.

64. Preston, *Dinosaurs in the Attic*, 23.

65. Osborn, *History, Plan, and Scope*, 34–35.

66. Preston, *Dinosaurs in the Attic*, 24–33; Jonaitis, *From the Land of the Totem Poles*, 207.

67. Osborn, *History, Plan, and Scope*, 37–39; Hellman, *Bankers, Bones, and Beetles*, 62; "Mrs. Jesup Leaves $8,450,000 to Public," *New York Times*, June 25, 1914; *AMNH Annual Report for 1915*, 28.

4. Robert Peary, the Journey to the North Pole, and the Cape York Meteorites

1. Josephine Peary, *Snow Baby*, 58–66; Peary, *Northward over the Great Ice*, 2:559–61; "Biggest Greenland Meteorite Ends Its Travels," *New York Times*, October 9, 1904.

2. Peary, *Northward over the Great Ice*, 2:145, 554–56.

3. Mills, *Exploring Polar Frontiers*, 511; Peary, *Northward over the Great Ice* 1:xxxiv–xxxvi.

4. Bryce, *Cook & Peary*, 20.

5. In this chapter, the standard modern spelling is used for Inuit names, and the spelling that Peary used will be placed in the notes. For example, Peary spelled "Qisug" as "Kessuh."

6. Peary, *Northward over the Great Ice*, 2:127–28.

7. Henderson, *True North*, 75–76, 89; Peary, *Northward over the Great Ice*, 1:395–96; Josephine Peary, *My Arctic Journal*, 217.

8. Henderson, *True North*, 89; Josephine Peary, *My Arctic Journal*, 217.

9. Josephine Peary, *Snow Baby*, 23; "A Very Remarkable Baby," *New York Times*, October 7, 1894.

10. Josephine Peary, *Snow Baby*, 16.

11. Peary, *Northward over the Great Ice*, 2:75–76.

12. Peary, *Northward over the Great Ice*, 2:85–120; Mills, *Exploring Polar Frontiers*, 512; Bryce, *Cook & Peary*, 131–32; Green, *Peary*, 120–22; Fleming, *Ninety Degrees North*, 296; Henderson, *True North*, 92–93.

13. Tallakoteah.

14. Peary, *Northward over the Great Ice*, 2:127–49.

15. E-Klay-I-Shoo.

16. Green, *Peary*, 125.

17. Bryant, *The Peary Auxiliary Expedition*, 23; Peary, *Northward over the Great Ice*, 2:155, 556.

18. *Journal of the American Geographical Society*, "The Greenland Scientific Expedition of 1895," 224; *Northward over the Great Ice*, 2:535.

19. Henderson, *True North*, 97; Bryce, *Cook & Peary*, 135; Green, *Peary*, 125.

20. "Little Miss Marie Ahnighito Peary," *New York Times*, September 26, 1894; "A Very Remarkable Baby," *New York Times*, October 7, 1894; Josephine Peary, *Snow Baby*, 37–38.

21. *Journal of the American Geographical Society*, "The Greenland Scientific Expedition of 1895," 126–28.

22. Peary, *Northward over the Great Ice*, 2:556; *Journal of the American Geographical Society*, "The North Greenland Expedition," 300–1.

23. *Journal of the American Geographical Society*, "The Greenland Scientific Expedition of 1895," 128–33.

24. Brown, *Morris Ketchum Jesup*, 188–92.

25. "Her Point of View," *New York Times*, May 5, 1895; *New York Times*, May 8, 1895, untitled story on p. 4; "Lieut. Peary's Wife Lectures," *New York Times*, May 12, 1895; "City and Vicinity," *New York Times*, May 27, 1895; "The Heart of the House," *New York Times*, June 2, 1895; Green, *Peary*, 132–33.

26. Brown, *Morris Ketchum Jesup*, 192; *AMNH Annual Report for 1895*, 11–12.

27. Sharp and Sullivan, *The Dashing Kansan*, 79–90; "From the Frozen Seas," *New York Times*, October 2, 1895.

28. Salisbury, "The Arctic Expedition of 1895," 16560.

29. "Peary and His Party Return," *New York Times*, September 22, 1895.

30. *Journal of the American Geographical Society*, "The North Greenland Expedition," 304.

31. Mills, *Exploring Polar Frontiers*, 512; *Journal of the American Geographical Society*, "The North Greenland Expedition," 302–36; "Peary and His Party Return," *New York Times*, September 22, 1895; "From the Frozen Seas," *New York Times*, October 2, 1895; Green, *Peary*, 133–44; Peary, *Northward over the Great Ice*, 2:507–24, 535–49, 562–68.

32. "Mrs. Peary to Meet Her Husband," *New York Times*, September 28, 1895.

33. "Lieut. Peary Starts for New-York," *New York Times*, October 1, 1895; "Will Never See the Pole," *New York Times*, October 2, 1895.

34. Peary, *Northward over the Great Ice*, 1:xlvii–xlix.

35. "Lieut. Peary in Washington," *New York Times*, October 6, 1895.

36. "From the Frozen Seas," *New York Times*, October 2, 1895.

37. Robinson, *Dark Companion*, 114–20. That Henson's work at the museum was far from steady can be seen in the letters from Henson to Peary from the Robert E. Peary collection of the National Archives, in Washington, DC. For example, November 1, 1895: "I don't think that I will be working at the museum but a few days more." September 29, 1896: "I would like to work at the museum again this winter if I could get the employment there again. Will you write to Mr. Wallace and ask him if he could give me employment for the winter?" Letters from October through December 1896 indicate that Henson is on a tour performing on stage with arctic sled dogs in Chicago, Philadelphia, and Baltimore (October 17, 18, 20, 24, November 5, 7, 25, December 3, 10). From the November 7 letter: "Mr. Peary is it impossible for me to get work at the museum this winter?" January 16, 1897: "I have been looking for work and cannot find anything to do." Henson's letters continue to show he is having difficulties finding employment (January 31, March 27, April 9). However, on June 27, Henson writes, "I went to work at the museum Thursday morning for two weeks." The letters do indicate that

Henson did have frequent interactions with the museum on behalf of Peary and often show the museum for his return address. It's hard to know what to make of the return address, since the September 29, 1886 letter ("I would like to work at the museum again this winter") has the museum for the return address.

38. Sharp and Sullivan, *The Dashing Kansan*, 107–13.

39. Peary, *Northward over the Great Ice*, 1:xlvii–xlix; Green, *Peary*, 146; Henderson, *True North*, 109; "Will Command the Dolphin," *New York Times*, April 17, 1896; "Peary Is Going North Again," *New York Times*, April 18, 1896; "Engineer Peary's Detail," *New York Times*, April 22, 1896; Hellman, *Bankers, Bones, and Beetles*, 82–83; Peary, *Northward over the Great Ice*, 1:xlix.

40. *Journal of the American Geographical Society*, "Record of Geographical Progress," 278.

41. Peary, *Northward over the Great Ice*, 2:568–74.

42. *Journal of the American Geographical Society*, "Record of Geographical Progress," 279.

43. Peary, *Northward over the Great Ice*, 1:xlix.

44. Peary, *Northward over the Great Ice*, 1:li–liii.

45. Peary, *Northward over the Great Ice*, 1:li–liii; Peary, *Nearest the Pole*, 295; Green, *Peary*, 163–67; Henderson, *True North*, 111–12; Hellman, *Bankers, Bones, and Beetles*, 83–84; Brown, *Morris Ketchum Jesup*, 193–95.

46. AMNH Department of Anthropology, file 1896–38, letter of Franz Boas to Robert Peary, May 24, 1897; cited in Harper, *Give Me My Father's Body*, 25.

47. Josephine Peary, *Snow Baby*, 54–56.

48. Mene.

49. Harper, *Give Me My Father's Body*, 17–18.

50. Peary, *Northward over the Great Ice*, 2:574–89.

51. Henson, *Negro Explorer*, 11.

52. "Returned from the Arctic," *New York Times*, September 27, 1897; "Back from the Far North," *New York Times*, October 1 1897; "The Big Meteorite Landed," *New York Times*, October 3, 1897.

53. Harper, *Give Me My Father's Body*, 17.

54. Harper, *Give Me My Father's Body*, 18.

55. "Back from the Far North," *New York Times*, October 1, 1897; "The Big Meteorite Landed," *New York Times*, October 3, 1897. Peary, *Northward over the Great Ice*, 2:594, states that it was a seventy-five-ton derrick.

56. Harper, *Give Me My Father's Body*; "Minik, the Lost Eskimo," *American Experience*, PBS, https://www.thirteen.org/programs/american-experience/american-experience-minik-the-lost-eskimo-preview.

57. Peary, *Nearest the Pole*, 296.

58. Peary, *Nearest the Pole*, 326; Hellman, *Bankers, Bones, and Beetles*, 86.

59. Henson, *Negro Explorer*, 12.

60. Peary, *Nearest the Pole*, 305–10.

61. Peary, *Nearest the Pole*, 285; Brown, *Morris Ketchum Jesup*, 195.

62. Peary, *Nearest the Pole*, 285.

63. Kirkpatrick, *Snow Baby*, 16–17; Josephine and Marie Peary, *Children of the Arctic*, 13–15; Peary, *Nearest the Pole*, 287.

64. Kirkpatrick, *Snow Baby*, 17–26; Josephine Peary and Marie Peary, *Children of the Arctic*, 40–88; Peary, *Nearest the Pole*, 287.

65. Henson, *Negro Explorer*, 49.

66. Henderson, *True North*, 136–40; Peary, *Nearest the Pole*, 287; Josephine Peary and Marie Peary, *Children of the Arctic*, 105–7.

67. Peary, *Nearest the Pole*, 101, 287–88, 344, 349.

68. Peary, *Nearest the Pole*, 355–72.

69. Hellman, *Bankers, Bones, and Beetles*, 85.

70. Henderson, *True North*, 161.

71. "To Cart 70-Ton Lady through the Streets," *New York Times*, October 1, 1904; "Biggest Greenland Meteorite Ends Its Travels," *New York Times*, October 9, 1904.

72. "The Toilet of a Meteorite," *New York Times*, May 18, 1906.

73. Brown, *Morris Ketchum Jesup*, 196; Peary, *Nearest the Pole*, 289.

74. Peary, *Nearest the Pole*, 10–11.

75. Henson, *Negro Explorer*, 13.

76. Peary, *Nearest the Pole*, xiii; Peary, *North Pole*, 13–14.

77. Peary, *North Pole*, 14.

78. Henderson, *True North*, 187.

79. Peary, *North Pole*, 15.

80. Peary, *North Pole*, 16.

81. Peary, *North Pole*, 25–27.

82. Iggiannguaq (Peary's spelling: Egingwah), Sigluk (Seegloo), Uutaaq (Ootah), and Ukkujaaq (Ooqueah).

83. Hellman, *Bankers, Bones, and Beetles*, 86.

84. Henderson, *True North*, 243.

85. Henderson, *True North*, 253. Message to Bumpus: Hellman, *Bankers, Bones, and Beetles*, 83. Message to Roosevelt: Roosevelt, *African Game Trails*, 288.

86. "A Remarkable Exhibit at the Natural History Museum Illustrating Arctic Life and Adventure," *New York Times*, October 17, 1909; *American Museum Journal*, "Achievement in Polar Exploration."

87. Hellman, *Bankers, Bones, and Beetles*, 84; Preston, *Dinosaurs in the Attic*, 40–41; *AMNH Annual Report for 1909*, 37, 50, 56; *AMNH Annual Report for 1910*, 70, 71; *AMNH Annual Report for 1911*, 86, 87.

88. "54 Tons of Meteorites Will Be Moved through the Streets to New Planetarium," *New York Times*, July 8, 1935.

89. "A Meteor Weighs In," *New York Times*, February 12, 1956; Sanka Knox, "Peary Meteorite Weighs 34 Tons," *New York Times*, February 15, 1956; "Science Notes," *New York Times*, September 9, 1956.

90. "Star Attraction Gets New Home," *New York Times*, September 14, 1979; Malcolm W. Browne, "Biggest Meteorite Is Star of Museum's New Hall," *New York Times*, May 1, 1981.

91. John Noble Wilford, "New Hall for Meteorites Old Beyond Imagining," *New York Times*, September 19, 2003.

5. The Osborn Years (1908–1933)

1. Rainger, *Agenda for Antiquity*, 47.
2. Rainger, *Agenda for Antiquity*, 47; Bickmore, "Autobiography," 2:39–40.
3. "Zoological Society's Officers," *New York Times*, May 18, 1895; *AMNH Annual Report for 1927*, 2.
4. Osborn, *History, Plan, and Scope*, 157–59.
5. Osborn, *History, Plan, and Scope*, 155.
6. Osborn, *History, Plan, and Scope*, 150–51.
7. Osborn, *History, Plan, and Scope*, 151.
8. Osborn, *History, Plan, and Scope*, 160.
9. Osborn, *History, Plan, and Scope*, 162.
10. Osborn, *History, Plan, and Scope*, 155.
11. Osborn, *History, Plan, and Scope*, 162–64.
12. Osborn, *History, Plan, and Scope*, 160, 164–65.
13. Osborn, *History, Plan, and Scope*, 151–53.
14. Osborn, *History, Plan, and Scope*, 149; *AMNH Annual Report for 1910*, 19; Higgins & Quasebarth, *Planetarium & North Side Project*, 17.
15. Osborn, *History, Plan, and Scope*, 150–51; *AMNH Annual Report for 1910*, 19; *AMNH Annual Report for 1911*, 20.
16. *AMNH Annual Report for 1915*, 18–19; "History Museum Has a Park Plan," *New York Times*, February 8, 1916; "Now It Is Central Park," *New York Times*, February 9, 1916. That this plan was hatched "behind the scenes" is indicated by the fact that the plan wasn't mentioned in the AMNH annual reports until 1916. *AMNH Annual Report for 1915* (published May 1, 1916), 18–19. The report introduced the topic, saying, "A plan of very great importance for the future scientific and artistic development of the City of New York was suggested to the President some years ago by a member of our Board, *whose name is withheld*" [emphasis added]. Osborn drops further hints about the origins of the plan in several *New York Times* articles published *decades later*. Three examples, with emphasis added: "The superb new space between the two museums, which, with the aide of Commissioner William Williams of the City Water Board, I succeeded in transferring from Aqueduct purposes and restoring to Central Park *in the Spring of 1911*" (Henry Fairfield Osborn, "The Inter-Museum Plan," letter to the editor, *New York Times*, April 18, 1930); ". . . development of this Central Park reservoir space, *as suggested by Archer M. Huntington in 1911* . . ." (Henry Fairfield Osborn, "The Reservoir Plan," letter to the editor, *New York Times*, June 5, 1930); ". . . redemption of the Southern Reservoir as proposed by the AMNH in the year 1912 . . . without any

assistance from the department of parks, but with the cooperation of Water Supply and its commissioner, Mr. William Williams. . . . New plans for this central space, which would still be a reservoir . . . had it not been for *the suggestion of Archer M. Huntington in 1912* . . ." (Henry Fairfield Osborn, "Reservoir Plan Opposed," letter to the editor, *New York Times*, February 16, 1931). On March 10, 1912, an article appeared in the *New York Times* quoting then park commissioner Charles B. Stover at length concerning the idea of using the space from the soon-to-be obsolete Lower Reservoir for a connecting link between the two museums. The article makes no mention of Henry Fairfield Osborn, Archer M. Huntington, or William Williams.

17. *AMNH Annual Report for 1911*, 20, 22.

18. *AMNH Annual Report for 1912*, 21; *AMNH Annual Report for 1913*, 28.

19. Kennedy, "Philanthropy and Science," 191.

20. *AMNH Annual Report for 1915*, 15–16.

21. *AMNH Annual Report for 1911*, 18; *AMNH Annual Report for 1915*, 15; *AMNH Annual Report for 1927*, 4; "Contract of 1878," in *AMNH Annual Report for 1878*, 21–26.

22. *AMNH Annual Report for 1915*, 16.

23. *AMNH Annual Report for 1916*, 19–20; "$1,000,000 Wing to Be Built on Museum Here," *New York Times*, November 5, 1916.

24. *AMNH Annual Report for 1916*, 23.

25. *AMNH Annual Report for 1918*, 17; Sherwood, *Free Education*.

26. *AMNH Annual Report for 1920*, 18–19.

27. *AMNH Annual Report for 1918*, 18.

28. In addition to the numerous connections between Roosevelt and the museum detailed in this book, he also undertook an expedition to South America on behalf of the museum from 1913–1914 and gifted the museum with many specimens he collected throughout his life, starting in 1871.

29. "Report of the Roosevelt Memorial Commission," 1922, 12, in "New York Legislative Documents, Volume 14," https://books.google.com/books?id=qMYaAQAAIAAJ; "Osborn on Roosevelt Commission," *New York Times*, June 4, 1920.

30. *AMNH Annual Report for 1921*, 18.

31. *AMNH Annual Report for 1927*, 5–6; Higgins & Quasebarth, *Planetarium & North Side Project*, 19. *AMNH Annual Report for 1921*, 239, 219.

32. *AMNH Annual Report for 1927*, 6.

33. Higgins & Quasebarth, *Planetarium & North Side Project*, 19.

34. *AMNH Annual Report for 1923*, 30.

35. Higgins & Quasebarth, *Planetarium & North Side Project*, 19.

36. *AMNH Annual Report for 1926*, 1.

37. "Museum Dedicates School of Service," *New York Times*, January 18, 1928.

38. "Report of the Roosevelt Memorial Commission," 1922, 13–15, in "New York Legislative Documents, Volume 14," https://books.google.com/books?id=qMYaAQAAIAAJ; "Osborn on Roosevelt Commission," *New*

York Times, June 4, 1920; "Great Roosevelt Memorial," *New York Times*, March 12, 1922; "Proposed State Memorial by Roosevelt," *New York Times*, March 19, 1922; "Roosevelt Board at Odds over Site," *New York Times*, February 7, 1924.

39. "Roosevelt Memorial to Be in New York City; Senate Committee Kills Bill for Albany Site," *New York Times*, March 12, 1924; "Seek Memorial to Roosevelt," *New York Times*, March 19, 1924; "Favors New York Site for Roosevelt Shrine," *New York Times*, March 20, 1924. Walker's role is described in Henry Fairfield Osborn, "The Roosevelt Memorial," letter to the editor, *New York Times*, April 19, 1930.

40. "Seek Memorial to Roosevelt," *New York Times*, March 19, 1924; "Roosevelt Memorial Here," *New York Times*, April 10, 1924; "Governor Approves Roosevelt Memorial," *New York Times*, May 7, 1924.

41. 1930 Roosevelt Memorial Plans," 11, 22, https://www.nycgovparks .org/news/reports/archive#ov; Osborn, *History, Plan, and Design of the New York State Roosevelt Memorial*; cited in Stern, Gilmartin, and Mellins, *New York 1930*, 136.

42. The competing architects also included Gordon & Kaelber, Edward B. Green & Son, J. H. Freedlander, Helmle & Corbett, H. Van Buren Magonigle, and York & Sawyer. Stern, Gilmartin, and Mellins, *New York 1930*, 135.

43. *AMNH Annual Report for 1927*, 9.

44. *AMNH Annual Report for 1929*, 22, 24.

45. "Refuse Roosevelt Fund," *New York Times*, February 3, 1927; *AMNH Annual Report for 1929*, 22.

46. *AMNH Annual Report for 1928*, 15.

47. January 8, according to *AMNH Annual Report for 1928*, 16. January 9, according to *AMNH Annual Report for 1927*, 5.

48. *AMNH Annual Report for 1928*, 16.

49. Higgins & Quasebarth, *Planetarium & North Side Project*, 32; "Planetarium for New York," *New York Times*, August 12, 1928.

50. *AMNH Annual Report for 1928*, 16.

51. *AMNH Annual Report for 1932*, 9–12.

52. *AMNH Annual Report for 1932*, 11.

53. *AMNH Annual Report for 1932*, 12; "Rothschild Birds Are Whitneys' Gift," *New York Times*, November 15, 1932.

54. "Osborn to Retire as Museum Head,"*New York Times*, May 1, 1931.

55. *AMNH Annual Report for 1931*, 59; *AMNH Annual Report for 1932*; "Roosevelt Honored in Nation's Eulogies," *New York Times*, October 28, 1931.

56. *AMNH Annual Report for 1930*, 51.

57. *AMNH Annual Report for 1932*, 23, 32, 76.

58. These included the Columbus Avenue entrance pavilion, the amphitheater in the north transept space, the Astronomic Hall, and a northeast corner pavilion. *AMNH Annual Report for 1932*, 34, 58.

59. "Davison Is Named to Head Museum," *New York Times*, January 10, 1933; *AMNH Annual Report for 1933*, 54.

60. AMNH guide, 1933, 32.

61. *The New York State Theodore Roosevelt Memorial, Dedicated January 19, 1936*, prepared by George N. Pindar (1936), 17–52, https://archive.org/details/newyorkstate00newy/page/n0; *AMNH Annual Report for 1936*, 3, 57.

62. "Giannini Is Honored," *New York Times*, June 26, 1935; "Roosevelt Memorial to Be Dedicated Here," *New York Times*, January 12, 1936; "President Honors Cousin Here Today," *New York Times*, January 19, 1936; *AMNH Annual Report for 1936*, 57; "Giannini, Vittorio, 1903–1966," *Social Networks and Archival Context*, http://socialarchive.iath.virginia.edu/ark:/99166/w6qr54jn.

63. *AMNH Annual Report for 1936*, 3; "Akeley Memorial Dedicated by 2,000," *New York Times*, May 20, 1936.

64. Davison, "Future Plans for the Akeley African Hall," 86; Quinn, *Windows on Nature*, 166.

65. *AMNH Annual Report for 1933*, 3–4; *AMNH Annual Report for 1939*, 8; Robert W. Brown, "Birds 'Fly' in Museum," *New York Times*, June 4, 1939.

66. *AMNH Annual Report for 1936*, 2.

67. "Widow to Unveil Statue," *New York Times*, October 27, 1940; *AMNH Annual Report for 1940*, 5–6.

68. *The New York State Theodore Roosevelt Memorial, Dedicated January 19, 1936*, 9–12; Historical Designation Report, Landmarks Preservation Commission, July 22, 1975, no. 3, LP-0889; William Neuman, "Planned Review of Statues Leaves de Blasio to Parse Role of History and Culture," *New York Times*, August 31, 2017; William Neuman, "Mayor's Panel Will Seek Guidelines on Monuments," *New York Times*, September 9, 2017; "Review of City's Monuments Treads Carefully," *New York Times*, January 13, 2018.

69. Rosenzweig and Blackmar, *Park and the People*, 439.

70. "Fear Park Misuse in Osborn's Plans," *New York Times*, February 9, 1916; "The Natural History Museum," *New York Times*, October 8, 1916.

71. Rosenzweig and Blackmar, *Park and the People*, 426–35.

72. *AMNH Annual Report for 1930*, 2–9.

73. "Hearing Before the Committee of the Whole of the Board of Estimate and Apportionment," in "1930 Roosevelt Memorial Plans," 24, https://www.nycgovparks.org/news/reports/archive#ov.

74. Nathan Straus Jr., "Park Invasion," letter to the editor, *New York Times*, April 22, 1930.

75. Henry Fairfield Osborn, "The Inter-Museum Plan," letter to the editor, *New York Times*, April 18, 1930; Henry Fairfield Osborn, "The Roosevelt Memorial," letter to the editor, *New York Times*, April 19, 1930; Nathan Straus Jr., "Park Invasion," letter to the editor, *New York Times*, April 22, 1930; Henry Fairfield Osborn, "Mr. Osborn Explains," letter to the editor, *New York Times*, May 19, 1930; Henry Fairfield Osborn, "The Reservoir Plan," letter to the

editor, *New York Times*, June 5, 1930; Henry Fairfield Osborn, "Reservoir Plan Opposed," letter to the editor, *New York Times*, February 16, 1931; W. B. Van Ingen, "Central Park Plans," letter to the editor, *New York Times*, February 27, 1931; Benjamin T. Fairchild, "Plans for Central Park," letter to the editor, *New York Times*, March 5, 1931; Carl Arthur Beck, "A Matter for Experts," letter to the editor, *New York Times*, March 7, 1931; William W. Niles, "Central Park Plans," letter to the editor, *New York Times*, April 1, 1931.

76. "Herrick Opposes Central Park Promenade to Link Art and Natural History Museums," *New York Times*, April 11, 1930; "Offer Plaza Plan for Reservoir Site," *New York Times*, April 22, 1930; "Plan for Reservoir Adopted by Herrick," *New York Times*, June 3, 1930.

77. "Denies He Opposes Tribute to Roosevelt," *New York Times*, October 15, 1930; "Protests $500,000 for Park Project," *New York Times*, October 22, 1930.

78. *AMNH Annual Report for 1932*, 20.

79. "Roosevelt Returns to Work at Albany," *New York Times*, December 14, 1931; "Roosevelt Presses Fight for Economy," *New York Times*, December 16, 1931.

80. *AMNH Annual Report for 1931*, 13; *AMNH Annual Report for 1932*, 18.

81. Rosenzweig and Blackmar, *Park and the People*, 439–42; "New Design for Roosevelt Arch Approach Omits Esplanade to Assure Park Harmony," *New York Times*, March 12, 1932.

82. *AMNH Annual Report for 1932*, 18.

83. *AMNH Annual Report for 1933*, 15.

84. Rosenzweig and Blackmar, *Park and the People*, 448–449.

85. "Roosevelt Arch to Rise Here Soon," *New York Times*, March 20, 1935; "New Plan for Approach to Roosevelt Memorial Building" (standalone photo on p. 25), *New York Times*, March 22, 1935; "Park Plaza Plans Shelved by Moses," *New York Times*, May 16, 1935.

86. Moses, *Public Works*, 55.

87. Moses, *Public Works*, 56.

88. "Park Plaza Plans Shelved by Moses," *New York Times*, May 16, 1935.

89. Moses, *Public Works*, 56.

90. Moses, *Public Works*, 56–57.

6. The Akeley African Hall: From the Elephant in the Room to the Seven-Hundred-Pound Gorilla

1. Wallace, *Gathering of Wonders*, 12.

2. Preston, *Dinosaurs in the Attic*, 80.

3. Wallace, *Gathering of Wonders*, 12–13.

4. Preston, *Dinosaurs in the Attic*, 80.

5. Akeley, *In Brightest Africa*, 7; *AMNH Annual Report for 1889*, 8, 20, 46; Preston, *Dinosaurs in the Attic*, 132–135.

6. *AMNH Annual Report for 1973–1974* 12, 31; *AMNH Annual Report for 1992–1993*, 8, 69.

7. Hellman, *Bankers, Bones, and Beetles*, 137.

8. Quinn, *Windows on Nature*, 15.

9. Hellman, *Bankers, Bones, and Beetles*, 137.

10. Alexander, *Museum in America*, 40; Wallace, *Gathering of Wonders*, 13.

11. Hellman, *Bankers, Bones, and Beetles*, 143–44; Clark, "The Image of Africa," 69; Clark, *Good Hunting*, 14–15; Akeley, *In Brightest Africa*, 18; Barton, "Adventures of an Artist Explorer," 50–51.

12. Williams, "The Museum Trademark," 3; AMNH guide, 1920, 93; McCutcheon, *In Africa*, 77, 168; Roosevelt, *African Game Trails*, 345; Akeley, "Elephant Hunting on Mount Kenya," 36.

13. Wallace, *Gathering of Wonders*, 13–14; Preston, *Dinosaurs in the Attic*, 80; Alexander, *Museum in America*, 40.

14. Akeley, *In Brightest Africa*, 158–59.

15. Kennedy, "Philanthropy and Science," 184.

16. "Explorers See Roosevelt," *New York Times*, November 21, 1908.

17. Roosevelt, *African Game Trails*, 3.

18. Delia Akeley, *Jungle Portraits*, 82; Quinn, *Windows on Nature*, 18; Rexer and Klein, *125 Years*, 112.

19. McCutcheon, *In Africa*, 134.

20. Roosevelt, *African Game Trails*, 287–88; Peary, *North Pole*, vii.

21. Barton, "Adventures of an Artist Explorer," 51–53.

22. Akeley, *In Brightest Africa*, 160–63; Clark, *Good Hunting*, 35–38; McCutcheon, *In Africa*, 135–63; Roosevelt, *African Game Trails*, 340–45.

23. McCutcheon, *In Africa*, 200–12.

24. Akeley, *In Brightest Africa*, 44–52; Carl Akeley to Hermon Bumpus, July 20, 1910, quoted in *American Museum Journal*, "Adventure with an African Elephant," 186.

25. Akeley, *In Brightest Africa*, 42; Clark, *Good Hunting*, 45.

26. Virginia Pope, "Roosevelt and Akeley Honored in the Museum," *New York Times*, June 30, 1929; Quinn, *Windows on Nature*, 31; Akeley, *In Brightest Africa*, 42; Glenn Collins, "Long Live the Elephants, Long Dead," *New York Times*, June 4, 2004; AMNH guide, 1939, 96.

27. Akeley, *In Brightest Africa*, 252; Quinn, *Windows on Nature*, 33.

28. Akeley, *In Brightest Africa*, 252.

29. Osborn, *History, Plan, and Scope*, 165.

30. Akeley, *In Brightest Africa*, 251–59; *AMNH Annual Report for 1914*, 30–31; *American Museum Journal*, "New African Hall Planned by Carl E. Akeley," 175–87.

31. Akeley, *In Brightest Africa*, 252; *AMNH Annual Report for 1913*, 27, 37; AMNH guides, 1911, 49; 1913, 11; 1914, 70.

32. *American Museum Journal*, "Museum Notes," April 1914, 166; "New African Hall in Museum Model," *New York Times*, April 23, 1914.

33. Akeley, *In Brightest Africa*, 164–74.

34. Quinn, *Windows on Nature*, 166; McCleary, "He Makes Them Look Alive," 36–37.

35. *AMNH Annual Report for 1917*, 46–47.

36. *AMNH Annual Report for 1921*, 31, 44; AMNH guide, 1921, 67.

37. *AMNH Annual Report for 1919*, 215. AMNH guides 1920–1930, e.g., 1920 (93) and 1930 (84).

38. *AMNH Annual Report for 1920*, 19, 20.

39. Akeley, *In Brightest Africa*, 254.

40. Bradley, "In Africa with Akeley," 161.

41. "The Secret Sci-Fi Life of Alice B. Sheldon," *NPR*, https://www.npr.org/templates/story/story.php?storyId=6468136.

42. Akeley, "Gorillas," 437.

43. Akeley, *In Brightest Africa*, 230.

44. "Desired Burial in Africa," *New York Times*, December 2, 1926.

45. Akeley, *In Brightest Africa*; Akeley, "Gorillas"; Bradley, "In Africa with Akeley"; Bradley, *On Gorilla Trail*.

46. Akeley, "Gorillas," 437.

47. Akeley, *In Brightest Africa*, 216.

48. Akeley, *In Brightest Africa*, 248.

49. Wallace, *Gathering of Wonders*, 18–19.

50. Akeley, "Gorillas," 431.

51. Akeley, *In Brightest Africa*, 265–66.

52. Andrews, *Beyond Adventure*, 137.

53. *AMNH Annual Report for 1922*, 98, 99, 138; Akeley, *In Brightest Africa*, 251–67.

54. "There will be forty of these realistic groups." Akeley, *In Brightest Africa*, 257; "The plans of the thirty-six groups were considered up to the very last moment by the President and Mr. Akeley before Mr. Akeley's departure on his last journey to Africa." *AMNH Annual Report for 1927*, 13.

55. Andrews, *Beyond Adventure*, 138; *AMNH Annual Report for 1925*, 50; Preston, *Dinosaurs in the Attic*, 83; Mary Akeley, *Carl Akeley's Africa*, 3.

56. Johnson, "Camera Safaris," 47; *AMNH Annual Report for 1923*, 31.

57. Akeley, "Africa's Great National Park," 526; "Mrs. Akeley Shows Film," *New York Times*, February 9, 1934.

58. Preston, *Dinosaurs in the Attic*, 90–92; Akeley, "Africa's Great National Park," 529–32; Akeley, "The African Hall Expedition," 176–77.

59. Akeley, *Carl Akeley's Africa*, 2.

60. Clark, "The Image of Africa," 70; Clark, *Good Hunting*, 62–64; Barton, "Adventures of an Artist Explorer," 62–63.

61. "Mrs. Akeley Is Now a Museum Assistant," *New York Times*, September 18, 1927; "Museum Speeds Akeley Memorial," *New York Times*, May 26, 1929.

62. Akeley, "Africa's Great National Park"; Wallace, *Gathering of Wonders*, 20; Rexer and Klein, *125 Years*, 117.

63. In addition to her works listed in the bibliography, see, for example, her articles "Into the Abode of Gnomes and Fairies," *New York Times*, January 26, 1930; and "Wildlife Sanctuary Created in Congo," *New York Times*, March 15, 1931.

64. "Mrs. Akeley Going to Observe Zulus," *New York Times*, June 17, 1935; "Dr. Mary Akeley Returns," *New York Times*, February 29, 1936; "Dr. Akeley Describes How Africans Live," *New York Times*, March 7, 1936.

65. "Museum Speeds Akeley Memorial," *New York Times*, May 26, 1929.

66. *AMNH Annual Report for 1931*, 6; Virginia Pope, "Roosevelt and Akeley Honored in the Museum," *New York Times*, June 30, 1929.

67. Davison, "Elephants, Lions, and Airplanes," 105.

68. "5 Elephants Slain by Davison Party," *New York Times*, September 5, 1933; "Mrs. Davison Shoots Lion and Leopard in Africa for Museum Collection Here," *New York Times*, October 9, 1933; Davison, "Elephants, Lions, and Airplanes," 105.

69. *AMNH Annual Report for 1936*, 3; "Akeley Memorial Dedicated by 2,000," *New York Times*, May 20, 1936. Speeches were given by President Davison, Daniel Pomeroy, and Mary Jobe Akeley, whose speech was read by someone else because she had laryngitis. The hall was thrown open to the public the following day.

70. Davison, "Future Plans for the Akeley African Hall," 86; Quinn, *Windows on Nature*, 166.

71. Shane Dixon Kavanaugh, "A Quest to Track Down Immortalized Gorilla Turf," *New York Times*, November 22, 2010; Shane Dixon Kavanaugh, "From a Gorilla Diorama to the Real African Turf," *New York Times*, January 3, 2011; AMNH, "Finding the Site of an Iconic Museum Diorama," https://www.amnh.org/explore/news-blogs/news-posts/finding-the-site-of-an-iconic-museum-diorama; AMNH, "Revisiting Akeley's Gorillas," https://www.youtube.com/watch?v=JsrEOKzxL5A; "November 2010: Revisiting Akeley's Gorillas," https://www.youtube.com/watch?v=KM8_NUXpkxY; Stephen Quinn, "Lost in Paradise," *Artists for Conservation*, https://www.artistsforconservation.org/blog-entry/stephen-quinn/lost-paradise; "How an Artist Saved the Mountain Gorilla," *Artists for Conservation*, https://www.artistsforconservation.org/programs/flag-expeditions/expedition/11/how-artist-saved-mountain-gorilla.

7. The Evolution of the Dinosaur Exhibits

1. Wallace, *The American Museum of Natural History's Book of Dinosaurs*, 18; Osborn, *History, Plan, and Scope*, 77.

2. Wallace, *Gathering of Wonders*, 172–73; Preston, *Dinosaurs in the Attic*, 65–67; Dingus and Norell, *Barnum Brown*, 53; Norell, Gaffney, and Dingus, *Discovering Dinosaurs*, x, xi.

3. Norell, Dingus, and Gaffney, *Discovering Dinosaurs*, 103.

4. *AMNH Annual Report for 1899*, 24; *AMNH Annual Report for 1895*, 16; Norell, Gaffney, and Dingus, *Discovering Dinosaurs*, ix, xi; Matthew, "Allosaurus," 3.

5. Norell, Dingus, and Gaffney, *Discovering Dinosaurs*, 103; Matthew, "The Mounted Skeleton of Brontosaurus," 64.

6. Matthew, "The Mounted Skeleton of Brontosaurus," 63.

7. Norell, Dingus, and Gaffney, *Discovering Dinosaurs*, 112–13; Matthew, "Allosaurus," 3–5.

8. Norell, Dingus, and Gaffney, *Discovering Dinosaurs*, 156–57; Brown, "The Trachodon Group," 50–56; *American Museum Journal*, "Museum News Notes," 89.

9. Norell, Dingus, and Gaffney, *Discovering Dinosaurs*, 114–16.

10. Milner, "Bringing Back the Dinosaurs," 8.

11. Osborn, "Tyrannosaurus, Restoration and Model of the Skeleton."

12. *AMNH Annual Report for 1915*, 72.

13. According to the *AMNH Annual Report for 1917*, "The skeleton of the giant Tyrannosaurus has been removed from its temporary place in the Hall of the Age of Man and installed in the Dinosaur Hall, where it properly belongs" (87). The AMNH guide, 1917, places it in the Hall of the Age of Man (109). The AMNH guide, 1918, places it in Dinosaur Hall (106).

14. AMNH guides, 1918 (105), 1919 (107), 1920 (107), 1921 (107), 1922 (107).

15. Norell, Dingus, and Gaffney, *Discovering Dinosaurs*, 117.

16. W. H. Ballou, "The Dinosaurs Are Moving," *New York Times*, December 28, 1924; Diana Rice, "Dinosaurs Now 'at Home' in Their Museum Hall," *New York Times*, March 13, 1927.

17. *AMNH Annual Report for 1923*, 90; Norell, Dingus, and Gaffney, *Discovering Dinosaurs*, 172; Wallace, *The American Museum of Natural History's Book of Dinosaurs*, 109.

18. Norell, Dingus, and Gaffney, *Discovering Dinosaurs*, 146.

19. *AMNH Annual Report for 1932*, 60.

20. Andrews, *This Business of Exploring*, xv.

21. Hellman, *Bankers, Bones, and Beetles*, 171–87; Preston, *Dinosaurs in the Attic*, 94–108; Rexer and Klein, *125 Years*, 52–66; Wallace, *The American Museum of Natural History's Book of Dinosaurs*, 47–61; Wallace, *Gathering of Wonders*, 199–201, 204.

22. AMNH guide, 1928, 97.

23. Dingus, *Next of Kin*, 73; Jane Cobb, "Living and Leisure," *New York Times*, April 16, 1939; "Fossil Skeletons Shown This Week," *New York Times*, April 16, 1939; *AMNH Annual Report for 1938*, 2; *AMNH Annual Report for 1939*, 5.

24. Dingus, *Next of Kin*, 73; Robert K. Plumb, "Museum Dedicates Brontosaur Hall," *New York Times*, May 22, 1953; AMNH guide, 1953, 56.

25. Norell, Dingus, and Gaffney, *Discovering Dinosaurs*, 181–83.

26. Dingus, *Next of Kin*, 80; Robert K. Plumb, "Footprints in Stone Offer Clues to a 120,000,000-Year Mystery," *New York Times*, April 24, 1952; Norell, Dingus, and Gaffney, *Discovering Dinosaurs*, 183.

27. Norell, Dingus, and Gaffney, *Discovering Dinosaurs*, 183.

28. Dingus, *Next of Kin*, 101; Sanka Knox, "Museum 'Exalts' Its Dinosaur King," *New York Times*, July 25; AMNH guide, 1956, 65–68.

29. Dingus, *Next of Kin*, 16–17, 45, 88, 108; Malcolm W. Browne, "Dinosaur Displays Closing for Renovation," *New York Times*, November 29, 1990; Glenn Collins, "Clearing a New Path for T. Rex and Company," *New York Times*, December 1, 1991; Malcolm W. Browne, "New Dinosaur Exhibit Underscores Disputes within Paleontology," *New York Times*, May 23, 1995; John Noble Wilford, "The Dinosaurs Reappear in Top Form," *New York Times*, June 2, 1995; Lowell Dingus email to Colin Davey, August 3, 2012; Ralph Appelbaum interview by Colin Davey, June 21, 2016.

30. Malcolm W. Browne, "Dinosaur Displays Closing for Renovation," *New York Times*, November 29, 1990; Glenn Collins, "Clearing a New Path for T. Rex and Company," *New York Times*, December 1, 1991; John Noble Wilford, "The Dinosaurs Reappear in Top Form," *New York Times*, June 2, 1995; Gaffney, Dingus, and Smith, "Why Cladistics?"; Gould, "Evolution by Walking."

31. Norell, Dingus, and Gaffney, *Discovering Dinosaurs*, 103–4; Milner, "Bringing Back the Dinosaurs," 9.

32. Norell, Dingus, and Gaffney, *Discovering Dinosaurs*, 117–18; Milner, "Bringing Back the Dinosaurs," 8.

33. Wallace, *Gathering of Wonders*, 202–6; Norell, Dingus, and Gaffney, *Discovering Dinosaurs*, 209–13; Dingus, *Next of Kin*, 109, 112.

8. The Years 1936 to 1999

1. Higgins & Quasebarth, *Planetarium & North Side Project*, 21–23.

2. Stern, Fishman, and Mellins, *New York 1960*, 662–64; Higgins & Quasebarth, *Planetarium & North Side Project*, 23; *AMNH Annual Report for 1942*, 21; "Museum of Natural History Here Will Be Modernized after the War," *New York Times*, January 12, 1943; "Topics of the Times," *New York Times*, January 13, 1943; Doris G. Tobias, "Museum Plans Disapproved," letter to the editor, *New York Times*, January 15, 1943; Henry Weil, "Unpleasant Comparisons," letter to the editor, *New York Times*, January 15, 1943; Eva Pratt, "New Museum Plans Approved," letter to the editor, *New York Times*, January 19, 1943; Rufus Graves Mather, "Museum Plans Opposed," letter to the editor, *New York Times*, January 27, 1943.

3. Higgins & Quasebarth, *Planetarium & North Side Project*, 23; John Darnton, "City Postpones Park Fund Deal," *New York Times*, April 13, 1973; Boyce Rensberger, "Museum Will Open Hall of Gems," *New York Times*,

May 19, 1976; Paul Goldberger, "Design Notebook," *New York Times*, April 14, 1977.

4. Thomas A. Lesser email to Colin Davey, April 28, 2017; Dingus, *Next of Kin*, 17.

5. Historical Designation Report, Landmarks Preservation Commission, August 24, 1967, no. 2, LP-0282.

6. Historical Designation Report, Landmarks Preservation Commission, July 22, 1975, no. 3, LP-0889.

7. National Register designation 76001235.

8. National Register designation 82001189.

9. Historical Designation Report, Landmarks Preservation Commission, April 24, 1990.

10. *AMNH Annual Report for 1972*, 7, 31.

11. *AMNH Annual Report for 1972*, 6, 24.

12. *AMNH Annual Report for 1974*, 7, 14.

13. *AMNH Annual Report for 2000*, 18, 31, 43, 60.

14. Quinn, *Windows on Nature*, 91, 167–68; Russell Owen, "Wild Life Vistas along Central Park," *New York Times*, March 29, 1942; "Preview Wednesday Opens Museum Show," *New York Times*, April 3, 1942; "History Museum Opens New Hall," *New York Times*, April 9, 1942; "Museum Finishes 20-Year Project," *New York Times*, May 19, 1954.

15. Murray Schumach, "Museum Trades Man-Made Whale for Bigger One," *New York Times*, November 15, 1968; "Hall of Ocean Life Is Opening Today at History Museum," *New York Times*, February 26, 1969; *AMNH Annual Report for 1973*, 24, 37. The AMNH guide, 1967, shows the Biology of Mammals Hall and includes a picture of the whale after its completion in 1907. Museum guides from 1911 to 1936 refer to the hall as Mammals of the World and from 1939 to 1967 as Biology of Mammals. The floorplan of the 1972 museum guide (8–9) shows no exhibit at the location of the Biology of Mammals Hall. Subsequent floorplans indicate that the location is used for temporary exhibits.

16. Quinn, *Windows on Nature*, 142–43, 169; Glenn Collins, "Rescuing the Diorama from the Fate of the Dodo," *New York Times*, February 3, 2003.

17. *AMNH Annual Report for 1970*, 3; AMNH guide, 1972, 10 (floorplan); Boyce Rensberger, "Museum Opens Pacific Exhibit," *New York Times*, May 19, 1971.

18. "Margaret Mead Hall for American Museum," *New York Times*, November 26, 1984; "At New Mead Hall, a Bygone World," *New York Times*, December 21, 1984.

19. Boyce Rensberger, "Museum Will Open Hall of Gems," *New York Times*, May 19, 1976; Paul Goldberger, "Design Notebook," *New York Times*, April 14, 1977.

20. John Noble Wilford, "Showing Why a Rain Forest Matters," *New York Times*, May 29, 1998; "In the Hall of Biodiversity," *New York Times*,

June 1, 1998; Glenn Collins, "Step Right Up and Watch the Amazing Vanishing Species!" *New York Times*, June 2, 1998.

9. From the Beginning of Time to October 2, 1935

1. "'Tour of Sky' Opens Planetarium; 800 Get a New Vision of Universe," *New York Times*, October 3, 1935.

2. "'S.R.O.' at Planetarium," *New York Times*, October 4, 1935.

3. "Throngs Wait in Line to See Planetarium," *New York Times*, October 6, 1935.

4. Werner, *From the Aratus Globe*, 14–16.

5. Werner, *From the Aratus Globe*, 20–22.

6. Werner, *From the Aratus Globe*, 23; Marché, *Theaters of Time and Space*, 11.

7. "To Cart 70-Ton Lady Through the Streets," *New York Times*, October 1, 1904; "The Toilet of a Meteorite," *New York Times*, May 18, 1906.

8. *AMNH Annual Report for 1903*, 11.

9. Tobin, "Deconstructing James Lord Brown," 57–58; Richard Tobin email to Colin Davey, April 13, 2018.

10. "The Toilet of a Meteorite," *New York Times*, May 18, 1906.

11. "The Toilet of a Meteorite," *New York Times*, May 18, 1906; *AMNH Annual Report for 1908*, 18; AMNH guide, 1911, 35; Hodgins, "A Huge Planetarium," 30.

12. *AMNH Annual Report for 1908*, 16, 18, 19; Osborn, *History, Plan, and Scope*, 155.

13. *AMNH Annual Report for 1908*, 19; Osborn, *History, Plan, and Scope*, 162, 165.

14. *AMNH Annual Report for 1912*, 30.

15. The foyer's solar system model appears in the 1911 AMNH guide, published in November (14). In both AMNH guides for 1913 (a and b), it is gone.

16. *AMNH Annual Report for 1912*, 31–32.

17. *AMNH Annual Report for 1913*, 28.

18. AMNH guide, 1913b, 43. The astronomical clock appears in the AMNH guide for 1913a (3); the 1913b guide, published in July, indicates it is gone.

19. *AMNH Annual Report of 1916*, 23; *AMNH Annual Report of 1920*, 20; *AMNH Annual Report of 1921*, 20; Marché, "Theaters of Time and Space," 115; Lawrence and Milner, "Forgotten Cosmic Designer," 100.

20. *AMNH Annual Report of 1921*, 117.

21. Henry Fairfield Osborn to Carnegie Foundation, May 1925; cited in Lawrence and Milner, "Forgotten Cosmic Designer," 100.

22. *AMNH Annual Report of 1922*, ix; Marché, "Theaters of Time and Space," 217.

23. *AMNH Annual Report of 1923*, xxii; *AMNH Annual Report of 1924*, 32.

24. Butler, "An Ideal Astronomic Hall," 393.

25. Barton, "He Brought the Stars to America," 59–63; Lockwood, "Clyde Fisher Naturalist and Teacher," 111–13; Menke, "Planetarium Lifeline," 54–58; Green, *Te Ata*, 90–151.

26. *AMNH Annual Report for 1924*, 32–34.

27. *AMNH Annual Report for 1925*, xviii, 24, 31.

28. Lawrence and Milner, "Forgotten Cosmic Designer," 100; Pasachoff and Olson, "Eclipse Art"; Pasachoff and Olson, "The Solar Eclipse Mural Series by Howard Russell Butler."

29. *AMNH Annual Report for 1924*, 32–33.

30. Marché, *Theaters of Time and Space*, 13.

31. Higgins & Quasebarth, *Planetarium & North Side Project*, 24.

32. Werner, *From the Aratus Globe*, 29.

33. Hagar, *Planetarium*, 174; Werner, *From the Aratus Globe*, 27, fig. 16; Marché, *Theaters of Time and Space*, 12.

34. Fisher, "The New Projection Planetarium," 405, 409.

35. Memorandum by acting director George H. Sherwood, Central Archives, 1178.5, AMNH Library; cited in Marché, "Theaters of Time and Space," 217; Fisher, "The New Projection Planetarium," 405; "Museum to Make the Known Universe Visible," *New York Times*, May 2, 1926.

36. Fisher, "The New Projection Planetarium," 405.

37. Marché, "Theaters of Time and Space," 217.

38. *AMNH Annual Report for 1925*, 34; "Eclipse Paintings Shown at Museum," *New York Times*, March 25, 1926.

39. John W. Harrington, "Amateurs of Astronomy Are Active in New York," *New York Times*, December 16, 1934; *AMNH Annual Report for 1927*, 37–38; Patrick Rizzo, "A History of the First Forty Years of the Amateur Astronomers Association," https://www.aaa.org/articles/a-history-of-the -first-forty-years-of-the-amateur-astronomers-association.

40. Fisher to Sherwood, March 19, Central Archives, 1178.5, AMNH Library; cited in Marché, "Theaters of Time and Space," 218.

41. Higgins & Quasebarth, *Planetarium & North Side Project*, 32; "Planetarium for New York," *New York Times*, August 12, 1928.

42. *AMNH Annual Report for 1928*, 38; *AMNH Annual Report for 1930*, 42–43.

43. Burns and Sanders, *New York*, 413–14.

44. "Davison Is Named to Head Museum," *New York Times*, January 10, 1933; *AMNH Annual Report for 1933*, 54.

45. Silber, "Why Did FDR's Bank Holiday Succeed?"

46. "Science: Rotated Halls," *Time*, March 27, 1933.

47. "Gov. Lehman Acts to Spur Aid Jobs," *New York Times*, January 28, 1933; "Gov. Lehman Sets Up Committee to Push Job Relief by R.F.C.," *New York Times*, February 2, 1933; "R.F.C. Will Confer on New York Loans," *New York Times*, February 3, 1933; "State Board to Ask $150,000,000 of R.F.C.," *New York Times*, February 4, 1933; "R.F.C. Loan Hearing Today," *New York*

Times, February 6, 1933; "$98,250,000 Works Approved by State as R.F.C. Projects," *New York Times*, February 7, 1933; Caro, *Power Broker*, 345.

48. James Butkiewicz, "Reconstruction Finance Corporation," *EH.Net Encyclopedia*, July 19, 2002, https://eh.net/encyclopedia/reconstruction -finance-corporation.

49. Marcus H. Heyman to American Museum of Natural History, August 17, 1932, Central Archives, 1178.5, AMNH Library; cited in Marché, "Theaters of Time and Space," 116.

50. There are several comprehensive books that cover Moses's career in great detail. In chronological order: Moses' own autobiographical volume, *Public Works: A Dangerous Trade* (1970), has 952 pages. The Pulitzer Prize–winning *The Power Broker: Robert Moses and the Fall of New York* (1974) by Robert Caro has 1,280 pages. More recently, his career was revisited in the richly illustrated *Robert Moses and the Modern City: The Transformation of New York* (2007), ed. Hilary Ballon and Kenneth T. Jackson, who managed to keep it down to 336 extra-wide pages. The Hayden Planetarium is mentioned, in passing, two times in *The Power Broker* (508, 568) and not at all in *Robert Moses and the Modern City*. Moses devotes over three pages to it in his *Dangerous Trade* (50–53). Moses's work was so massive that each of these books necessarily had to allow parts of the story to fall through the cracks. For example, Moses's rivalry with Jane Jacobs over the fate of Greenwich Village, which was omitted from *The Power Broker* because of a lack of space, recently became the topic of an entire 231-page book, *Wrestling with Moses*, by Anthony Flint (2009).

51. Mitchell, *The American Experiment with Government Corporations*, 30.

52. Caro, *Power Broker*, 15.

53. Moses, *Public Works*, 703; "The RFC under Hoover and Roosevelt," *CQ Researcher*, July 17, 1935, https://library.cqpress.com/cqresearcher/docu ment.php?id=cqresrre1935071700; Olson, *Saving Capitalism*.

54. "Roosevelt's Message on Muscle Shoals," *New York Times*, April 11, 1933.

55. "TVA: From the New Deal to a New Century," https://www.tva .com/abouttva/history.htm.

56. Mitchell, *The American Experiment with Government Corporations*, 32.

57. "Planetarium Plan Revived by Museum," *New York Times*, April 6, 1933.

58. "Planetarium Plan Revived by Museum," *New York Times*, April 6, 1933; "Sales Tax Passed by Legislature; to Quit Monday," *New York Times*, April 9, 1933; "Three New 'Authorities,'" *New York Times*, April 20, 1933; "Governor Signs Saratoga Bill," *New York Times*, April 20, 1933; "Museum Votes Planetarium Plan; Approval by City and R.F.C. Needed," *New York Times*, May 20, 1933; "Act on Planetarium," *New York Times*, May 26, 1933; "City Planetarium Favored by Board," *New York Times*, May 24, 1933; "Planetarium Site Voted," *New York Times*, May 27, 1933.

59. "Asks $350,000,000 as Outlay in State on Public Works," *New York Times*, June 6, 1933.

"Public Works Here," *New York Times*, June 6, 1933.

60. Moses, *Public Works*, 51.

61. "Planetarium Here Assured by Loan," *New York Times*, June 27, 1933.

62. Advisory committee to F. Trubee Davison, April 18, 1933, Central Archives, 1178.5, AMNH Library; Clyde Fisher to F. Trubee Davison, April 25, 1933, Central Archives, 1178.5, AMNH Library; "Museum Votes Planetarium Plan; Approval by City and R.F.C. Needed," *New York Times*, May 20, 1933; "The Proposed Planetarium," *New York Times*, May 22, 1933; "Planetarium Here Assured by Loan," *New York Times*, June 27, 1933; Higgins & Quasebarth, *Planetarium & North Side Project*, 32–34.

63. George H. Sherwood to Carl Zeiss, Inc., October 11, 1933, Central Archives, 1178.5, AMNH Library; cited in Marché, "Theaters of Time and Space," 117.

64. Hellman, *Bankers, Bones, and Beetles*, 209.

65. Hellman, *Bankers, Bones, and Beetles*, 209–10.

66. Marché, *Theaters of Time and Space*, 35; "Banker to Religion via Stars," *Time*, January 15, 1934.

67. Hellman, *Bankers, Bones, and Beetles*, 210.

68. Hellman, *Bankers, Bones, and Beetles*, 210.

69. F. Trubee Davison to John D. Rockefeller III, November 17, 1933, Central Archives, 1178.5, AMNH Library; cited in cited in Marché, "Theaters of Time and Space," 117–18; Charles Hayden to F. Trubee Davison, November 20, 1933, Central Archives, 1178.5, AMNH Library.

70. "$150,000 by Hayden for Planetarium," *New York Times*, January 5, 1934.

71. Moses, *Public Works*, 50; Hellman, *Bankers, Bones, and Beetles*, 210; Caro, *Power Broker*, 568.

72. Marché, *Theaters of Time and Space*, 29–31.

73. Moses, *Public Works*, 50–51.

74. "Bids Are Opened for Museum Unit," *New York Times*, May 12, 1934; American Museum of Natural History Planetarium Authority, "Contract Papers for Construction of a Planetarium Building in Manhattan Square, City of New York/The American Museum of Natural History Planetarium Authority," 1934, 1, Rare Book Collection, PC-1-C, AMNH Library.

75. "Ceremonies Are Held at Planetarium Site," *New York Times*, May 29, 1934.

76. "Planetarium Is Delayed," *New York Times*, March 21, 1935; Higgins & Quasebarth, *Planetarium & North Side Project*, 35; Pape, "Thin Concrete Shell Dome for New York Planetarium," 105–7; Faunce, "Problems of Construction," 208–9.

77. Caro, *Power Broker*, 402–25.

78. For more technical information about the dome's construction, see Pape, "Thin Concrete Shell Dome for New York Planetarium," 105–8; Bertin, "Centering for the Planetarium Shell Dome," 108–9; Hines and Billington,

"Anton Tedesko," 1639–50; Faunce, "Problems of Construction," 207–16; Higgins & Quasebarth, *Planetarium & North Side Project*, 49–51.

79. "Star-Projector Arrives," *New York Times*, January 27, 1935.

80. "Museum Unpacks 'Heavens' Machine," *New York Times*, July 9, 1935.

81. "54 Tons of Meteorites Will Be Moved Through the Streets to New Planetarium," *New York Times*, July 8, 1935.

82. Caro, *Power Broker*, 143–322; recruitment of Davison: 176–77; Davison quote: 185.

83. Francis X. Clines, "Rockefeller Halts Efforts to Build L.I. Sound Bridge," *New York Times*, June 21, 1973.

84. "WNET Reports: A Conversation with Robert Moses," interview by Robert Sam Anson, 1977, https://www.pbs.org/wnet/blueprintamerica/reports/the-next-american-system/video-the-master-builder-1977/925.

85. "Guide to the F. Trubee Davison Papers," comp. William E. Brown Jr., May 1982, http://drs.library.yale.edu:8083/fedora/get/mssa:ms.0601/PDF; Hellman, *Bankers, Bones, and Beetles*, 214.

10. Robert Moses and the Norman Bel Geddes Report

1. According to the AMNH Annual Report for 1935, "indications are that the debt for construction will be paid in less than the time allowed in the contract" (38).

2. Anticipated attendance is based on "Report of Engineers Advisory Board," June 22, 1933, Central Archives, 1178.5, AMNH Library, 3. Attendance figures compiled by Thomas A. Lesser from the museum's Annual Reports.

3. "Financial Report on Application of American Museum of Natural History Planetarium Authority for a Loan of $740,000," June 22, 1933, Central Archives, 1178.5, AMNH Library, 3.

4. "Organization Profile Report," Charles Hayden Foundation, prepared for Colin Davey, October 3, 2012.

5. "Planetarium Visits Drop," *New York Times*, May 4, 1939; Attendance figures compiled by Thomas A. Lesser from the museum's Annual Reports.

6. Robert Moses to A. Perry Osborn, June 4, 1941; Robert Moses to Norman Bel Geddes, October 14, 1941; both in Harry Ransom Center, University of Texas, box 29, folder 444.1–2, http://norman.hrc.utexas.edu/nbg-public/details.cfm?ID=366.

7. Moses, Public Works, 3; "City Bill Faces Fight," *New York Times*, January 4, 1934; "Democrats Block Moses Bill," *New York Times*, January 5, 1934; "La Guardia Pleads for His Park Plan," *New York Times*, January 7, 1934; "City Bill Faces Fight," *New York Times*, January 4, 1934; W. A. Warn, "Bill to Reform Charter up at Albany as Lehman Speeds City Economy Act," *New York Times*, January 18, 1934; "Smith Hails Moses as City

Parks Head," *New York Times*, January 19, 1934; "La Guardia Fills Three Cabinet Posts," *New York Times*, January 19, 1934; "Commissioner Moses," *New York Times*, January 20, 1934.

8. AMNH Annual Report for 1933, 55.

9. Flint, Wrestling with Moses, 35.

10. Moses, Public Works, 41–43.

11. "Museums Too Musty for Moses; He Says They Intimidate Visitors," *New York Times*, March 3, 1941.

12. Robert Moses to A. Perry Osborn, June 4, 1941, Harry Ransom Center, University of Texas, box 29, folder 444.1–2.

13. Norman Bel Geddes to Roy Chapman Andrews, October 8, 1941, Central Archives, 1178.5, AMNH Library; James Dawson (senior park director under Moses) to Wayne Faunce (vice director AMNH), October 11, 1941, Central Archives, 1178.5, AMNH Library; Robert Moses to Norman Bel Geddes, October 14, 1941, Harry Ransom Center, University of Texas, box 29, folder 444.1–2.

14. Robert Moses to Norman Bel Geddes, October 14, 1941, Harry Ransom Center, University of Texas, box 29, folder 444.1–2.

15. Wayne Faunce to Norman Bel Geddes, November 14, 1941, Harry Ransom Center, University of Texas, box 29, folder 444.1–2.

16. "Job Diary, Norman Bel Geddes & Company, Inc.," November 19, 1941 (5), November 18, 1941 (6), November 19, 1941 (7), November 25, 1941 (8), November 27, 1941 (10a–10b), December 4, 1941 (11), December 9, 1941 (12), December 10, 1941 (13), December 11, 1941 (14), December 12, 1941 (15), December 15, 1941 (16), December 23, 1941 (17), Harry Ransom Center, University of Texas, box 29, folder 444.1–2; Norman Bel Geddes to Wayne Faunce, November 17, 1941, Central Archives, 1178.5, AMNH Library; "Minutes of Meeting Norman Bel Geddes & Company, Inc.," November 19, 1941; "Minutes of Meeting Norman Bel Geddes & Company, Inc.," November 27, 1941; Norman Bel Geddes, "Miscellaneous Notes on Planetarium Job," November 27, 1941; "Minutes of Meeting Norman Bel Geddes & Company, Inc.," December 2, 1941; William H. Barton (planetarium curator) to Joseph Brent (account executive for Norman Bel Geddes & Company, Inc.) December 5, 1941, all in Harry Ransom Center, University of Texas, box 29, folder 444.1–2.

17. "Job Diary, Norman Bel Geddes & Company, Inc.," January 6, 1942 (18), January 7, 1942 (19), January 8, 1942 (20), January 13, 1942 (22), January 14, 1942 (23), Harry Ransom Center, University of Texas, box 29, folder 444.1–2.

18. "Wayne Faunce to AMNH trustees, January 17, 1942; Wayne Faunce to Morton Macartney (chief, self-liquidating division, RFC), January 24, 1942; Wayne Faunce to Edgar A. Doubleday (executive vice president of the Charles Hayden Foundation), January 24, 1942; Edgar A. Doubleday to

Wayne Faunce, January 26, 1942, all in Central Archives, 1178.5, AMNH Library.

19. Norman Bel Geddes & Co., Preliminary Report to the Hayden Planetarium Authority.

20. "Job Diary, Norman Bel Geddes & Company, Inc.," January 21, 1942, 25, Harry Ransom Center, University of Texas, box 29, folder 444.1–2; Erle V. Daveler (vice president Charles Hayden Foundation) to Wayne Faunce, January 29, 1942, Central Archives, 1178.5, AMNH Library; "Job Diary, Norman Bel Geddes & Company, Inc." February 3, 1942, 30–30a, Harry Ransom Center, University of Texas, box 29, folder 444. 1–2; Morton Macartney (chief, self-liquidating division RFC) to Waynce Faunce, February 14, 1942, Central Archives, 1178.5, AMNH Library; Ellsworth B. Buck (president of the Board of Education from 1942 to 1944 and AMNH ex-officio trustee) to Wayne Faunce, June 2, 1942, Central Archives, 1178.5, AMNH Library.

21. James L. Clark to A. Perry Osborn, April 21, 1942, Central Archives, 1178.5, AMNH Library; A. Perry Osborn to James L. Clark, April 28, 1942, Central Archives, 1178.5, AMNH Library; A. Perry Osborn to Norman Bel Geddes, April 28, 1942, Harry Ransom Center, University of Texas, box 29, folder 444.1–2.

22. Moses, Public Works, 51–52.

23. Hellman, *Bankers, Bones, and Beetles*, 215; Moses, Public Works, 52; "Organization Profile Report," Charles Hayden Foundation.

24. "Organization Profile Report," Charles Hayden Foundation.

25. Caro, "The City-Shaper," 48.

26. Moses, Public Works, 43; Robert Moses, "The City's Museums—A Fresh Appraisal," *New York Times*, November 13, 1949; Robert Moses, "The City's Museums: Some Prescriptions," *New York Times*, November 20, 1949.

27. Program of the American Museum–Hayden Planetarium Reopening Ceremonies, January 29, 1960, 10–11.

28. Moses, Public Works, 53.

11. The Golden Age of Spaceflight and the Hayden Planetarium

1. McCurdy, *Space and the American Imagination*, 29; *American Enterprise*, "The Moon Landing Revisited," 88.

2. Stuhlinger and Ordway, *Wernher von Braun*, 17; Neufeld, *Von Braun*, 39.

3. Crouch, "Willy Ley," 158.

4. Neufeld, *Von Braun*, 232.

5. Miller and Durant, *The Art of Chesley Bonestell*, 54–55.

6. Miller and Durant, *The Art of Chesley Bonestell*, 63.

7. Mason, "Space Travel," *Wired*, December 19, 2011; The Hayden Letters, https://www.flickr.com/photos/amnh/sets/72157628295324859; Meyer Berger, "'Space Fever' Hits the Small-Fry," *New York Times*, March 16, 1952;

Clyde Haberman, "Delays? Try Booking a Flight to the Moon," *New York Times*, February 23, 2007.

8. Terry, *Honest Weight*, 238; *AMNH Annual Report for 1950*, 36.

9. *AMNH Annual Report for 1950–51*, 35.

10. Ley, *Rockets, Missiles, and Space Travel*, 331.

11. Crouch, "Willy Ley," 161.

12. McCurdy, *Space and the American Imagination*, 35–36.

13. Invitation and program to the First Annual Symposium on Space Travel at the Hayden Planetarium; "Platforms in Sky Now Seen Feasible," *New York Times*, October 13, 1951; McCurdy, *Space and the American Imagination*, 36.

14. "Platforms in Sky Now Seen Feasible," *New York Times*, October 13, 1951.

15. Neufeld, *Von Braun*, 255.

16. Stuhlinger and Ordway, *Wernher von Braun*, 112.

17. "Platforms in Sky Now Seen Feasible," *New York Times*, October 13, 1951.

18. *AMNH Annual Report for 1951*.

19. McCurdy, *Space and the American Imagination*, 37–38.

20. Liebermann, "The *Collier's* and Disney Series," 135.

21. Neufeld, *Von Braun*, 256; Stuhlinger and Ordway, *Wernher von Braun*, 112.

22. Stuhlinger and Ordway, *Wernher von Braun*, 113.

23. Neufeld, *Von Braun*, 256.

24. Stuhlinger and Ordway, *Wernher von Braun*, 112.

25. Whipple, "Recollections of Pre-Sputnik Days," 128–29.

26. Stuhlinger and Ordway, *Wernher von Braun*, 113.

27. Neufeld, *Von Braun*, 257–59.

28. Tooker, "Line Forms Here for Trip to Moon."

29. Ward, *Dr. Space*, 89.

30. Neufeld, *Von Braun*, 270; William L. Laurence, "2 Rocket Experts Argue 'Moon' Plan," *New York Times*, October 14, 1952.

31. "Dreams of Space: A List of Nonfiction Children's Books about Spaceflight, 1945–1975," http://dreamsofspace.nfshost.com/spacebookdraft07July-webpage.htm; Meyer Berger, "'Space Fever' Hits the Small-Fry," *New York Times*, March 16, 1952; Frost, *Rocket Away!*; Phyllis Fenner, "Moon Ahead!" *New York Times*, May 31, 1953.

32. *AMNH Annual Report for 1952*; *AMNH Annual Report for 1953*.

33. *Collier's*, February 28, 1953; March 7, 1953; March 14, 1953; June 27, 1953; April 30, 1954.

34. *AMNH Annual Report of 1954*, 53; Rosen, *The Viking Rocket Story*, 7. The copies of *The Viking Rocket Story* given away at the exhibit's opening contained a bookplate saying "This book is presented with the compliments of the Martin Company of Balitimore, Maryland at the opening of Viking

Hall, the Hayden Planetarium, New York, June 30, 1955." The bookplate can be seen at https://www.worthpoint.com/worthopedia/1955-rosen -viking-rocket-story-signed-462184610.

35. "Sputnik and The Dawn of the Space Age," http://history.nasa.gov/ sputnik; "The International Geophysical Year," http://www.nas.edu/history/igy; Stuhlinger and Ordway, *Wernher von Braun*, 126–28; Neufeld, *Von Braun*, 294–98; Constance McLaughlin Green and Milton Lomask, "*Vanguard, a History*," chap. 3, https://history.nasa.gov/SP-4202/chapter3.html.

36. McCurdy, *Space and the American Imagination*, 47; *American Enterprise*, "The Moon Landing Revisited," 88.

37. Robert Moses to Norman Bel Geddes, October 4, 1955, Harry Ransom Center, University of Texas, box 29, folder 444.1–2, http://norman.hrc .utexas.edu/nbgpublic/details.cfm?ID=366.

38. Neufeld, *Von Braun*, 285–290, 295, 301, 317.

39. Neufeld, *Von Braun*, 311–23, 327; "Sputnik and The Dawn of the Space Age," http://history.nasa.gov/sputnik; "Chronology of Sputnik/Vanguard/ Explorer Events 1957–58," https://history.nasa.gov/sputnik/chronology.html.

40. *AMNH Annual Report for 1957*, 44.

41. McCurdy, *Space and the American Imagination*, 58; *American Enterprise*, "The Moon Landing Revisited," 88.

42. Crouch, "Willy Ley," 161–62.

43. Nancy Hicks, "Planetariums Ride High on Space Success," *New York Times*, July 25, 1969.

44. *AMNH Annual Report for 1967*, 26; *AMNH Annual Report for 1970*, 42; Richard F. Shepard, "Going Out Guide," *New York Times*, July 19, 1972.

45. *AMNH Annual Report for 1968–69*, 18, 42.

46. Nancy Hicks, "Planetariums Ride High on Space Success," *New York Times*, July 25, 1969.

12. A Visit to the Original Hayden Planetarium

1. "Planetarium Puts Heavens on Walls," *New York Times*, February 10, 1953.

2. AMNH guide, 1953, 39.

3. *Sky & Telescope*, May 1953, 175.

4. *Sky & Telescope*, May 1953, 175.

5. *Sky & Telescope*, May 1953, 175.

6. *AMNH Annual Report for 1952*, 51–52.

7. "Planetarium Completes Last 3 of Mural Illusions of Other Worlds," *New York Times*, February 1, 1955.

8. *AMNH Annual Report for 1963*, 25–26.

9. Frank H. Winter, "The First Rocket Built for Space," https://www .airspacemag.com/daily-planet/first-rocket-built-space-180969273.

10. John Noble Wilford, "Preparations for Moon Shot Proceeding Smoothly," *New York Times*, December 18, 1968; *AMNH Annual Report for 1988*, 13.

11. Re taped lectures: HP guides, 1937 (15), 1945 (11), 1947 (11), 1950 (9), 1952 (9), 1953 (9), 1954 (9), 1961 (n.p.); "The lecturer, often in a tux, would first come to that theater and do a short presentation on the orrery, and then lead the crowd up the stairs to the Sky Theater for the planetarium show." Thomas A. Lesser email to Colin Davey, August 27, 2015.

12. "The Talk of the Town," *New Yorker*, January 11, 1958.

13. *AMNH Annual Report for 1959*, 42; "The Talk of the Town," *New Yorker*, January 11, 1958.

14. *AMNH Annual Report for 1970*, 20; *AMNH Annual Report for 1971*, 18; *AMNH Annual Report for 1972*, 17; Higgins & Quasebarth, *Planetarium & North Side Project*, 38, 39.

15. Murray Schumach, "New World Due at Planetarium," *New York Times*, January 20, 1959; "Organization Profile Report," Charles Hayden Foundation, prepared for Colin Davey, October 3, 2012; Paula Chamberlain (wife of Joseph Chamberlain) email to Colin Davey, January 19, 2011.

16. James Marsden, "New Stars Above," *New York Times*, January 24, 1960.

17. *Program of the American Museum–Hayden Planetarium Reopening Ceremonies*, January 29, 1960.

18. Sandra Blakeslee, "New Star at the Planetarium Is a More Sophisticated Projector," *New York Times*, October 3, 1969; "Organization Profile Report," Charles Hayden Foundation, prepared for Colin Davey, October 3, 2012.

19. *Audio-Visual Communications*, "Multi-Media: Heaven on Earth," 24–28.

20. *AMNH Annual Report for 1963*, 25–26; "Progress in Astronomy to Be Shown," *New York Times*, June 30, 1964. Asimov's attendance: Gordon Ashby interview by Colin Davey, January 4, 2011.

21. *AMNH Annual Report for 1963*, 25–26.

22. Philip Benjamin, "Role of Computers in Astronomy Shown in Planetarium's Exhibit," *New York Times*, September 13, 1958; HP guide, 1961 (n.p.); *AMNH Annual Report for 1958*, 44; *AMNH Annual Report for 1959*, 43.

23. "Mathematica: A World of Numbers . . . and Beyond," https://en.wikipedia.org/wiki/Mathematica:_A_World_of_Numbers..._and_Beyond.

24. Much of the information in this section is drawn from Gordon Ashby interview by Colin Davey, January 4, 2011.

25. *AMNH Annual Report for 1968*, 19.

26. *AMNH Annual Report for 1974*, 14.

27. Terry, *Honest Weight*, 238; *AMNH Annual Report for 1950*, 36.

28. *AMNH Annual Report for 1960*, 31; *AMNH Annual Report for 1968*, 18.

13. The Rose Center for Earth and Space

1. *AMNH Annual Report for 1974*, 14; Dickstein, "Laserium"; 1976 Laserium program: https://www.patrickmccray.com/wp/wp-content/uploads/2015/01/1976-Laserium-program.pdf.

2. Glenn Collins, "Voyaging a Universe on Beams of Light," *New York Times*, January 4, 1991.

3. Cooper, "Sphere of Influence," 53; *AMNH Annual Report for 1992*, 18; James S. Sweitzer email to Colin Davey, April 30, 2018; Dennis Davidson email to Colin Davey, August 24, 2018.

4. William H. Honan, "Barnard's President to Head Museum of Natural History," *New York Times*, June 29, 1993; Jeannette Walls, "New York Intelligencer," *New York*, December 21–28, 1992.

5. *AMNH Annual Report for 1993*, 8.

6. William H. Honan, "Barnard's President to Head Museum of Natural History," *New York Times*, June 29, 1993.

7. Ellen Futter via Eugenia Levenson email to Colin Davey, June 8, 2018.

8. Dena Kleiman, "Trustee, 30, Likely for Barnard Post," *New York Times*, July 8, 1980; "Ellen Futter Appointed Barnard's Acting Head," *New York Times*, July 11, 1980; Edward B. Fiske, "Acting Head Chosen by Barnard for Post of President," *New York Times*, May 7, 1981.

9. William H. Honan, "Barnard's President to Head Museum of Natural History," *New York Times*, June 29, 1993.

10. Neil deGrasse Tyson emails to Colin Davey, April 17 and April 19, 2016.

11. Tyson, *The Sky Is Not the Limit*, 28, 29.

12. Tyson, *The Sky Is Not the Limit*, 35.

13. Neil deGrasse Tyson interview by Colin Davey, September 24, 2013.

14. Fleischer et al., *Polshek Partnership Architects*, 154; Cooper, "Sphere of Influence," 53.

15. Cooper, "Sphere of Influence," 53; Neil deGrasse Tyson email to Colin Davey, April 19, 2016.

16. Neil deGrasse Tyson email to Colin Davey, April 19, 2016.

17. Dennis Davidson email to Colin Davey, August 24, 2018.

18. Cooper, "Sphere of Influence," 55.

19. Ralph Appelbaum interview by Colin Davey, June 21, 2016; Fleischer et al., *Polshek Partnership Architects*, 156–59; Cooper, "Sphere of Influence," 50–55.

20. Ralph Appelbaum interview by Colin Davey, June 21, 2016; Dennis Davidson email to Colin Davey, August 24, 2018; James S. Sweitzer email to Colin Davey, April 30, 2018; Neil deGrasse Tyson email to Colin Davey, April 17, 2016.

21. Cooper, "Sphere of Influence," 50.

22. Paul Goldberger, "Natural History Museum Plans Big Overhaul," *New York Times*, January 27, 1995.

23. James Barron, "Its Stars Eclipsed, Hayden Is Cleared for Demolition," *New York Times*, November 22, 1995; "Organization Profile Report," Charles Hayden Foundation, prepared for Colin Davey, October 3, 2012.

24. *AMNH Annual Report for 1990*, 4.

25. Joyce Purnick, "A Mystery Gift to a Museum Loses Its Mask," *New York Times*, November 7, 1996.

26. James S. Sweitzer email to Colin Davey, April 30, 2018; Dennis Davidson email to Colin Davey, August 24, 2018.

27. Sweitzer, "Theater of the Stars"; Robertson, "Stargazing"; Nelson, "New Technology for a New Museum," 85–88; Abbott, Emmart, and Wyatt, "Virtual Universe"; James S. Sweitzer email to Colin Davey, April 30, 2018.

28. Candy Schulman, "Daddy's Dome," *New York Times*, January 12, 1997.

29. David Gelernter, "The End of Dignity," *New York Times*, March 5, 1995; James Barron, "Its Stars Eclipsed, Hayden Is Cleared for Demolition," *New York Times*, November 22, 1995; Christopher Gray, "A Remnant of the 1930s, and Its Sky, Will Fall," *New York Times*, August 18, 1996; N. R. Kleinfield, "Down-to-Earth Fight over Planetarium," *New York Times*, October 22, 1996; Stephanie Calmenson, "$39 Million for What?" letter to the editor, *New York Times*, October 26, 1996; Michael Henry Adams, "Maintain a Landmark," letter to the editor, *New York Times*, October 26, 1996; Candy Schulman, "Daddy's Dome," *New York Times*, January 12, 1997; Veliz, "Renaissance or Regret?"

30. Salvatore Arena, "Group Seeing Stars over Museum Plan," *New York Daily News*, January 21, 1997; "Metro News Briefs," *New York Times*, February 27, 1997; Salvatore Arena and Anne E. Kornblut, "Judge's Hit Leaves Foes Seeing Stars," *New York Daily News*, February 27, 1997.

31. *AMNH Annual Report for 1994*, 6.

32. John Noble Wilford, "Shaping Restless Planet Earth," *New York Times*, June 11, 1999; Ralph Appelbaum interview by Colin Davey, June 21, 2016.

33. Cooper, "Sphere of Influence," 55; *AMNH Annual Report for 2000*, 8.

Epilogue: The Gilder Center for Science, Education, and Innovation

1. American Museum of Natural History, "Project News," https://www.amnh.org/about-the-museum/richard-gilder-center-for-science-education-and-innovation/project-news.

2. American Museum of Natural History Press Center, "AMNH to Design All-New Halls of Gems and Minerals," https://www.amnh.org/about-the-museum/press-center/amnh-to-design-all-new-halls-of-gems-and-minerals.

3. "Opponents File Suit to Block Museum Expansion Approval, Saying It Will Cause Catastrophic Environmental Damage," April 2, 2018, https://

www.westsiderag.com/2018/04/02/opponents-file-suit-to-block-museum
-expansion-approval-saying-it-will-cause-catastrophic-environmental
-damage; Alex Israel, "Museum Moves *New York Times* Time Capsule to Be
Opened in the Year 3000," July 20, 2018, https://www.westsiderag.com/
2018/07/20/museum-moves-new-york-times-time-capsule-to-be-opened
-in-the-year-3000; Carol Tannenhauser, "Museum of Natural History
Closes Part of Surrounding Park for New Building as Opposition Heads to
Court," September 20, 2018, https://www.westsiderag.com/2018/09/20/
museum-of-natural-history-construction-begins; Carol Tannenhauser,
"Hearing on Challenge to Museum Expansion Hinges on a Single Letter,"
October 2, 2018, https://www.westsiderag.com/2018/10/02/hearing-on
-challenge-to-museum-expansion-hinges-on-a-single-letter; "Judge Issues
Temporary Restraining Order against Construction and Tree Removal for
Museum of Natural History Addition," October 29, 2018, https://www
.westsiderag.com/2018/10/29/judge-issues-temporary-restraining-order
-against-construction-and-tree-removal-for-museum-of-natural-history
-addition; "Museum Gets Court Permission to Start Basic Site Work for
New Building, with Limits; Both Sides Declare Victory," November 3, 2018,
https://www.westsiderag.com/2018/11/03/museum-gets-court-permission
-to-start-basic-site-work-for-new-building-with-limits-both-sides-declare
-victory; https://www.saveourpark.nyc/news.

4. "Museum of Natural History Wins Lawsuit Allowing it to Proceed
With Expansion," December 10, 2018, https://www.westsiderag.com/2018/
12/10/museum-of-natural-history-wins-lawsuit-allowing-it-to-proceed
-with-expansion.

Bibliography

Archives

American Museum of Natural History annual reports are available online at the AMNH website: https://digitallibrary.amnh.org/handle/2246/6178. New York Parks Department annual reports, historical reports, press releases, and minutes of meetings cited in this volume, including BCCP (Central Park Commissioners) and BCDPP (Department of Public Parks) documents, are available online at the NYC Parks Department website: https://www.nycgovparks.org/news/reports/archive. The above archive does not contain the tenth and fourteenth annual BCCP reports. The tenth annual BCCP report can be found in this archive, which contains the ninth through eleventh annual reports: https://books.google.com/books?id=WKwWAAAAYAAJ&dq=%22tenth+annual+report+of+the+board+of+commissioners+of+the+central+park%22. The fourteenth annual BCCP report can be found in this archive, which contains the twelfth through fourteenth annual reports: https://books.google.com/books?id=nqwWAAAAYAAJ&vq=%22fourteenth+report%22&dq=fourteen+report+of+the+commissioners+of+the+central+park. If the document cited does not appear in that electronic archive, a URL is provided in the note.

Museum Guides

The American Museum of Natural History publishes an official guide to its collections. These pamphlets are frequently revised, updated, and replaced by newer versions. Over the years they have varied by title, by whether they credit an author, by publisher, etc. The guides referenced in this book are listed here

by year and in the notes by "AMNH guide," followed by year of publication
and pagination information.

1904.   *A General Guide to the American Museum of Natural History*. Published
by the museum as supplement to the *American Museum Journal* 4, no. 1
(January 1904). Guide Leaflet no. 13.

1911.   *General Guide to the Exhibition Halls of the American Museum of Natural
History*. By George H. Sherwood. American Museum of Natural History Guide Leaflet no. 35.

1912a. *American Museum of Natural History Key to Building and Collections*.
American Museum of Natural History.

1912b. *American Museum of Natural History Key to Building and Collections*. 2nd
ed. American Museum of Natural History.

1913a. *American Museum of Natural History Key to Building and Collections*. 3rd
ed. American Museum of Natural History.

1913b. *General Guide to the Exhibition Halls of the American Museum of Natural
History*. By Frederic A. Lucas, assisted by members of the museum
staff. American Museum of Natural History Guide Leaflet no. 37.

1914.   *General Guide to the Exhibition Halls of the American Museum of Natural
History*. By Frederic A. Lucas, assisted by members of the museum
staff. American Museum of Natural History Guide Leaflet no. 40.

1916.   *General Guide to the Exhibition Halls of the American Museum of
Natural History*. By Frederic A. Lucas, assisted by members of the
museum staff. American Museum of Natural History Guide Leaflet
no. 44.

1917.   *Guide to the Nature Treasures of New York City: American Museum of Nat-
ural History, New York Aquarium, New York Zoological Park and Botanical
Garden, Brooklyn Museum, Botanic Garden and Children's Museum*. By
George N. Pindar, assisted by Mabel H. Pearson and G. Clyde Fisher.
Published for the American Museum of Natural History by Charles
Scribner's Sons.

1918.   *General Guide to the Exhibition Halls of the American Museum of Natural
History*. Frederic A. Lucas, assisted by members of the museum staff.
American Museum of Natural History Guide Leaflet no. 47.

1919.   *General Guide to the Exhibition Halls of the American Museum of Natural
History*. Ed. of 1919. By Frederic A. Lucas, assisted by members of the
museum staff. American Museum of Natural History.

1920.   *General Guide to the Exhibition Halls of the American Museum of Natural
History*. Ed. of 1920. By Frederic A. Lucas, assisted by members of the
museum staff. American Museum of Natural History.

1921.   *General Guide to the Exhibition Halls of the American Museum of Natural
History*. Ed. of 1921. By Frederic A. Lucas, assisted by members of the
museum staff. American Museum of Natural History.

1922. *General Guide to the Exhibition Halls of the American Museum of Natural History*. 9th ed. By Frederic A. Lucas, assisted by members of the museum staff. American Museum of Natural History.

1927. *Guide to the Present Exhibition Halls of the American Museum of Natural History: For Use during the Rearrangement of the Collections*. Ed. of 1927. By Frederic A. Lucas. American Museum of Natural History.

1928. *General Guide to the Exhibition Halls of the American Museum of Natural History*. 13th ed. By Frederic A. Lucas, assisted by members of the museum staff. American Museum of Natural History.

1929. *General Guide to the Exhibition Halls of the American Museum of Natural History*. 14th ed. By Frederic A. Lucas, assisted by members of the museum staff. American Museum of Natural History.

1930. *General Guide to the Exhibition Halls of the American Museum of Natural History*. 15th ed. By Frederic A. Lucas, revised by members of the museum staff. American Museum of Natural History.

1931. *General Guide to the Exhibition Halls of the American Museum of Natural History*. 16th ed. By Frederic A. Lucas, revised by members of the museum staff. American Museum of Natural History.

1932. *General Guide to the Exhibition Halls of the American Museum of Natural History*. 17th ed. By Frederic A. Lucas, revised by members of the museum staff. American Museum of Natural History.

1933. *General Guide to the Exhibition Halls of the American Museum of Natural History*. 18th ed. By Frederic A. Lucas, revised by members of the museum staff. American Museum of Natural History.

1934. *General Guide to the Exhibition Halls of the American Museum of Natural History*. 19th ed. By Frederic A. Lucas, revised by members of the museum staff. American Museum of Natural History.

1935. *General Guide to the Exhibition Halls of the American Museum of Natural History*. 20th ed. By Frederic A. Lucas, revised by members of the museum staff. American Museum of Natural History.

1936. *General Guide to the Exhibition Halls of the American Museum of Natural History*. 21st ed. By Frederic A. Lucas, revised by members of the museum staff. American Museum of Natural History.

1939. *Exhibition Halls of the American Museum of Natural History*. By Roy Waldo Miner, assisted by members of the museum staff. American Museum of Natural History.

1943. *General Guide to the Exhibition Halls of the American Museum of Natural History*. 2nd ed. completely revised. By Roy Waldo Miner, assisted by members of the museum staff. American Museum of Natural History Science Guide no. 118.

1945. *General Guide to the Exhibition Halls of the American Museum of Natural History*. 3rd ed. completely revised. American Museum of Natural History Science Guide no. 118.

1949. *General Guide to the Exhibition Halls of the American Museum of Natural History.* 5th ed. American Museum of Natural History Science Guide no. 118.

1953. *General Guide to the American Museum of Natural History.* Rev. ed. American Museum of Natural History Science Guide no. 118.

1956. *General Guide to the American Museum of Natural History.* Rev. ed. American Museum of Natural History Science Guide no. 118.

1958. *General Guide to the American Museum of Natural History.* Rev. ed. American Museum of Natural History Science Guide no. 118.

1962. *General Guide to the Exhibits.* American Museum of Natural History.

1964. *General Guide to the Exhibits.* American Museum of Natural History.

1967. *A Pictorial Guide to the American Museum of Natural History.* American Museum of Natural History. Unpaginated.

1972. *The American Museum of Natural History: An Introduction.* American Museum of Natural History.

1984. *Official Guide to the American Museum of Natural History.* By Georg Zappler. American Museum of Natural History.

1993. *Official Guide: Images from Around the American Museum of Natural History.* American Museum of Natural History.

2001. *American Museum of Natural History: The Official Guide.* Scala Publishers, Ltd.

Planetarium Guides

These guides are referenced in the notes as "HP Guide," followed by year of publication. Note that all the guides from 1945 to 1961 have "copyright 1945" on their title page. Years listed here refer to the year following the "revised edition" statement.

1935. *The Book of the Hayden Planetarium.* American Museum of Natural History.

1937. *The Hayden Planetarium.* American Museum of Natural History.

1945. *The Hayden Planetarium.* American Museum of Natural History.

1947. *The Hayden Planetarium.* American Museum of Natural History.

1952. *The Hayden Planetarium.* American Museum of Natural History.

1953. *The American Museum–Hayden Planetarium.* American Museum of Natural History.

1954. *The American Museum–Hayden Planetarium.* American Museum of Natural History.

1961. *American Museum–Hayden Planetarium.* American Museum of Natural History. Unpaginated.

Books and Articles

Abbott, Brian, Carter Emmart, and Ryan Wyatt. "Virtual Universe." *Natural History* 113, no. 3 (April 2004): 44–49.

Ackerman, Kenneth D. *Boss Tweed: The Corrupt Pol Who Conceived the Soul of Modern New York*. Viral History Press, 2011.

Akeley, Carl E. "Elephant Hunting on Mount Kenya." *American Museum Journal* 15, no. 7 (November): 322–38.

———. "Gorillas—Real and Mythical." *Natural History* 23, no. 5 (September–October 1923): 428–47.

———. *In Brightest Africa*. Garden City Publishing, 1920.

Akeley, Delia. *Jungle Portraits*. Macmillan, 1930.

Akeley, Mary L. Jobe. "The African Hall Expedition." *Natural History* 27, no. 2 (March–April 1927): 176–77.

———. "Africa's Great National Park." *Natural History* 29, no. 6 (November–December 1929): 525–32.

———. *Carl Akeley's Africa: The Account of the Akeley-Eastman-Pomeroy African Hall Expedition of the American Museum of Natural History*. Blue Ribbon Books, 1929.

———. "In the Land of His Dreams: The Last Chapter of Carl Akeley's 1926 African Expedition." *Natural History* 27, no. 6 (November–December 1927): 525–32.

Alexander, Edward P. *The Museum in America: Innovators and Pioneers*. AltaMira Press/Sage Publications, 1997.

American Architect and Building News. "Competitive Design for the American Museum of Natural History, New York, N.Y., Mr. R. H. Robertson, Architect, New York, N.Y." *American Architect and Building News* 26, no. 709 (July 27, 1889): 37, plate.

American Enterprise. "The Moon Landing Revisited." *American Enterprise* 5, no. 4 (July–August 1994): 88–91.

American Museum Journal. "Achievement in Polar Exploration: The Exhibit of the Peary Arctic Club." *American Museum Journal* 9, no. 7 (November 1909): 199–211.

———. "Adventure with an African Elephant." Signed "M.C.D.," probably Mary Cynthia Dickerson. *American Museum Journal* 10, no. 6 (October 1910): 186–87.

———. "Museum News Notes." *American Museum Journal* 8, no. 6 (October 1908): 88–94.

———. "Museum Notes." *American Museum Journal* 14, no. 4 (April 1914): 166–68.

———. "New African Hall Planned by Carl E. Akeley." *American Museum Journal* 14, no. 5 (May 1914): 175–87.

Andrews, Roy Chapman. *Beyond Adventure*. Duell, Sloan and Pearce, 1954.

———. *This Business of Exploring*. G. P. Putnam's Sons, 1935.

Audio-Visual Communications. "Multi-Media: Heaven on Earth." *Audio-Visual Communications*, January 1983, 24–28.

Barton, D. R. "Adventures of an Artist Explorer." *Natural History* 49, no. 1 (January 1942): 50–53, 62–63.

———. "He Brought the Stars to America." *Natural History* 46, no. 1 (June 1940): 59–63.

Bertin, R. L. "Centering for the Planetarium Shell Dome." *Engineering News-Record* 115, no. 4 (July 25, 1935): 108–9.

Bickmore, Albert. "An Autobiography with a Historical Sketch of the Founding and Early Development of the American Museum of Natural History." Unpublished manuscript, 1908.

Bradley, Mary Hastings. "In Africa with Akeley." *Natural History* 27, no. 2 (March–April 1927): 161–72.

———. *On the Gorilla Trail*. D. Appleton, 1922.

Brown, Barnum. "The Trachodon Group." *American Museum Journal* 8, no. 4 (April 1908): 50–56.

Brown, William Adams. *Morris Ketchum Jesup: A Character Sketch*. Charles Scribner's Sons, 1910.

Bryant, Henry G. *The Peary Auxiliary Expedition of 1894*. Philadelphia, 1895.

Bryce, Robert M. *Cook & Peary: The Polar Controversy, Resolved*. Stackpole, 1997.

Burns, Ken, and James Sanders, with Lisa Ades. *New York: An Illustrated History*. Knopf, 1999.

Butler, Howard Russell. "An Ideal Astronomic Hall." *Natural History* 26, no. 4 (July–August 1926): 392–98.

Caro, Robert. "The City-Shaper." *New Yorker*, January 5, 1998, 38–55.

———. *The Power Broker: Robert Moses and the Fall of New York*. Knopf, 1974.

Choate, Joseph H. "Reminiscences of a Founder of the American Museum." *American Museum Journal* 17, no. 5 (May 1917): 285–87.

Clark, James L. *Good Hunting: Fifty Years of Collecting and Preparing Habitat Groups for the American Museum*. University of Oklahoma Press, 1966.

———. "The Image of Africa." *Natural History* 37, no. 1 (January 1936): 69–80.

Colbert, E. H., and K. Beneker. "The Paleozoic Museum in Central Park, or the Museum That Never Was." *Curator: The Museum Journal* 2, no. 2 (April 1959): 137–50.

Cooper, Henry S. F., Jr. "Sphere of Influence." *Natural History* 109, no. 1 (February 2000): 50–59.

Crouch, Tom D. "Willy Ley: Chronicler of the Early Space Age." In *Realizing the Dream of Flight: Biographical Essays in Honor of the Centennial of Flight, 1903–2003*, ed. V. P. Dawson and M. P. Bowles, 155–62. NASA, 2005.

Curator: The Museum Journal. "Theodore Roosevelt Park: 1807–1958." *Curator: The Museum Journal* 3, no. 2 (April 1960): 161–82.

Curran, Kathleen. "A Forgotten Architect of the Gilded Age: Josiah Cleaveland Cady's Legacy." *Watkins Exhibition Catalogs*, paper 20. Trinity College, 1993. http://digitalrepository.trincoll.edu/exhibitions/20.

Davison, F. Trubee. "Elephants, Lions, and Airplanes." *Natural History* 34, no. 2 (March–April 1934): 105–16.

———. "Future Plans for the Akeley African Hall." *Natural History* 37, no. 1 (January 1936): 86–89.

Dickstein, Martin. "Laserium: Light with Music." *DB: The Sound Engineering Magazine* 9, no. 6 (June 1975): 16–19.

Dingus, Lowell. *Next of Kin: Great Fossils at the American Museum of Natural History*. Rizzoli, 1996.

Dingus, Lowell, and Mark Norell. *Barnum Brown: The Man Who Discovered Tyrannosaurus Rex*. University of California Press, 2011.

Faunce, Wayne M. "Problems of Construction." *Natural History* 36, no. 3 (October 1935): 207–16.

Fisher, Clyde. "The New Projection Planetarium." *Natural History* 26, no. 4 (July–August 1926): 402–10.

Fleischer, Joseph L., Timothy P. Hartung, Duncan R. Hazard, Richard M. Olcott, James S. Polshek, Susan T. Rodriguez, and Todd H. Schliemann. *Polshek Partnership Architects*. Princeton Architectural Press, 2005.

Fleming, Fergus. *Ninety Degrees North: The Quest for the North Pole*. Granta, 2001.

Flint, Anthony. *Wrestling with Moses: How Jane Jacobs Took on New York's Master Builder and Transformed the American City*. Random House, 2009.

Foord, John. *The Life and Public Services of Andrew Haswell Green*. Doubleday, Page, 1913.

Frost, Frances. *Rocket Away!* McGraw-Hill, 1953.

Gaffney, Eugene S., Lowell Dingus, and Miranda K. Smith. "Why Cladistics?" *Natural History* 104, no. 6 (June 1995): 33–35.

Goldberger, Paul. *The City Observed: New York, a Guide to the Architecture of Manhattan*. Vintage/Random House, 1979.

Goldman, David. "Benjamin Waterhouse Hawkins and his New York City Paleozoic Museum." Prehistoric Times 63, (December–January 2003). https://www.copyrightexpired.com/hawkins/nyc/Benjamin_Waterhouse_Hawkins.html.

Gould, Stephen Jay. "Evolution by Walking." *Natural History* 104, no. 3 (March 1995): 10–15.

Green, Fitzhugh. *Peary: The Man Who Refused to Fail*. G. P. Putnam's Sons, 1926.

Green, Richard. *Te Ata: Chickasaw Storyteller, American Treasure*. University of Oklahoma Press, 2002.

Hagar, Charles F. *Planetarium: Window to the Universe*. Carl Zeiss, 1980.

Harper, Kenn. *Give Me My Father's Body: The Life of Minik, the New York Eskimo*. Washington Square/Simon & Schuster, 2001.

Hawkins, Benjamin Waterhouse. "Report of Progress of Work Accomplished at the Palaeozoic Museum, in the Central Park, New York." March 16, 1871. In *Proceedings of the Lyceum of Natural History in the City of New York*, 1:179–88. New York: The Society, 1874.

Heckscher, Morrison H. *Creating Central Park*. Metropolitan Museum of Art/ Yale University Press, 2011. Reprint of *The Metropolitan Museum of Art Bulletin*, Winter 2008.

———. *The Metropolitan Museum of Art: An Architectural History. Metropolitan Museum of Art Bulletin*, Summer 1995.

Hellman, Geoffrey. *Bankers, Bones, and Beetles: The First Century of the American Museum of Natural History*. Natural History Press, 1969.

Henderson, Bruce. *True North: Peary, Cook, and the Race to the Pole*. Norton, 2005.

Henson, Matthew A. *A Negro Explorer at the North Pole*. Frederick A. Stokes, 1912.

Higgins & Quasebarth. *American Museum of Natural History: Planetarium & North Side Project; Background Research Report*. For Polshek and Partners. Prepared by Christopher Neville. With William J. Higgins and Christopher Jenks. October 5, 1995.

Higgins Quasebarth and Partners. *American Museum of Natural History: Richard Gilder Center for Science, Education, and Innovation; Historic Preservation Background Research Report*. September 1, 2016.

Hines, Eric M., and David P. Billington. "Anton Tedesko and the Introduction of Thin Shell Concrete Roofs in the United States." *Journal of Structural Engineering* 130, no. 11 (November 2004): 1639–50.

Hodgins, George Sherwood. "A Huge Planetarium." *Scientific American* 101, no. 2 (July 10, 1909): 30.

Howe, Winfred E. *A History of the Metropolitan Museum of Art: With a Chapter on the Early Institutions of Art in New York*. New York, 1913.

Johnson, Martin. "Camera Safaris." *Natural History* 37, no. 1 (January 1936): 47–62.

Jonaitis, Aldona. *From the Land of the Totem Poles: The Northwest Coast Indian Art Collection at the American Museum of Natural History*. American Museum of Natural History/University of Washington Press, 1988.

Journal of the American Geographical Society of New York. "The Greenland Scientific Expedition of 1895." *Journal of the American Geographical Society of New York* 27, no. 1 (1895): 126–33.

———. "The Greenland Scientific Expedition of 1895." *Journal of the American Geographical Society of New York* 27, no. 2 (1895): 221–25.

———. "The North Greenland Expedition." *Journal of the American Geographical Society of New York* 27, no. 3 (1895): 300–6.

———. "Record of Geographical Progress." *Journal of the American Geographical Society of New York* 28, no. 3 (1896): 273–89.

Kelby, Robert Hendre. *The New-York Historical Society, 1804–1904*. New-York Historical Society, 1905.

Kennedy, John Michael. "Philanthropy and Science in New York City: The American Museum of Natural History, 1868–1968." PhD diss., Yale University, 1968.

Kirkpatrick, Katherine. *The Snow Baby: The Arctic Childhood of Admiral Robert E. Peary's Daring Daughter*. Holiday House, 2007.

Klutsch, Anita. "Andrew Haswell Green: The Father of Greater New York and His Dual Vision of a Cultivated and Consolidated Metropolis." PhD diss., Ludwig Maximilian University of Munich, 2012.

Lawrence, Jenny, and Richard Milner. "Forgotten Cosmic Designer." *Natural History* 109, no. 1 (February 2000): 100.

Ley, Willy. *Rockets, Missiles, and Space Travel.* Rev. ed. Viking, 1957.

Liebermann, Randy. "The *Collier's* and Disney Series." In *Blueprint for Space: Science Fiction to Science Fact,* ed. Frederick I. Ordway III and Randy Liebermann, 135–146. Smithsonian Institute Press, 1992.

Lockwood, Marian. "Clyde Fisher Naturalist and Teacher." *Sky and Telescope* 8, no. 5 (March 1949): 111–13.

Marché, Jordan Dale, II. *Theaters of Time and Space: American Planetaria, 1930–1970.* Rutgers University Press, 2005.

———. "Theaters of Time and Space: The American Planetarium Community, 1930–1970." PhD diss., Indiana University, 1999.

Mason, Betsy. "Space Travel: The Interplanetary Tours Reservation Desk." *Wired,* December 19, 2011. http://www.wired.com/2011/12/space-tour-reservations.

Matthew, W. D. "Allosaurus, a Carnivorous Dinosaur, and Its Prey." *American Museum Journal* 8, no. 1 (January 1908): 2–5.

———. "The Mounted Skeleton of Brontosaurus." *American Museum Journal* 5, no. 2 (April 1905): 62–70.

Mazaraki, George Alexander. "The Public Career of Andrew Haswell Green." PhD diss., New York University, 1966.

McCleary, Elliot. "He Makes Them Look Alive." *The Rotarian* 97, no. 4 (October 1960): 36–39.

McCurdy, Howard E. *Space and the American Imagination.* Smithsonian Institution Press, 1997.

McCutcheon, John T. *In Africa: Hunting Adventures in the Big Game Country.* Bobbs-Merrill, 1910.

McWilliams, Stewart A. "Frank M. Chapman: A Scientist Who Has Shared His Knowledge." *Natural History* 28, no. 6 (November–December 1928): 663–64.

Menke, David H. "Planetarium Lifeline: Clyde Fisher and the Hayden Planetarium." *The Planetarian* 16, no. 2 (April 1987): 54–58.

Miller, Ron, and Frederick C. Durant III. *The Art of Chesley Bonestell.* Paper Tiger, 2001.

Mills, William James. *Exploring Polar Frontiers: A Historical Encyclopedia.* 2 vols. ABC-CLIO, 2003.

Milner, Richard. "Bringing Back the Dinosaurs." *Natural History* 104, no. 5 (May 1995): 6–10.

Mitchell, Jerry. *The American Experiment with Government Corporations.* Routledge, 1999.

Moses, Robert. *Public Works: A Dangerous Trade.* McGraw-Hill, 1970.

The Museums in the Park: Should They Be Open on Sunday? New York: Rufus Adams, 1885.

Nelson, Robert J. "New Technology for a New Museum." In *Rose Center for Earth and Space: A Museum for the Twenty-First Century,* 78–95. American Museum of Natural History/Abrams, 2001.

Neufeld, Michael J. *Von Braun: Dreamer of Space, Engineer of War.* Vintage/Random House, 2007.

Norell, Mark, Lowell Dingus, and Eugene Gaffney. *Discovering Dinosaurs: Evolution, Extinction, and the Lessons of Prehistory.* Rev. ed. University of California Press. 2000.

Norell, Mark, Eugene Gaffney, and Lowell Dingus. *Discovering Dinosaurs: In the American Museum of Natural History.* Knopf, 1995.

Norman Bel Geddes and Company, Inc. *Preliminary Report to the Hayden Planetarium Authority.* 1942.

Olson, J. *Saving Capitalism: The Reconstruction Finance Corporation and the New Deal, 1933–1940.* Princeton, NJ: Princeton University Press.

Osborn, Henry Fairfield. *History, Plan, and Scope of the American Museum of Natural History.* Irving Press, 1910.

———. "Tyrannosaurus, Restoration and Model of the Skeleton." *Bulletin of the American Museum of Natural History* 32 (1913): 91–92.

———. "The Vanishing Wildlife of Africa." *Natural History* 27, no. 6 (November–December 1927): 515–24.

Pape, Paul F. "Thin Concrete Shell Dome for New York Planetarium." *Engineering News-Record* 115, no. 4 (July 25, 1935): 105–8.

Pasachoff, Jay, and Roberta Olson. "Eclipse Art." *Nature* 508, no. 7496 (April 17, 2014): 314–315.

———. "The Solar Eclipse Mural Series by Howard Russell Butler." In *Inspiration of Astronomical Phenomena VIII: City of Stars. Proceedings of a Conference Held at the American Museum of Natural History, New York, United States, July 7–12, 2013,* ed. Brian Patrick Abbott. ASP Conference Series 501. San Francisco: Astronomical Society of the Pacific.

Peary, Josephine Diebitsch. *My Arctic Journal: A Year among Ice-Field and Eskimos.* Contemporary Publishing, 1893.

———. *Snow Baby: A True Story with True Pictures.* Frederick A. Stokes, 1901.

Peary, Josephine Diebitsch, and Marie Ahnighito Peary. *Children of the Arctic.* Frederick A. Stokes, 1903.

Peary, Robert E. *Nearest the Pole: A Narrative of the Polar Expedition of the Peary Arctic Club in the S.S. Roosevelt, 1905–1906.* Doubleday, Page, 1907.

———. *The North Pole: Its Discovery in 1909 under the Auspices of the Peary Arctic Club.* Frederick A. Stokes, 1910.

———. *Northward over the Great Ice: A Narrative of Life and Work along the Shores and upon the Interior Ice-Cap of Northern Greenland in the Years 1886 and 1891–1897.* 2 vols. Frederick A. Stokes, 1898.

Peary, Robert E., and Marie Ahnighito Peary. *Snowland Folk: The Eskimos, the Bears, the Dogs, the Musk Oxen, and Other Dwellers in the Frozen North.* Frederick A. Stokes, 1904.

Peck, Robert McCracken. "The Art of Bones." *Natural History* 117, no. 10 (December 2008–January 2009): 24–29.

Preston, Douglas J. *Dinosaurs in the Attic: An Excursion into the American Museum of Natural History.* St. Martin's Press, 1993.

Quinn, Stephen Christopher. *Windows on Nature.* American Museum of Natural History/Abrams, 2006.

Rainger, Ronald. *An Agenda for Antiquity: Henry Fairfield Osborn and Vertebrate Paleontology at the American Museum of Natural History, 1890–1935.* University of Alabama Press, 1991.

"Report of the Roosevelt Memorial Commission." State of New York Legislative Document (1922) 48. J. B. Lyon, 1922.

Rexer, Lyle, and Rachel Klein. *American Museum of Natural History: 125 Years of Expedition and Discovery.* American Museum of Natural History/Abrams, 1995.

Robertson, Barbara. "Stargazing." *Computer Graphics World* 23, no. 2 (February 2000): 32–35.

Robinson, Bradley, with Matthew Henson. *Dark Companion: The Story of Matthew Henson.* Rev. ed. Fawcett, 1967.

Roosevelt, Theodore. *African Game Trails: An Account of the African Wanderings of an American Hunter-Naturalist.* John Murray, 1910.

Rosen, Milton. *The Viking Rocket Story.* American ed. Faber and Faber, 1955.

Rosenzweig, Roy, and Elizabeth Blackmar. *The Park and the People: A History of Central Park.* Cornell University Press, 1992.

Rubbinaccio, Michael. *New York's Father Is Murdered! The Life and Death of Andrew Haswell Green.* Pescara, 2012.

Salisbury, Rollin D. "The Arctic Expedition of 1895, and Lieutenant Peary's Work." *Scientific American Supplement* 15, no. 1036 (November 9, 1895): 16560.

Schuyler, Montgomery. "The Romanesque Revival in New York." *Architectural Record* 1, no. 1 (July–September 1891): 7–38.

Scribner's Monthly. "An American Museum of Art: The Designs Submitted by Wm. H. Beard." *Scribner's Monthly* 2, no. 4 (August 1871): 409–15.

Sharp, Bill, and Peggy Sullivan. *The Dashing Kansan: The Amazing Adventures of a Nineteenth-Century Naturalist and Explorer.* Harrow, 1990.

Sherwood, George Herbert. *Free Education by the American Museum of Natural History in Public Schools and Colleges: History and Status of Museum Instruction and Its Extension to the Schools of Greater New York and Vicinity.* American Museum of Natural History, 1920.

Silber, William L. "Why Did FDR's Bank Holiday Succeed?" *FRBNY Economic Policy Review*, July 2009. https://www.newyorkfed.org/medialibrary/media/research/epr/09v15n1/0907silb.pdf.

Sky and Telescope. "Hayden Planetarium Black-light Murals." *Sky and Telescope* 12, no. 7 (May 1953): 175.

Stern, Robert A. M., David Fishman, and Thomas Mellins. *New York 1960: Architecture and Urbanism between the Second World War and the Bicentennial.* Monacelli, 1995.

Stern, Robert A. M., David Fishman, and Jacob Tilove. *New York 2000: Architecture and Urbanism between the Bicentennial and the Millennium.* Monacelli, 2006.

Stern, Robert A. M., Gregory Gilmartin, and John Montague Massengale. *New York 1900: Metropolitan Architecture and Urbanism, 1890–1915.* Rizzoli, 1983.

Stern, Robert A. M., Gregory F. Gilmartin, and Thomas Mellins. *New York 1930: Architecture and Urbanism between the Two World Wars.* Rizzoli, 1987.

Stern, Robert A. M., Thomas Mellins, and David Fishman. *New York 1880: Architecture and Urbanism in the Gilded Age.* Monacelli, 1999.

Stuhlinger, Ernst, and Frederick I. Ordway III. *Wernher von Braun: Crusader for Space.* Rev. ed. Krieger, 1996.

Sweitzer, James S. "Theater of the Stars." *Natural History* 109, no. 1 (February 2000): 60–61.

Terry, Bob. *Honest Weight: The Story of Toledo Scale.* Xlibris, 2000.

Tobin, Richard Leonard. "Deconstructing James Brown Lord: A Monograph." MS thesis, Columbia University, 2012.

Tooker, L. G. "Line Forms Here for Trip to Moon." *Popular Science* 161, no. 2 (August 1952): 82–84, 226–40.

Tyson, Neil deGrasse. *The Sky Is Not the Limit.* 2nd ed. Prometheus, 2004.

Vail, R. W. G. *Knickerbocker Birthday: The Sesqui-Centennial Birthday of the New-York Historical Society, 1804–1954.* New-York Historical Society, 1954.

Veliz, Claudio. "Renaissance or Regret?" *Astronomy* 25, no. 1 (January 1997): 20.

Wallace, Joseph. *The American Museum of Natural History's Book of Dinosaurs and Other Ancient Creatures.* Simon & Schuster, 1994.

———. *A Gathering of Wonders.* St. Martin's Press, 2000.

Ward, Bob. *Dr. Space: The Life of Wernher von Braun.* Naval Institute Press, 2005.

Werner, Helmut. *From the Aratus Globe to the Zeiss Planetarium.* Rev. ed. Trans. A. H. Degenhardt. Verlag Gustav Fischer, 1957.

Whipple, Fred L. "Recollections of Pre-Sputnik Days." In *Blueprint for Space: Science Fiction to Science Fact,* ed. Frederick I. Ordway III and Randy Liebermann, 127–34. Smithsonian Institute Press, 1992.

White, Norval. *New York: A Physical History.* Atheneum/Macmillan, 1987.

Williams, Patricia M. "The Museum Trademark." *Field Museum of Natural History Bulletin* 39, no. 1 (January 1968): 2–5.

Index

Colin Davey's life was shaped by frequent visits to the American Museum of Natural History and the Hayden Planetarium as a child. He is a scientist, software engineer, martial artist, and author of *Learn Boogie Woogie Piano* (Boogie Woogie Press, 1998). Colin was the historical content consultant for and appeared in the AMNH documentary "Stories in the Sky: A History of Planetariums."

Thomas A. Lesser was Scientific Assistant and Intern Astronomer (1974–76) and Senior Lecturer (1975–82) at the Hayden Planetarium. He has also held several positions at the American Museum of Natural History, including Manager of Development.

Select titles from Empire State Editions

ESE

Patrick Bunyan, *All Around the Town: Amazing Manhattan Facts and Curiosities, Second Edition*

Salvatore Basile, *Fifth Avenue Famous: The Extraordinary Story of Music at St. Patrick's Cathedral.* Foreword by Most Reverend Timothy M. Dolan, Archbishop of New York

William Seraile, *Angels of Mercy: White Women and the History of New York's Colored Orphan Asylum*

Andrew J. Sparberg, *From a Nickel to a Token: The Journey from Board of Transportation to MTA*

New York's Golden Age of Bridges. Paintings by Antonio Masi, Essays by Joan Marans Dim, Foreword by Harold Holzer

Anthony D. Andreassi, C.O., *Teach Me to Be Generous: The First Century of Regis High School in New York City.* Foreword by Timothy Michael Cardinal Dolan, Archbishop of New York

Daniel Campo, *The Accidental Playground: Brooklyn Waterfront Narratives of the Undesigned and Unplanned*

Gerard R. Wolfe, *The Synagogues of New York's Lower East Side: A Retrospective and Contemporary View, Second Edition.* Photographs by Jo Renée Fine and Norman Borden, Foreword by Joseph Berger

Joseph B. Raskin, *The Routes Not Taken: A Trip Through New York City's Unbuilt Subway System*

Phillip Deery, *Red Apple: Communism and McCarthyism in Cold War New York*

North Brother Island: The Last Unknown Place in New York City. Photographs by Christopher Payne, A History by Randall Mason, Essay by Robert Sullivan

Richard Kostelanetz, *Artists' SoHo: 49 Episodes of Intimate History*

Stephen Miller, *Walking New York: Reflections of American Writers from Walt Whitman to Teju Cole*

Tom Glynn, *Reading Publics: New York City's Public Libraries, 1754–1911*

Craig Saper, *The Amazing Adventures of Bob Brown: A Real-Life Zelig Who Wrote His Way Through the 20th Century*

R. Scott Hanson, *City of Gods: Religious Freedom, Immigration, and Pluralism in Flushing, Queens.* Foreword by Martin E. Marty

Dorothy Day and the Catholic Worker: The Miracle of Our Continuance. Edited, with an Introduction and Additional Text by Kate Hennessy, Photographs by Vivian Cherry, Text by Dorothy Day

Mark Naison and Bob Gumbs, *Before the Fires: An Oral History of African American Life in the Bronx from the 1930s to the 1960s*

Robert Weldon Whalen, *Murder, Inc., and the Moral Life: Gangsters and Gang-busters in La Guardia's New York*

Joanne Witty and Henrik Krogius, *Brooklyn Bridge Park: A Dying Waterfront Transformed*

Sharon Egretta Sutton, *When Ivory Towers Were Black: A Story about Race in America's Cities and Universities*

Pamela Hanlon, *A Wordly Affair: New York, the United Nations, and the Story Behind Their Unlikely Bond*

Britt Haas, *Fighting Authoritarianism: American Youth Activism in the 1930s*

David J. Goodwin, *Left Bank of the Hudson: Jersey City and the Artists of 111 1st Street*. Foreword by DW Gibson

Nandini Bagchee, *Counter Institution: Activist Estates of the Lower East Side*

Carol Lamberg, *Neighborhood Success Stories: Creating and Sustaining Affordable Housing in New York*

Susan Celia Greenfield (ed.), *Sacred Shelter: Thirteen Journeys of Homelessness and Healing*

Elizabeth Macaulay Lewis and Matthew M. McGowan (eds.), *Classical New York: Discovering Greece and Rome in Gotham*

Susan Opotow and Zachary Baron Shemtob (eds.), *New York After 9/11*

Andrew Feffer, *Bad Faith: Teachers, Liberalism, and the Origins of McCarthyism*

**For a complete list, visit
www.fordhampress.com/empire-state-editions.**